Conor Mark Jameson has wr [...]
The Ecologist, *Africa Geo[...]*
magazine, *Birdwatch* and *Birdwatching* magazines and has been
a scriptwriter for the BBC Natural History Unit. He is a columnist
and feature writer for *Birds* magazine, and has worked in
conservation for 20 years, in the UK and abroad. He was born
in Uganda to Irish parents, brought up in Scotland, and now lives
in England. He lives in a village an hour north of London, with a
garden that Google Earth indicates may be reverting to woodland.

CONOR MARK JAMESON
Silent Spring
Revisited

BLOOMSBURY

LONDON · BERLIN · NEW YORK · SYDNEY

*This is for my family, friends and colleagues,
for supporters of nature everywhere, and, of
course, for Rachel Carson.*

First published in Great Britain 2012
Published in paperback in Great Britain 2013

A CIP catalogue record for this book is
available from the British Library

Bloomsbury Publishing Plc
50 Bedford Square
London
WC1B 3DP

www.bloomsbury.com

Bloomsbury Publishing, London, New Delhi, New York and Sydney

Commissioning editor: Julie Bailey
Page design and typesetting by Susan McIntyre

ISBN (paperback) 978 1 4081 9407 2
ISBN (hardback) 978 1 4081 5760 2
ISBN (ePub) 978 1 4081 5761 9

Printed in Great Britain by CPI Group (UK) Ltd, Croydon, CR0 4YY

10 9 8 7 6 5 4 3 2 1

MIX
Paper from
responsible sources
FSC® C020471

Contents

This grand show is eternal. It is always sunrise somewhere; the dew is never all dried at w; a shower is forever falling; vapor ever rising. Eternal sunrise, eternal sunset, eternal dawn and gloaming, on seas and continents and islands, each in its turn, as the round earth rolls.

John Muir, *John of the Mountains*, 1938

Prologue

In a book about the dawn chorus, about songbirds and birdsong, the Peregrine Falcon might not be the obvious place to start, but bear with me. For one thing, you don't have to ponder for long the question 'What is a songbird?' or 'What combines to make the dawn chorus?' to realise that these are broader concepts than they may have appeared at first glance. All birds are songbirds. Either they all sing, or none of them do, if 'song' is what you choose to call the utterances they make to attract attention to themselves or express any from a broad spectrum of emotions. We think of Peregrines as predators, but all our birds – bar one or two of our finch species – are predators for at least part of their life cycle. They eat meat, and sometimes they eat each other.

That said, I don't begin with the Peregrine Falcon because I especially value how it sounds, although clearly its voice is part of the essential drama of a Peregrine in its fullest glory. But one way or another the Peregrine Falcon is a central character in this narrative; one of many, as I hope will become clear.

The inspiration for this story arose from a combination of life-affirming circumstances. It was a Sunday morning for one thing, always a good place to start, in my book. It was shortly after dawn. A sunlit dawn too, with the pure beams of piercing new daylight angling in across the hedge tops to illuminate the humble stage of my back garden. It was the beginning of April, and Mother's Day for good measure. It was also my first chance to sit out in a deckchair so far this year. I had an essay to finish writing, and had some books propped around me as I worked through a bit of additional research. The piece is called 'Looking for J. A. Baker', and is about the author and his classic sixties book, *The Peregrine*.

The Peregrine is a love story of sorts, about the author's relationship with this ever-intriguing wild bird. But the story has baggage. Nature-loving readers have often doubted what the author *really saw*. I love this book, I should make clear, and in my essay I am exploring the question of whether these doubts have been justified, sifting the available evidence. There has been something of a schism in interpretation, between those of a literal, scientific outlook on one side, and those of an artistic, cultural persuasion on the other. Both camps are concerned with truth, but truths of different kinds.

Just like *Silent Spring*, *The Peregrine* has become something of an article of faith for nature writers, and devotees of nature writing. In writing the book, Baker, like his subject, has attained almost mythic, prophet status, and deservedly so. *The Peregrine* has played its part in inspiring many of the leading conservationists of today, and supporters of conservation. Its literary quality is not in dispute. It was originally published to critical acclaim, and a Duff Cooper Prize.

Baker is an intriguing and mysterious figure, and he wrote his beguiling book at a time (several years before it was finally published in 1967, the year I was born) when the tragedy of what was happening to birds like the Peregrine Falcon through the misuse of agrochemicals was slowly becoming apparent to a wider public.

Not surprisingly, the reissue of *The Peregrine* in 2010, along with Baker's only other book, *The Hill of Summer*, and extracts from his notebooks, was greeted eagerly. With access to Baker's previously private diaries, editors Mark Cocker and John Fanshawe have been able to set the author's work in a fresh and revealing light. A third of the diaries are included in the new volume. They were made available by Baker's widow Doreen shortly before she died in 2006.

But with *The Peregrine* there is, as they say, an elephant in the room.

Most authorities, while recognising the quality of Baker's prose, will admit in private to misgivings about the reliability of what the author claims to have seen, to have known. The prevailing feeling is that Baker can't have been seeing Peregrines, if he was seeing anything at all.

Rereading the book today, I have some sympathy with this view. And to be troubled in this way isn't, I think, to miss the point of Baker's writing.

'He was a lovely man, and he was very certain that he was right,' one of his contemporaries has told me. He met Baker while both were on the set of the children's programme *Animal Magic*, at Christmas 1969. And for sure there is a mood of honesty and concern for truth that pervades Baker's words, taken as a whole.

So why the doubts? And is a reader entitled to have them? For one thing, goes the reasoning, Peregrine Falcons barely occurred in southern Britain at the time Baker wrote. His book is based on observations made in Essex over a decade from the mid-fifties. So *were* there Peregrine Falcons?

'If you look at a map of the distribution of the Peregrine in 1962,' wrote Lord Shackleton at the time, 'you will see that it has largely disappeared from the south of England. In the north of England Peregrines are still present in fair numbers, but although some pairs laid eggs, more than half of these failed. The position is similar in southern Scotland. In the Highlands and Islands there has been a fairly normal nesting season. Investigation of an egg taken from an abandoned nest near Perth showed that here again was poison.'

And what of Essex itself? I had a rummage in the archives of the Royal Society for the Protection of Birds (RSPB) and this produced a bundle of contemporary *Essex Bird Reports*. These reveal that in fact quite a lot of mostly wintering Peregrines were being reported in the county up to and during the Baker years. What was also unexpected, given the received wisdom, were Peregrine Falcon reports submitted by a certain JAB – Baker himself.

Baker's diaries begin in 1954, but the first 'JAB' Peregrine records aren't logged by the *Essex Bird Report* until 1957. It's possible (but I think unlikely) he was among the 'many observers' who had been seeing Peregrines wintering at two reservoirs – Abberton and Hanningfield – before 1957. But what's clear is that Peregrines *were* at large for a few years before Baker began to identify them.

He first began to notice what he took to be possible signs of Peregrines in the behaviour of other birds, and in the carcases he was finding. It is clear he was still getting to grips with raptor identification. His first diary records of Peregrine sightings don't correspond with the ones he reported in the *Essex Bird Report*, but it should be noted that he is said to have disposed of his diary entries for Peregrine in the course of writing his book.

To summarise, a graph of JAB's Peregrine reports plotted over time, alongside records from other observers, would show a peak in JAB's reports in the early sixties just as the other reports dwindled to isolated birds. So, just around the time when agrochemical poisoning was beginning to make its presence felt in the landscape, these wintering Peregrines apparently decreased in Essex as a whole, but were increasingly present in Baker's corner of the interior.

Assuming Baker was right about what he saw, how might this be explained? Might, for example, the birds have moved from the reservoirs, which were closely managed as wildfowl reserves, to Baker's patch?

A second doubt typically raised about the book is that Baker's descriptions don't fit the usually understood behaviour of Peregrines, or indeed, in some cases, the appearance of the bird, particularly its flight patterns.

Towards the book's conclusion, in the aggregated entries for the month of March, Baker writes at length about a 'golden tiercel' (the old falconry name for a male Peregrine), often seen in and around an orchard. The bird appears from his descriptions to be semi-tame, with a habit of hovering low, eating worms and mice, and – in case you are already thinking 'it's a Kestrel' – pouncing on Partridges in the grass, which Kestrels would not be large enough to do, and robbing Kestrels of their prey.

This bird not only allows Baker to approach, but also approaches him. It is described as large, it perches on wires, hunts by skimming low over the ground, shelters from the rain in tree holes, and is variously described as brown, buff, amber, reddish, bronze, gold, golden wheat and lion-coloured. Apart from anything, if Baker were working from other people's images or descriptions of the Peregrine, these are hardly the terms he is likely to have used.

But the reader is still entitled, particularly in light of our increasing familiarity with the species today, to conclude that this doesn't sound like a Peregrine: even a juvenile, visiting Scandinavian, much-habituated Peregrine from a bygone age. So what does it sound like?

Looking again closely at my copy of *The Peregrine* and these peculiar, detailed, loving descriptions of the bird, I had what felt like a moment of clarity, as a hypothesis dawned on me that just might clear up the confusion. There is a species that all of this fits, and could describe, and it's neither Peregrine nor Kestrel. It's Saker Falcon – *Falco cherrug*. Or even, at a push, Lugger Falcon – *Falco lugger*. Or possibly a hybrid of either of these with Peregrine Falcon. They can be cross-bred in captivity.

Take this description of his pet Lugger Falcon by Philip Glasier, renowned authority on falconry: 'This was a very odd bird, like a great big Kestrel, but with the soft brown plumage of the desert falcons such as the Sakers'.

But were these species in circulation at the time? Baker's decade straddles a period in which the owning of raptors had become what Gerald Summers called a 'craze'. Inspired by some high-profile (i.e. televised) exponents of the art, uninhibited by lack of insight and with no need for registration documents, would-be falconers were turning up everywhere.

'Loads and loads of different species were being brought in at this point and flogged through dealers and *Exchange and Mart*,' falconry and raptor expert Helen MacDonald tells me. 'Everything from Red-headed Falcons to Changeable Hawk-eagles to Black-collared Hawks.'

Gerald Summers recalls it like this: 'During the years 1965 to 1966 the new upsurge of enthusiasm for falconry reached its peak. Falconers and potential falconers of widely differing degrees of competence seemed to appear in practically every town and village in Britain. The consequent demand ... was almost insatiable.'

Summers also reported that 'a rash of hawk thefts broke out. Two peregrines were stolen from one establishment, several lugger falcons and a saker from another.'

It's clear that the latter two species were readily available in the marketplace at the time.

Falconry is a difficult art to master, some species more so than others. Sakers and Luggers are known to be problematic, and easy to lose, or to lose patience with. Raptor and falconry enthusiast Richard Hines provides this insight on Peregrine/Saker crosses:

'I knew someone who flew two Peregrine/Saker hybrids, and even though they were brilliant falconry hawks, he soon lost enthusiasm for them. Sakers migrate, and get restless at migration time. These birds would give up the chase and fly miles away. My friend put this down to the Saker in them. After travelling miles each time using telemetry to find the birds, he eventually sold them.'

Glasier added this, of his own Lugger Falcon: 'I gave it away finally ... like so many foreign species of falcons, it failed to make the grade.' He also recalled releasing a Peregrine one autumn in north Kent, across the mouth of the Thames from Baker's Essex, when a change in his circumstances meant he could no longer do the bird justice. It isn't difficult to imagine many others in this populous part of the country feeling compelled to do something similar.

A third aspect of *The Peregrine* that has puzzled readers is the curious number of dead birds that Baker found in the course of his searches: 619 are carefully itemised. He attributes them all to Peregrine predation, even those he finds dead in large groups, such as 30 (mainly Woodpigeons) in one place, 16 in another, and 49 in another.

But there is something that Baker, his editor, and many of his readers, appear to have overlooked, something that might be behind these unusual aggregations of avian death. It's well known that organo-chlorine pesticides persisted in the food chain in the post-war period, accumulating in the bodies of top-end predators like Peregrines, causing infertility and reproductive problems. What seems less well remembered is that these chemicals were sometimes directly lethal, killing birds of all kinds in large numbers.

This was what prompted me to take Rachel Carson's *Silent Spring* down from the shelf. Like many people, I own a copy of this book. It's another article of faith for environmentalists. But I couldn't at that time claim to have read it in full. It is dense with facts and figures, intense in its mission to catalogue evidence, to warn. It has 50 pages of references. It is a book that celebrates nature, but it is also a book about chemicals, chromosomes, cancer. Reading it now, in that spring Sunday morning deckchair, I noted this reflection on the year 1961, by Lord Shackleton, from his introduction to the book: 'Tens of thousands of birds were found littering the countryside, dead or dying in agony.' At the Queen's Sandringham Estate, at the opposite end of East Anglia from Baker's Chelmer Valley, he reported that 'over 142 bodies were collected in 11.5 hours of special survey counts, and hundreds more over a period of weeks.

'The list of dead birds included pheasants, red-legged partridges, partridges, woodpigeons and stock doves, greenfinches, chaffinches, blackbirds, song thrushes, skylarks, moorhens, bramblings, tree sparrows, carrion crows, hooded crows, goldfinches, and sparrow-hawks.' Just across the Wash, at Tumby in Lincolnshire, at another estate in 1961, 'over 6,000 dead birds were counted'.

These were clearly unusual times in the farmed countryside. Lord Shackleton also noted 'reports of a mysterious illness affecting foxes … coming in from all over the country until it was estimated that 1,300 foxes had been found dead'.

'One odd symptom,' he added, 'as the Nature Conservancy Council reported, was that sick foxes appeared to lose their fear of mankind.'

Perhaps this decline of Foxes, if not in itself a confirmed symptom of chemical poisoning, might go some way to explaining the unusual number of bird corpses lingering in the environment, unscavenged.

These pivotal times for the environmental movement coincided with the RSPB's move from London to its new, larger, rural headquarters in a rambling Victorian country house at Sandy, Bedfordshire that is today still its well-known UK base, and my place of work. The Society was foremost among those pushing hard for Parliament to take urgent action on these lethal pesticides. A voluntary agreement on control was rapidly reached. Farmers and landowners were urged to refrain from using certain of these products on seeds, and only in extreme circumstances in autumn. The impact on birds seemed to lessen after the *annus horribilis* of 1961, but not to cease. It went on being what Julian Huxley called, in his preface to *Silent Spring*'s British edition, 'an ecological tragedy'. As Shackleton noted, 'many deaths were reported from widely separated places'.

But not reported by Baker, it seems. Perhaps by the time his book was edited and published, in 1967, the likely link between his observed bird corpses and this widespread carnage had been forgotten. Perhaps poisoning might even explain the unusual or lethargic behaviour of closely studied raptors of the time. *The Essex Bird Report* noted in its 1961 editorial the 'moribund hobby found at Lexden' in August. Sparrowhawks were all but wiped out, and Kestrels reduced to just a handful of pairs across the entire county. A year later the *Report* told its readers: 'It is generally conceded that the use of poisonous sprays and seed dressings is mainly responsible, directly or indirectly, for the decline on the part of these resident species.'

As I was reading this sobering introduction to *Silent Spring*, and the quote from Julian Huxley's brother Aldous, a literary hero to me, that 'we are losing half the subject matter of English poetry', I looked up from where I sat, towards the sky. Just at that moment a Swallow, the first of spring, dashed into view over the roof of the house, did a breathless circuit above me and the garden, racing, swimming in air, exuberant as a puppy, then disappeared from view again more or less at the point at which it had entered the scene. A sudden injection of reckless joy.

The returning spring migrant carries with it a hint of the miraculous; the more so with each passing year. For me their impact, if anything, increases. That, in a nutshell, is the thrill of these birds, the message of hope that they carry, that they symbolise. Except that it's more than symbolic, it is what they are, not just what they mean. Planet health.

I don't mind admitting that I shed a tear at that Swallow, or perhaps for us, for that little piece of inspiration for poetry in English, or any other language for that matter.

As well as the Baker questions that had been gnawing at me for weeks, another one was by now forming in my mind. Where have we got to since *Silent Spring*? How well have we heeded Rachel Carson's warning?

In early March I had visited J. A. Baker's former haunts, the better, I hoped, to relate to the man and his milieu. I followed the river Chelmer upstream, through and past places where Baker spent much of his time, and had many of his close encounters with falcons. It's a rolling landscape of arable field and spinney, a typical lowland England scene, a place Peregrine might at any time pass over, even hunt across, but not the kind of place we expect them to loiter, even now, with nesting Peregrines crowning many of our inland cathedrals and other iconic city centre buildings all across the land.

Baker was not a wealthy man, with the luxury of much free time. He had a full-time job as an office manager. His Peregrines were only present in winter – the months of short days. And he travelled only on foot, and by bicycle. Walking by the Chelmer I found no Peregrine, but I did find one bird casualty – the remains of a drake Mallard. Looking more closely at the feathers, I could see the tell-tale bite marks of the mammal that plucked it.

So what do I think Baker saw? I believe what Baker wrote was based on real observations. Perhaps not as many as he described so seductively. But I think what he actually saw lies somewhere between escaped and semi-tame exotic birds and the gaps he filled in, in his mind's eye, to explain the huge number of dead birds he was finding, the kills he was mostly missing. Baker, like many of us, was largely confined in daylight hours to an office, to a desk, to smoky meeting rooms, the canteen. Meanwhile his Peregrines worked their magic, whether in the sky, or in his imagination, or somewhere in between.

I believe Baker was filling a vacuum, in his own knowledge, and in public knowledge. He was answering a need of his own, and of his publishers, and readers. And above all he was helping his subject – a bird that looked to be in serious trouble, in real danger of widespread oblivion.

Baker's legacy is real and lasting, evidenced in the fact that we're still talking about it 50 years on, and cases like me are still trying to get inside his head. He showed us how to relay feelings as well as bald records, how to write up notes, how to *look*, how to *listen*. I would urge any sceptic to read the book again. Read the last month of entries, thinking liberated falconry birds. Read about the dead birds, and think toxins. Above all, read the whole, and bear in mind that Peregrines were around, and feel the passion.

People who know more about the man, the period, the area and the bird may be able to give further insights. I just want to draw attention to some factors that might have been overlooked, and that might – just might – hold clues to the mystery and enigma of Baker's immortalised falcons.

Baker's *Essex Bird Report* records cease in 1969, the year *The Hill of Summer*, his second book, was published; the year this publicity-shy, diffident man met Roger Upton on the set of *Animal Magic*. (Did he appear on the show? I don't think so – I received a copy of it from a friend, who works at the BBC, but it has no sound, and I could see no one who resembled Baker.) He was by now incapacitated by rheumatoid arthritis.

Reports of Peregrines began to increase again as the seventies progressed, including birds reported by other people from inland areas. Librarian Ian Dawson drew my attention to an article by Baker in a 1971 issue of *Birds* magazine. It is a bleak lament for the loss of wilderness in our lives due to 'modern barbarity' and the 'lullaby language of indifferent politicians', and for the 'vile years to come'.

I spent time at the seafront at Maldon, Essex, gazing over the estuary, Baker's 'ancient bird-haunted coast', wondering if a Peregrine might show; watching, as Baker did, the gulls, the waders, the corvids, the pigeons, for any early hint from them that a *falconiforme* might be at large. Not that this would prove or disprove anything, of course …

I paused at a signboard depicting the local birds. It faces the river channel, where the Chelmer and Blackwater, the rivers that mark roughly the boundaries of Baker's core search area, enter the North Sea. Sara, my wife, and I couldn't help noting no Peregrine on this board, and none that we saw beyond it.

But there is a statue of a man, gazing out to sea. Not Baker, but Byrhtnoth, the man who led a small Saxon army in AD 991 against a much greater army of invading Vikings. A valiant, defiant, white-haired warrior of 60, Byrhtnoth gave the order for his troops to march into a battle few can have believed they could win. At that signal, a *hafoc* (hawk) – perhaps a Peregrine – was released, to inspire his fighters ...

A line from the famous old poem, *The Battle of Maldon*, I offer here as a dedication, and a mark of the greatest respect, to Mr J. A. Baker.

> 'He let then fly from his hand his beloved hawk towards its home, and went forth to battle.'

I could have guessed then at the parallels of Baker's story with Rachel Carson's life and motives, but not at the true extent of them. But I was to find out.

* * *

I set out to write this book, to attempt to answer questions that others have asked, and that I myself, even though I've given a large part of my life to conservation, still ask. Questions like: was Rachel Carson right? What has become of the birds, and of birdsong?

The opinions and feelings expressed in this story are entirely my own, as are any omissions, which I hope can be forgiven in the spirit in which the tale has been prepared.

American playwright and author Arthur Miller once said, 'I write as much to discover as to explain.' Fifty years are a lot to cover in one story. If this book works only to make the reader curious to know more about what we do to our natural world, then it will have served its purpose.

CMJ, Bedfordshire
Spring 2012

Introduction

Rachel Carson was born in May 1907 on her family's small farm in Springdale, Pennsylvania. She showed an early gift for story-writing, and a love of the natural world, especially the sea. She was originally a student of English, but switched to science, which women at that time were not often encouraged to do. Her hopes of studying for a doctorate were undone by the need to support her wider family, so she took on teaching roles and, later, jobs in government research bodies. In the fifties she wrote a trilogy of best-selling books about the marine environment, before turning her attention to studying the environmental impacts of synthetic pesticides.

Silent Spring is said to have been the spark that ignited the modern-day environmental movement. It certainly marked a step change in the wider public's concern about the well-being of wild birds. I'm not old enough to recall personally the mood of the times around its publication, but the name of the book and its author Rachel Carson have been present in my life for as long as I've been conscious. Since the day of its publication in 1962, the book – the concept – has had a kind of life of its own, a presence. Perhaps shadow is a better description. The idea of a silenced spring is both a 'doomsday' scenario and the contemplation of descent to a kind of purgatory. Carson has taken on the status of a prophet, creator of a new testament for our ecological times.

'It was pleasant to believe ... that much of Nature was forever beyond the tampering reach of man: he might level the forests and dam the streams, but the clouds and the rain and the wind were God's,' Carson wrote in 1958, at the outset of her project.

Having witnessed this belief system being challenged, she added:

> It seems time someone wrote of life in the light of the truth as it
> now appears to us ... As man approaches the 'new heaven and the
> new earth' – or the space-age universe, if you will, he must do so
> with humility rather than with arrogance. And along with humility,
> I think there is still a place for wonder.

Coming at the time they did, as the post-war boom years of the fifties
turned the corner into the much more uncertain sixties, Carson's
words were a sort of reality check for a developed world in serious
danger of becoming overdeveloped, which was threatening to get just
a little too far ahead of itself in the headlong rush to modernise, to
grow, to get wealthy, to live a little after the traumas of war and the
hardships of rationing. A Western world rapidly becoming bloated
on its own success. Birds – and more specifically the corpses of
birds – had become collateral damage of this unintentional war of
production: the nagging conscience telling that all was not well. If
something dawned on society at the start of the sixties, it was that
progress had natural limits.

Carson blew the whistle in the USA, and the reverberations were
felt globally. And while the world would not be the same place without
her contribution, she was not the only one – and nor was she the first –
to take up the cause. The role of the RSPB and its partners is a central
strand through this story in the British and Irish context.

By common consensus the sixties had promised much. In Britain,
Conservative Prime Minister Harold Macmillan had just finished
assuring the nation we'd 'never had it so good'. No one ever seriously
challenged him on that point, at least not in any way that received
much coverage. The lean years of the thirties and the brutal ones that
quickly followed were still fresh in the public mind. A lot of people of
my parents' generation were nostalgic about the baby boom years of
the rock 'n' rolling fifties. It isn't hard to see why.

The RSPB was then a small but reasonably influential organisation
with a handful of staff operating out of an office in the blitzed but
regenerating ruins of central London. It had fewer than 10,000
members. Much of its time and energy in the years up to the turn
of the decade had been devoted to bringing prosecutions against the
illegal trade in wild birds. They were good at it. In 40 of the cases
brought, only one had been lost. These were small but important

victories in the scheme of things that were soon to follow. Little can its personnel have suspected just how dramatically the organisation's priorities were to change as the decade turned, in step with the dizzyingly turbulent times.

By 1960, world population exceeded 3 billion people for the first time. Macmillan gave what at the time was an oft-quoted and far-reaching 'winds of change' speech in South Africa. It was a landmark moment in the empire's moves to 'decolonise' the world. A succession of countries would receive their independence from Britain in the coming years in the wake of his pledge. His words would have particular resonance for expatriate Britons, including my own family, who would hear them from the midst of one of these colonies – Uganda. My parents had emigrated there in 1957, from Ireland. My dad took up a government teaching post at a school near Kampala and my mum began to raise a family. Like migrant birds they had swapped the vagaries of the north-west European climate for sunny winters in the verdant, forested plateau of central East Africa. But instead of returning after one winter, they stayed for ten years, with an interlude of two years in Zanzibar in the early sixties. Those African years would help to shape and develop my parents' love of nature, and concern for the environment, and for people.

The issues that Rachel Carson was soon to describe may have seemed a far cry from the tropical paradise of the Ugandan uplands, but of course many of the birds affected by developments in Europe are shared by both continents. *Silent Spring* was among the titles my parents received through their membership of a book club, the spines of which lined one of the walls of our family home in Scotland when they finally returned to Britain in the late sixties. I think it is from this that the words 'silent spring' were imprinted on my impressionable young mind.

The early sixties also witnessed rapid change across the Atlantic. The youthful John F. Kennedy scraped home in the US presidential elections at the turn of the decade. He was said to embody a new spirit of youth and hope. My generation missed Kennedy, of course, but I knew families who still had statuettes to this iconic figure in their living rooms in west-central Scotland 20 years later. By common consent Kennedy had not sounded as convincing in the TV head-to-head as his opponent Richard Nixon, but it seemed that such issues of substance were no longer critical, in an increasingly televisual age. He sure looked the part, with his glamorous wife Jackie pregnant alongside him. The broad-smiling young couple caught the mood of the times, of youth and boom and optimism. The US and therefore the world economy had been buoyant since World War II, and ploughed millions of dollars into rebuilding Europe through the Marshall Plan. East and West were consolidating their polarity, with the finishing touches being put to the Berlin Wall.

The space race and the arms race were in full swing. In 1961 the USA put a chimpanzee into space, but it's arguable whether this counted as true parity with the Russians, who already had a higher primate – Yuri Gagarin – orbiting the Earth. Either way, this was the first time a primate of any kind had seen our beautiful planet from a distance beyond our atmosphere. Science and the 'white heat' of Western technology were pulling out all the stops to get to the moon before the opposition.

Eager for eye-witness accounts, I've quizzed a few people about this period. One retired couple gave me their recollections of the time. She spoke of her prevailing fear about nuclear war. He recalled fondly the Austin A40 his new-found prosperity had enabled him to buy.

On the pop culture front, and continuing the theme of new prosperity, footballers were battling to enhance their lot in life by breaking the glass ceiling of the maximum wage. The Beatles were on the rise, undergoing an image makeover from Brylcreme-quiffed rockers to mop-topped mods. With the USA waiting to be conquered, the Beatles and the Stones were two exports that would show the traffic wasn't all one way, where cultural imperialism was concerned. The people of Ayrshire, where my family would later relocate, were delighted when Elvis touched down at Prestwick Airport in spring 1960, in what turned out to be the only recorded sighting of E. Presley in the British Isles, witnessed by just a small crowd of privileged punters.

Architecture had entered a period known to some as the 'new brutalism'. Its central tenets and even this name might have been equally well applied to what was happening outside of towns, in the rural environment, where the agricultural revolution was progressing apace. The post-war crusade to ensure greater self-sufficiency in farm production was already under way, even though Britain's attempt to join Europe's Common Market on special terms was denied. But everything seemed to be swinging along quite nicely.

Environmentally, however, there was a problem. People had begun to notice that birds were dead, and dying. There is something peculiarly powerful about the image of a stricken bird, whether seen first-hand, photographed or simply described. The idea of dozens, even hundreds, of wild birds dying en masse was impossible to ignore, and was seized upon by the media. But it took a serious scientist with a gift for prose to pull together the evidence, the case, and present it in a readable narrative for the world. The stage was set for Rachel Carson. Throughout an intensive period of several years she had been amassing and arranging her evidence.

Silent Spring was first published in the USA in the autumn of 1962. Like most things American, it exported its message and had therefore already made a substantial impact beyond those shores, and in the UK and Europe, before its later publication by Hamish Hamilton in London in 1963.

The collateral damage from the new wave of synthetic insecticides that Carson described was being felt on a much wider scale in the USA than in other countries. But in Britain the conservation community, and within it the RSPB, was well aware of significant problems. They had already engineered political action to address these issues before *Silent Spring* landed, and in fact even before its publication in the States. The cause of conservation had already lurched from localised battles for the welfare and well-being of mistreated birds into an arena of widespread environmental contamination. It was no longer so much 'What are we doing to our birds?' as 'What are we doing to the planet?' And to ourselves in the process. The battle for the environment had already begun.

The Sixties

1961

I'm a rescuer, by instinct; a retriever of things. Some years ago our accounts department at the RSPB's Lodge headquarters had a clear-out, and I rescued a musty bundle of small booklets called *Bird Notes*. This was the title of a modest little black-and-white newsletter issued every couple of months by the RSPB until the mid-sixties. Digging them once again out of my archive in a back room at home, I found these provide a fascinating, blow-by-blow record of the pesticide saga unfolding at the time.

People had begun to find the corpses of birds, and birds in distress, in the fields of the farmed countryside around them, including right here, in this part of central south-eastern England. Take J. A. Baker's own chilling description of a stricken heron, most likely afflicted by poison as well as numbing cold:

> *December 24th*. Near the brook a heron lay in frozen stubble. Its wings were stuck to the ground by frost, and the mandibles of its bill were frozen together. Its eyes were open and living, the rest of it was dead. All was dead but the fear of man. As I approached I could see its whole body craving into flight. But it could not fly. I gave it peace, and saw the agonised sunlight of its eyes slowly heal with cloud.

Working with its partners in the British Trust for Ornithology (BTO) and the Game Research Association (GRA), the RSPB compiled and produced reports on incidents of what became known as bird-kill, from early 1960. It did the same again early the next year. If two years of data constitute a pattern, the bird death rate could already be said to be mounting. At least 260 incidents were reported in 1961, four times as many as the previous year. Around 40 different wild bird species were affected, along with mammals and domestic pigeons.

The state of the victims would usually leave a profound impression on the finder. 'Birds that were dying were often reported as standing about shivering,' *Bird Notes* reports. 'Others were described as "flapping around and gasping", "floundering about", "overbalancing".' All the birds seen in these conditions died. Other birds vomited coloured substances. Many were seen crashing to the ground. The symptoms clearly indicated death by poisoning.

The RSPB paid for analysis of some of the corpses, as many as could be afforded, but the cost of forensic laboratory time and expertise was prohibitive. The conclusions were clear and unanimous on the causes of death: poisoning.

Naturalists expressed particular concern about the poisoning of predatory birds and mammals that had consumed seed-eating species. Not that bigger birds and mammals have higher intrinsic value, but simply that this hinted strongly that the poisons were persisting in the food chain, passing from one organism to another. The RSPB spoke for all naturalists when it said: 'The presence of hawks and owls and wild and domestic animals such as cats and dogs amongst the kills gives some idea of the side effects of these poisons.'

The RSPB hosted a press conference to launch a damning report. Lord Hurcomb, who chaired the RSPB Council of trustees at that time, stated that the organisation believed most manufacturers of the chemicals and those involved in their use took a responsible view. He was less forgiving of the authorities. He declared that they had 'long been reluctant to admit these chemicals caused damage'.

The local and national press weren't slow to pick up on the story. The normally conservative broadsheet *Daily Telegraph* ran the emotive headline 'Birds slaughtered and the farm', and devoted an editorial to the story. *The Times* carried a rather sobering leader column:

No one denies that these chemical poisons have been valuable to farmers, but even they must be disturbed at what is happening. We know far too little about the balance of life to be able to guess what the effect of wholesale destruction of many species will be – but it might be both serious and unexpected. There is urgent need for a study of the whole problem, including the character of these poisons and the condition of their use, before the English countryside suffers an immeasurable impoverishment.

With public opinion informed, and armed with the data provided by concerned individuals such as 'farmers, gamekeepers, schoolkeepers and housewives', the joint committee of the three campaigning organisations submitted its findings to government.

The political response was immediate. In July 1961 the Minister for Agriculture, Fisheries and Food announced that three of the chemicals linked to bird deaths – named (like true sci-fi baddies) aldrin, dieldrin and heptachlor – were no longer to be used by farmers in treating grain that would be sown in springtime.

There remained a loophole, however. All three of the restricted chemicals could still be used in autumn and winter. This would be permissible if there was thought to be a threat to crops from an insect called the Wheat Bulb Fly. The new law would come into effect from the start of 1962, so progress of a kind was already being made in Britain while Rachel Carson was writing feverishly, with US publication of *Silent Spring* still six months away.

Although the *Telegraph* called it a 'major triumph ... scored by the wild life preservationists', there was disappointment in the conservation community that government had stopped short of an outright ban. The RSPB and its partners made clear their concern that the ban was voluntary. It was also noted that the ministry's labs, which would be expected to continue to investigate these incidents of chemical fallout, were badly under-resourced.

The same was said to be true of the government's own Nature Conservancy, which was expected to keep tabs on the longer-term effects of the toxins. The delayed effects of the poisons would be far less visible than the sudden and dramatic mass die-offs of wildlife that had set alarm bells off in the first place, and which made such compelling and visually arresting news.

'It is really rather ludicrous that only about half a dozen people are set aside to study a problem which is affecting the whole countryside,' lamented the RSPB's new chief Peter Conder. It was abundantly clear to Conder and to others that the effects of these toxins would not all be immediate and apparent. There had already been accounts of birds dying at least nine months after an orchard had been sprayed with the substances that killed them.

The RSPB also expressed concern that government had left out of the regulations some of the other chlorinated hydrocarbons, as they are known. These included DDT, lindane, endrin and methoxychlor. These substances, the RSPB noted presciently, 'are also dangerous, more particularly perhaps in their long term effects'.

1962

Pesticides weren't the only threat. 'Birds have many enemies; they still have too few friends,' the RSPB said. These enemies included 'bird-catchers who still carry out their illegal work with net and trap and bird-lime'.

RSPB members at the time were entitled to 'wear the tie or badge of the Society and avail yourself of its publications'. Member subscriptions were helping the RSPB to 'continue to track down and to expose and prosecute the small but active gang of unscrupulous lawbreakers who pillage birds' eggs to gloat over them privately in their cabinets'.

An initiative called the Common Birds Census was just being launched, a survey that aimed to provide a measure of changes in common bird numbers, year after year. 'Nobody gave it much of a chance,' *Bird Notes* would recall, several years later. 'It was thought to be too time-consuming, too dull and unexciting. Who wants to wander across the same tract of country a dozen times a season, year after year, painstakingly noting down the bread-and-butter birds?' Happily, 400 or so volunteers were happy to do the legwork. The system they set up would become the envy of conservationists in other European countries.

In the autumn of 1962, the RSPB called once again on its supporters and all naturalists to 'remain on the alert for kills of birds and mammals throughout the coming year'. Details were to be 'sent promptly' to the Society's Lodge headquarters, the slightly shabby but with room-to-grow country house and estate to which it had recently relocated, 50 miles north of London. It stands among pines, oaks and birches on a low promontory of greensand ridge elevated above the agricultural plains that dominate the landscape. With the ensuing mailbag began the lurch for the RSPB and for the budding conservation movement as a whole into environmentalism in its widest sense.

The greatly respected *British Medical Journal* ran a lengthy review of the pesticides situation, based on the evidence provided by the conservationists' reports. It concluded that the problem was urgent and in need of further scientific enquiry.

New regulations were in place, but soon afterwards, with evidence continuing to mount, the RSPB began to call even more strenuously for a complete ban on the three main chemicals proving directly lethal to wildlife. 'It appears', railed Peter Conder in *Bird Notes*, 'rather ridiculous to suppose that chemicals ... which kill large quantities of birds in spring are innocuous in autumn.'

Macmillan's government could ill afford to call this wrong. It lost a sequence of spring by-elections, and in the summer months the Prime Minister carried out a cull of ministers in what became known as the 'night of the long knives' – an attempt to revitalise the Cabinet and preserve his leadership. It bought him just over a year.

The ground was prepared for *Silent Spring*. Despite the events that preceded it, it took Rachel Carson's book to bring home the full extent of the issues involved, and raise widespread public awareness on both sides of the Atlantic, and even beyond. That it had been able to do so in the context of the time in which it was created says much about the extent of the problems it described, and the insight and persuasiveness of its creator. There was a great deal going on in the world to distract the mass media from the problems of mere farm chemicals and wildlife.

Vested interests in the USA 'tried to dismiss it as the emotional outburst of a sentimental woman', in the RSPB's words. Carson was subjected to campaigns of ridicule by pesticide manufacturers. In the face of this she remained stoic and resolute.

The bright new dawn of the turn of the decade had transformed rapidly into very choppy waters for the new US President, and for his counterparts overseas. The Cuban Missile Crisis had brought the planet perhaps as close to the brink of nuclear war as it has ever come. The world held its breath for a week late in the year as the brinkmanship was played out between the USA and Russia. To heighten the gloom Marilyn Monroe – poster girl of Hollywood and fashion – was found dead in her Los Angeles apartment, amid conspiratorial allegations of high-level political involvement. The thalidomide story broke, undermining trust in scientific progress. All of this and more formed the noisy backdrop against which the *Silent Spring* story would have to compete for ear-time. That it did so, and so successfully, seems all the more remarkable, in hindsight.

Also significantly, not least for my own family, Uganda gained its independence from the British Empire. For now life remained stable there, in that verdant equatorial Eden that Churchill had called 'the pearl of Africa'. In South Africa, meanwhile, an activist called Nelson

Mandela was sentenced to five years' imprisonment, later extended to life. Back in London that winter, a Dickensian 'pea-souper' smog descended, killing dozens of people.

1963

Silent Spring year would be a difficult one to follow for headlines, but 1963, as things turned out, was hardly any less eventful. With my parents moving their young brood to Zanzibar, where my dad had taken up another teaching job, the British Isles was in the grip of the cruellest winter in living memory. With much of the country ice- and snow-bound from the previous Christmas until March, the toll being taken on an already beleaguered wild bird population was by anyone's definition calamitous. All across the country birds were starving; freezing solid where they stood, or roosted, or fell. In these days before the widespread feeding of garden birds, there was little that many people could do to intervene.

A conference was held in Cambridge in the spring, on birds of prey. It brought together naturalists and falconers with farmers, landowners, hunters, pigeon keepers and gamekeepers, with representatives from the media and from abroad. In his 'reflections' on the conference, General Secretary of the British Falconers Club Michael Woodford noted the significance of the moment: 'Coming so soon after the publication of Rachel Carson's *Silent Spring*, this conference was particularly timely.'

'Delegates,' he went on, 'all of whom must have known or suspected that something is wrong, were plainly shocked to discover just how bad the situation is.'

The conference united falconers and conservationists in a common cause. Traditional disputes were put aside as 'the enormity and seriousness of the problem confronting us' began to sink in. Conflicts around egg collecting and illegal shooting and trapping and even the use of poisoned baits, as well as young birds being taken from the nest for captive rearing, began to seem 'insignificant compared with the slaughter being occasioned by the use of toxic chemicals on the land'.

Delegates were asking questions that the assembled experts from different walks of life between them could not answer. Could a bird that had been rendered infertile by ingesting these toxins eventually metabolise them, and become fertile again, assuming no more toxin was consumed? At this stage in the escalating crisis no one could say with any degree of certainty. The issue wasn't confined to the UK and

USA, where Ospreys and Bald Eagles were known to have suffered. A worrying absence of birds of prey was being reported from other countries.

The conference concluded by warning that continuance of present trends would lead to extinctions. In little more than a decade, the Sparrowhawk had all but disappeared from large areas of the lowland arable countryside. The Kestrel wasn't far behind. With these pressures, it had become virtually impossible to get a licence to take young birds of prey from nests in the wild for falconry purposes, still possible under the law until this time.

There was at least some heartening news to report. The RSPB, backed up by the widespread public concern that it was able to harness, persuaded government to give full protection to the nests of a long list of bird species excluded from the 1954 Protection of Birds Act: Blackbird, Chaffinch, Coot, Greenfinch, Black-headed Gull, Hedge Sparrow, Linnet, Moorhen, Robin, Skylark, Mistle Thrush, Song Thrush and Wren. Alongside the pesticides crisis, the severe winter had engendered intense public sympathy for the hardships being faced by birds. A second wave of compassion had swept the nation.

The RSPB continued to call upon the public to send in evidence of poisoning. The Society was by now also 'anxious to have information about lack of nesting success in circumstances which suggest that toxic chemicals have been the cause'. Birds living in and around gardens had begun to make up a growing proportion of these fatalities. Nests containing the corpses of nestlings were being reported, with parent birds sometimes dead on the nest.

The RSPB was critical of the advice on garden chemicals being issued by government. 'It is astonishing to find that the Ministry of Agriculture, Fisheries and Food has just published a booklet *Chemicals for the Gardener*, which purports to be a list of chemicals which can be safely used ...' The RSPB called on the ministry to withdraw the booklet immediately. The minister asked his advisory committee to look into it. The advisory committee then asked the RSPB for its evidence, and went off to deliberate.

I experienced an eerie echo of the 'bird-kill' era one morning recently, at The Lodge, when I got to work. I found several dead birds, of different species, close together in a grisly little gathering, in varying states of decomposition, on the reserve. Several conversations later, I had established the source. Even today, the RSPB receives dead birds in the post, neatly wrapped up (in most cases) and despatched to The Lodge by a vigilant public. The birds I found had been received in recent days by the enquiries department and left outside for later disposal. This made it all the easier to imagine the scene here 50 years ago, when rubber gloves would be issued to staff in the mail room at the RSPB, and parcel after macabre parcel would arrive in the post, full of bird corpses of different species, to be opened, logged, examined.

Since the previous death toll had been calculated and submitted in a report, 357 bodies of 74 species were sent in. There was no laboratory at The Lodge, then or now. Analysis was performed by a London firm of specialists and by the government chemist. New patterns were emerging. 'It would seem that more and more of the land and even the water courses have been poisoned.'

It was becoming more difficult to identify specific incidents against this overall backdrop of contamination. The birds were dead, the precise reasons were harder to pinpoint. A growing proportion of water birds, insect-eating birds and birds of prey were now numbered among the body count.

The RSPB itself was evolving apace under new chief Peter Conder, a man with an intriguing background. He had looked set for a lucrative career in the family advertising firm when World War II broke out in Europe. He was posted to France, armed like his comrades with weapons designed for World War I. With the Allies in retreat within a year, Conder's regiment didn't make it to Dunkirk, where rescue vessels were waiting. He was taken prisoner, among the troops who would face the 200-mile march under heavy guard through Belgium and the Netherlands to Germany, and later Poland, and a succession of prison camps. His five years in captivity, about which he almost never spoke, may have been traumatic in places but they were not entirely wasted. He used the time to nurture the interest in birds he had developed at school.

'I always kept records,' he would recall of the prison camps 12 years later when he finally stepped down as director. 'I turned books upside down and wrote between the lines, on toilet paper, or old cash books after I had rubbed out all the figures. I remember one camp in central Germany that was wonderful for migrating birds bound for north-east Russia.'

The surroundings were grim, and he made his observations and notes from vantage points on slag heaps. The freedom and beauty of the passing birds offered some form of release, some hope to hang on to. Conder was later moved to a camp in the south. 'An old officers' barracks,' he recalled, 'with hills, lots of trees and a river.' Here he became familiar with new species. 'We had icterine warblers, black redstarts, and many others like that.'

He became most attached to the Goldfinch, and made exhaustive notes on the comings and goings of these birds, on one occasion for 13 hours at a stretch. A pair nested just outside the barrack block. Conder's strange habits and note-taking did not pass unremarked, and twice he was hauled in for questioning by the camp commandant. Fortunately, he was allowed to keep his dog-eared notes, and this despite the fact that he used his status as resident ornithologist to act as lookout and decoy while some of his mates dug a tunnel.

Although his role as eyes and ears relieved him of tunnelling duties, he was included among the group who finally made a bid for life beyond the barbed-wire fence. He now found himself free as a bird, free as one of his cherished Goldfinches. This new-found sense of liberation lasted for all of an hour before he was rounded up with the others and marched back to camp. Birdwatching studies were curtailed for ten days while he brooded – like Steve McQueen's Captain Hilts, in *The Great Escape* – in solitary confinement: the cooler.

In camp he befriended two other bird-lovers, George Waterston and John Buxton. Waterston was invalided out of his prison camp and allowed to return to Scotland. He later became a leading figure in the RSPB and conservation movement. Buxton was studying Redstarts from his prison, and later published a celebrated book on the species, based on his meticulous studies of the birds breeding in and around the camp.

With the end of war and liberation, Conder returned to the London office of the family advertising business. It is impossible to imagine the frame of mind he must have been in. He allowed himself to be trapped there for just ten days before handing in his notice. 'It came as a bit of a shock to my pa,' he would later reflect, 'but I decided to take the risk and get out.'

He had given up a steady job at a time when these were hard to come by in a nation picking up the pieces after five years of war. He was contemplating a course of study when his old prison mate John Buxton got in touch. There was a job going as Warden on the uninhabited, tiny bird island of Skokholm, off the coast of Wales. Conder didn't hesitate, and ended up staying there for seven years.

'He was friendly to everyone who called,' one visitor remembered, 'although you got the impression he was far happier with birds than people.' He described himself as a loner, but returned to the London office life in 1955 when he became Assistant Secretary of the RSPB. His experience of the advertising business had already been a real asset. Once in the RSPB Director's chair, he began the task of welding together the team of experts needed to meet the challenges ahead for conservation. As an early task of modernisation he established and advertised the new post of Biologist, with a starting salary of £1,000 per year.

What remained of his wartime bird notes – and he had lost heart-breaking volumes of these – he later turned into a scientific paper on the inner world of the Goldfinch. This was published much later in the journal *Ibis*.

In the summer, the government's advisers at last shared their findings. The recommendation was for the use of the persistent toxins to be curtailed, and for the most noxious to be withdrawn from circulation, other than in certain very limited circumstances. It was the outcome the RSPB and others had been seeking. It was seen by the conservation community as an important step towards the elimination of all the persistent baddies – the chlorinated hydrocarbons – although they noted ruefully that the withdrawal would not be complete until 1965.

Some species were already in danger of extinction, and could ill afford another year of exposure to these threats. Nobody knew how long it would take for the disappearance of toxins already accumulated. Until the toxins were gone, territory-holding birds might continue to attempt to breed, and fail each time, bringing local extinction. The Society promised to maintain the utmost vigilance and called on the public to continue to do likewise, and to keep the corpses coming.

The end of the year brought a change of political leadership at the top. Harold Macmillan resigned as Prime Minister, on grounds of ill health. His government was by this time enmeshed in the scandal surrounding his Minister for War, John Profumo. An old-fashioned establishment figure was called forward to help restore some dignity to proceedings. And conservation could hardly have asked for a politician more sympathetic to the cause of birds than Sir Alec Douglas-Home, brother of Lord Home of the Hirsel, author of the autobiographical *Bird Man*. Sir Alec replaced Macmillan as leader of the Conservative Party, and assumed the mantle of Prime Minister.

On the other side of the Atlantic, and notwithstanding the grave concerns being felt at home, it was clear to most people that birds had been dying on a far greater scale in the USA than here, as might have been expected of a nation operating on the scale of a continent. Britons were also startled by the huge and disproportionate and even ruthless scale of the chemical use there, in the face of public protest.

By the time *Silent Spring* was published in Britain, late in 1963, Lord Shackleton was well placed in the book's guest introduction to speak of the impact it had already made, and what was already understood about the issue here. Birds higher up the food chain were starting to show worrying declines, although the sub-lethal effects on their fertility were yet to be established. There were also nods to the controversy *Silent Spring* had caused in the States. Julian Huxley, who contributed the short preface, was also in a position to note its impact. Huxley had a long track record as an environmental protectionist. He had headed a committee set up soon after the war to draw up plans for nature conservation in England and Wales, out of which the government's own Nature Conservancy was formed.

He summed up his views neatly and powerfully: 'Mass chemical control, besides being fostered by the profit motive, is another symptom of our exaggeratedly technological and quantitative approach.' The same might have been said of any aspect of human life or land use. It would be another year, for example, before the government's Forestry Commission, which had been up and running for nearly half a century, appointed a landscape adviser.

'It is,' Huxley pointed out, like all things, 'an ecological matter, and cannot be handed over entirely to the chemists.'

Shackleton and Huxley were anxious to be seen to be even-handed. One of the criticisms that had been quickly levelled by industry at Carson's approach was that her book lacked balance, and presented a very partisan case. The RSPB addressed this point in its own review of *Silent Spring*, and answered some of the author's critics:

> They have failed to fault her on the score of accuracy. Instead, they have concentrated on the charge that her book is emotional and one-sided, and, in particular that it contains no account of the benefits the use of toxic chemicals may bring. Many will feel that this is a pardonable omission, for the arguments so far, like the money and the big battalions, have largely been on one side. Nor have any of those with an interest in their use shown any great eagerness to stress possible drawbacks; in the USA, as in this country, it has

33

been largely left to the naturalists, hampered by lack of funds, to secure public recognition that the use of some chemicals could have harmful effects on wild life.

It needs to be stressed that Rachel Carson did acknowledge the potential and actual benefits of pest control technology, if used carefully and with due regard to the risks and side effects. What she spoke against was the culture of extermination. She was calling for a more holistic, controlled and balanced approach, for humility instead of arrogance.

She also spoke of the problems of pesticide use in domestic and other non-commercial situations. The new generation of synthetic insecticides causing such problems were largely a by-product of wartime and later research into chemical warfare agents. It was a lucrative industry with powerful vested interests. Between the end of the war and 1960, production of these substances had increased fivefold in the USA. Carson coined the term 'biocides'. She felt this more accurately described what these chemicals are – an assault on all life. The term didn't catch on more widely, but perhaps it should have done. For the chemicals didn't only kill the target pests, or even confine their effects to insects, as had now become all too clear.

Despite his other concerns around the space race, the arms race, the growing difficulty in Vietnam and with human rights on the streets of his major cities, and recognising the public mood and the political damage it could cause, President Kennedy had acted swiftly in responding to the publication of *Silent Spring*. He set up a special committee to report to him on all aspects of the problem. He spoke out unequivocally on the subject.

In May, after a lengthy enquiry, Kennedy's Science Advisory Committee published its pesticide report. According to the *New York Times*, 'It stressed that pesticides must be used to maintain the quality of the nation's food and health, but it warned against their indiscriminate use.' It called for more research into potential health hazards in the interim, and urged more judicious care in the use of pesticides in homes and in the field. Committee Chairman Dr Jerome B. Wiesner called the uncontrolled use of poisonous chemicals, including pesticides, 'potentially a much greater hazard' even than radioactive fallout.

The 1963 annual report of the Nature Conservancy issued in the autumn struck an optimistic note. 'It may now be said that conservation is at last visibly gathering impetus as a most important influence in national and international development,' it said. There had been what they'd nowadays call a paradigm shift. 'Now it is appreciated that in heavily populated countries nature conservation is not a synonym for protection; it nearly always entails management, which is the wise manipulation of the environment.' In other words, you couldn't just ring-fence a special place, exclude people, walk away and leave it to its own devices.

On the cultural front, the moral fabric of the British nation, still reeling from the Profumo affair and other spy scandals, had the publication of *Lady Chatterley's Lover*, and the filming of *Lolita*, to contend with. As birdsong diminished in the countryside, the signature tune for 1963 may have been a sombre, Bacharach-scripted love song by a flame-haired, mini-dress-wearing girl from Liverpool called Cilla Black. 'Anyone Who Had A Heart' topped the charts for several weeks and sold a million. It did even better than Dionne Warwick's original in the States. Dr Beeching announced the closure of more than 2,000 railway stations, to confirm the new supremacy of the motor car. In cinema, crowds were flocking to see the cheesily cheerful Cliff Richard and co, boarding that recommissioned double-decker bus for their wacky *Summer Holiday*. Implausible as it may seem, the RSPB would one day have a double-decker bus of its own.

And while birdsong may have been diminishing in the countryside and suburban gardens, people were discovering new, high-tech ways to enjoy it. This apology appeared alongside the regular updates on toxic chemicals being routinely issued by the RSPB: 'The series of bird-song records which the RSPB has produced jointly with the Dutch Bird-Protection Society continues to be in great demand, and we must apologise to members and others that the demand has more than once outrun the supply.' Interest in birds and birdsong, and scope for the public to enjoy them, even if only indirectly, was entering a new phase. By the end of the year the RSPB's membership had topped 20,000. It had doubled since 1960, and the start of the 'toxics war'.

And anyone present in the era hardly needs reminding that on 22 November President Kennedy was shot dead. For some months afterwards the political world reeled from this news.

1964

Just before sunset on a spring evening, 14 April 1964, in the town of Silver Spring, Maryland, Rachel Carson died. Barely a year had passed since publication of *Silent Spring* in Britain. Her death came as a shock to most people, including, it is recorded by biographer Linda Lear, many of her friends. 'Most were surprised, having no idea she had been seriously ill.' She was 56.

In fact she had been ill with cancer for several years, all through the research and writing of the book that would ensure her place in history. Reporting on her death, the *New York Times* carried an affectionate portrait. 'In manner, Miss Carson was a small, solemn-looking woman with the steady forthright gaze of a type that is sometimes common to thoughtful children who prefer to listen rather than to talk. She was politely friendly but reserved and was not given to quick smiles or to encouraging conversation even with her fans ... She was a rather solitary child. She never married.'

Prince Philip is said to have brought copies of *Silent Spring* back from a trip to the USA, to distribute to influential friends. He had a large wreath of red and white flowers delivered to the funeral. Presiding, the Reverend Duncan Howlett spoke of the 'strength, the simplicity and the serenity that marked her character', and of the 'extraordinary depth of insight and high poetic quality that marked her published writings'.

In early spring the RSPB spoke of the growing importance of securing what were then conceived as 'sanctuaries', and nowadays called nature reserves, in the face of mounting pressure from building programmes for roads and housing, and other development: 'It is essential that some thought be given to the setting aside of areas where our rich heritage of birds, and wild life generally, can live and breed in security for all time.'

Disturbingly, traces of biocides were now being discovered in the eggs of wild birds. Ten years had passed since the celebrated return of the once extinct Osprey to breed in Britain. As the nascent population of these iconic raptors in the Scottish Highlands was starting to spread and settle in new sites, a wave of publicity and dismay greeted the news that these strictly fish-eating birds were also being affected by toxins.

An Osprey egg from one of the precious pairs was taken under licence from a nest in Inverness-shire for laboratory analysis. The report on its contents read like a sinister roll call of dread toxins:

DDT, DDE and TDE. Toxin effects were becoming especially evident in larger birds like these, further along the food chain. Biocides were passing from organism to organism and accumulating in ever-greater concentrations in the tissues of each. The effects were sub-lethal, or non-deadly, but were found to be affecting the birds' ability to reproduce. This was exemplified by a peculiar case involving Peregrine Falcons and Kestrels, reported by renowned authority Derek Ratcliffe. He had been keeping a close eye on a Peregrine nest in south-west Scotland, as part of an ongoing study. It was a nest with four eggs, and one was taken, again under licence, for analysis. The Peregrines lost their remaining eggs, which appeared to have broken, or failed to hatch and been inadvertently broken by the parent birds, as was often the case when these toxins were present. A pair of Kestrels moved in and laid eggs in the same nest, but the larger Peregrines hadn't moved away. They ousted the Kestrels and resumed nest duties. Bizarrely, they went on to rear the four Kestrel chicks as their own.

Meanwhile, the RSPB patiently awaited the results of the inquiry by the Ministry of Agriculture's advisory committee. But there were changes afoot even in advance of those findings. Plant Protection's *Guide to Farmers 1964* had dropped any mention of aldrin, dieldrin and heptachlor. The RSPB called the development 'interesting'. It was reported that the leading agricultural supplier of the day had also dropped the products from its list.

The new mood of concern for afflicted birds was creeping into mainstream culture. The film *Mary Poppins* was released, featuring the song 'Feed the Birds'. An aged woman offers breadcrumbs for sale to passers-by, for tuppence a bag, from the steps of St Paul's Cathedral in London. The song was said to be Walt Disney's favourite, and the first one written about giving charity in such a way. The old lady might even be thought of as symbolic of conservation itself: helping people, helping birds. She certainly struck a chord with the nation, just a year after the arctic winter conditions that had caused such widespread hardship and suffering to birds and vulnerable people, as well as with Disney himself. He was said to ask lead actor Dick van Dyke to play this tune on the piano, at the end of each working week during shooting of the film. And he was heard to murmur, absently, 'That's what it's all about.'

After more than a decade of Conservative rule, Britain had a new government, with the narrow election of Harold Wilson and Labour to pick up the vexed question of pesticides. Wilson would inherit the task of tackling growing unease about what we were doing to the environment, among his portfolio of challenges in the developing decade. Edward Heath became leader of the Conservative Party. With the help of the public, the RSPB was continuing to ensure that the authorities were well provided with detailed reports.

The RSPB continued to expand. The first steps were being taken in the creation of the national network of nature clubs for young people. At the end of the year, the Society's Education Officer put the word out for volunteers to help young people learn more about birds, and to take them out in the field in different parts of the country. A tentative enquiry was also made to find volunteer teachers who might lead adult courses in ornithology.

The RSPB wasn't the only organisation producing birdsong recordings for sale in the growing market. The first long-playing record of bird calls, *A Tapestry of British Bird Song*, was released by the plummy nature enthusiast Victor C. Lewis. I became the proud owner of this record about 20 years ago when I turned up a copy in an antique shop. I have taken huge pleasure and amusement over the years in playing extracts of it to friends – not just of the bird songs themselves, but of the wonderful linking introductions and descriptions provided by Mr Lewis.

He speaks, as might be expected, given the era of its production, with a marvellous old-school BBC voice. He has obviously been coached well in the art of varying pitch and intonation, such that his voice rises and falls almost randomly, as though attempting to follow the modulations of the birds themselves. Or perhaps this was done later, in the mixing studio. It's a little difficult to capture on paper, but an example of the style may work best if presented as a little poem:

> The evening chorus
> is now in progress,
> and is led
> by one of our outstanding singers,
> whose performance
> is regarded by many
> as unique.
> Rich in quality,
> vigorous in delivery,
> it can only belong…
> to the Nightingale,
> the classic European songstah…
> [cue Nightingale]

I was pleased to discover a review of this seminal album in *Bird Notes*, praising the quality of the recordings. 'Some of them, such as those of woodlark and marsh warbler, are quite beautiful,' the reviewer reports. But he also warns readers of the album's limitations as an identification guide, 'because of the difficulties of picking out any one recording'.

Mr Lewis's voice isn't much to his liking. 'I feel that the commentator spoils the atmosphere of the recording and his script-reading voice becomes increasingly irritating.'

But the review is, on the whole, positive, and recommends the product. 'If,' the reviewer concludes, 'after a tiring day at the office, you wish to listen and relax for nearly an hour with bird songs and calls and do not mind a commentator introducing each species you should certainly buy this record.'

Popular as birdsong records might have been becoming, equivocal reviews like this made it even more unlikely they would threaten the chart toppers of the day. 'Mr Tambourine Man' by The Byrds was a big hit on both sides of the Atlantic and would be a signature tune of the times, capturing the folk-rock, flower-power mood that many would later associate with the year to come. Mary Quant was revolutionising British fashion tastes along mod-ish lines. The Beatles had a 'Ticket To Ride', and along with the Rolling Stones had a ticket to take America by storm. Boxer Cassius Clay, not yet reinvented as Muhammad Ali, was floating like a butterfly and stinging like a bee, one unencumbered by agrochemical fallout presumably, as he reduced Sonny Liston to tears on his way to the undisputed world heavyweight boxing crown.

1965

Dorothy Freeman honoured her friend Rachel Carson's wishes when she scattered the author's ashes to the wind on the rocky sea coast at Newagen, Maine. As she did so, she read some lines of poetry from T. S. Eliot's *Four Quartets*, his haunting meditation on time, which he considered his masterpiece, and for which he was awarded the Nobel Prize for Literature. Carson was a marine biologist by training, and had written three books about the sea in the fifties. In her own words: 'All at last return to the sea – to Oceanus, the ocean river, like the ever-flowing stream of time, the beginning and the end.'

The US-born Eliot died in early January, in his adoptive England.

* * *

The situation was deteriorating rapidly on the biocides front. Poisoned birds were being reported from new and unexpected places, habitats of all kinds. Carson would not have been surprised that the effects were now also being felt by and identified in birds at the coast and at sea. Organochlorine residues were evidently filtering from farm fields into rivers and on into the marine environment.

The volume of dead birds being received from members of the public was now so great that tough decisions had to be taken about which species to prioritise for analysis. By necessity, the ministry continued to be preoccupied with incidents of mass die-off, rather than the long-term effects. Of 127 bird-of-prey eggs examined at this time, all but four contained toxic residues.

Conservationists were by now almost entirely preoccupied with the pesticide threat. But the other – and what seem now relatively trivial – threats hadn't gone away, at the minor, local level. By way of an example of a widespread phenomenon, rarely resulting in court action, it was reported how in Scotland two teenagers had been caught killing Song Thrushes. The Sheriff told the boys to mend their ways, and to join the Junior Bird Recorders Club. The boys duly signed up.

The age of liberalisation was reflected within the evolving Society. The Junior Bird Recorders Club was in the process of being what they would nowadays call rebranded. It re-emerged as the more hip and contemporary Young Ornithologists' Club, or YOC. 'Many teenagers, quite understandably, objected to being called "junior",' explained the parent body RSPB, 'and "bird recording" is only one aspect of the club's many activities.'

Children under ten years old were to be admitted for the first time. This would put an end to the disappointment many (not to mention their parents) had been experiencing for years after being told they were not yet old enough to get involved. The member magazine *Junior Bird Recorder* was relaunched as *Bird Life*, a name it retains to this day.

Not so liberal as yet, the RSPB advertised the 'post of Warden (single man) for The Lodge, Sandy'. It wasn't spelt out exactly why the post-holder would need to be male, and single, but perhaps the location was considered too remote or basic for a wife or partner to tolerate. A Swan duly took up residence at The Lodge for several years: a – presumably single – man called Jack Swan landed the advertised job.

Spring 1965 marked an important anniversary. It was 75 years since the founding of the RSPB. A celebration dinner was held in London.

From the government side, the toast was provided by Lord Shackleton, by this time Minister for Defence, Royal Air Force.

'When one looks at the enormous powers there are today to alter irreversibly our environment,' he told the assembled audience, 'a Society such as yours is serving a wider purpose than bird protection; it is helping to teach a certain amount of humility and it is not only the layman but even certain scientists who need to learn humility.'

He returned to the theme of toxic chemicals: 'I wish someone would stop and listen to ornithologists, who have been nearly driven mad by people who ought to have taken their responsibilities seriously and have failed to do so.'

Responding, RSPB President Lord Hurcomb reflected on how the mission of the RSPB and conservation had changed since the Society's formation. He spoke of the realisation that it is not enough simply to protect a species, such as by preventing it from being hunted: 'We have, therefore, taken a very much wider view but nevertheless we are not afraid of keeping the word "protection" in our title,' he said.

The toast to 'the birds' was made by comedian and raconteur Frank Muir. A photograph in *Bird Notes* shows the three main speakers enjoying a glass of fizz and a smoke. While it does look as though the Society formed three-quarters of a century earlier by a 'band of women' (as *Bird Notes* describes them, and from which 'we had come a long way') had by now turned into something of a gentlemen's club, it is worth noting that actor and comedian Joyce Grenfell had been approached first to do the honours. She sent a note of apology, explaining that she was unavoidably detained by work, perhaps on her forthcoming film. She was well known for her roles in the St Trinian's movies, set in a school full of misbehaving boarding schoolgirls. A tradition linking ornithology and comics/comic actors was being established, which must be left for others better qualified to analyse ...

It wasn't just the youngsters who were busy recording the birds around them. The grown-ups were starting to coordinate their efforts better too. The RSPB began to issue advice to the lay birdwatcher about the potential value of their noted observations. Members were encouraged to make more careful and detailed notes, and to understand the value of repeating surveys to establish patterns over time – the longer the better, to allow for short-term natural fluctuations. All of this would be 'contributing something to the common store of knowledge'.

The RSPB launched *Birds* magazine, in the context of a greater number of publications providing what its predecessor *Bird Notes* offered. The new magazine would fulfil the demand for a more popular bird title: less specialist, less detailed. The passing of *Bird Notes* was of course painful for many, but the move appeared to encourage even greater loyalty among the membership. It retains the title to this day.

There was no shortage of people eager to see the now established and spruced-up headquarters and 50 acres of nature reserve and formal garden at The Lodge. The RSPB's membership had swelled to 29,000, with the new-look YOC boasting 10,000 young followers. Two Magpies were seen there in October – the first known records of the species for the reserve. It is not recorded whether anyone turned up to 'twitch' them, but it's a fairly safe bet that some people did. We take Magpies for granted now, but it's not difficult to imagine how impressive (not to mention lucky) a pair of Magpies must have looked to anyone who hadn't encountered the species before.

There was growing recognition of the importance of gardens as sanctuaries for wildlife in the context of an increasingly pressurised countryside. But of course many gardens were by this time subject to routine chemical dousing as well. To address this, the first leaflet was issued giving advice on garden chemicals. The RSPB also launched a project to collect information from the public on which berry-bearing plants were of most benefit to birds in a garden.

Conservation bodies continued to call for the voluntary ban on noxious pesticides to be made compulsory. Sheep dips were now under the spotlight. A number of proposals were put forward, including: compulsory surrender of all stocks of sheep dips containing organochlorine pesticides (which should not be dumped in rivers or the sea or used on land); a system to limit residues in food; more education for users of pesticides, among whom there was said to be 'widespread ignorance'; better labelling of toxic content in pesticides; and a legal requirement to keep records covering all persistent chemicals and the more lethal chemicals.

Autumn brought the second of what would become a series of study conferences aimed at future-gazing on the environment, entitled 'The Countryside in 1970'. It was of some small consolation that the number if not the severity of reported bird-kill incidents appeared at last to be lessening.

An RSPB publicity leaflet described oil pollution as 'this intolerable evil'. A new survey was launched, and by late in the year more than 200 volunteers had signed up to act as observers. More were needed, to ensure comprehensive coverage of the coastline. Volunteers were asked to spare an hour or two a fortnight to record incidents of oiling on beaches near where they lived. The results would be fed into an international monitoring effort. The timing was prescient. September brought the worst inshore oiling disaster yet to hit Britain. The German tanker *Seestern* haemorrhaged 1,700 tonnes of crude diesel oil into the Medway Estuary in Kent, washing its slick across the mouth of the river, a place where wildlife teems. Five thousand birds were oiled and killed, besides the less visible damage done to other marine animals and plants. The long-term damage could only be guessed at. In spite of this, the incident barely made the national press, in the new era of the Sunday colour supplement.

The music industry was providing plenty of material for the news as well as the showbiz pages. The US government rescinded all visas for British bands – mods and rockers alike – in an attempt to stem their malign influence. Mary Whitehouse set up the National Viewers' and Listeners' Association to keep tabs on the media's moral standards at home. The pirate station Radio Caroline set up operation just offshore to play the signature tunes of pop cultural rebellion.

1966

The flourishing Lodge nature reserve at this time extended to 50 acres around the house and gardens that accommodated a growing staff. It was then, as now, an idyllic place to work, if nature conservation is your passion. Almost a hundred nest-boxes had been installed, which not only helped certain species to nest, but also made easier the job of recording their attempts. A pair of Redstarts used one of these nest-boxes that spring, but when the nest was checked someone had the unpleasant task of reporting that the chicks were dead. The tiny corpses were duly packaged up and sent off for analysis. A similar fate had befallen a pair of Nuthatches which had also taken up residence in a nest-box.

Cuckoos were described at this time as locally 'very common'. Two young Cuckoos were found close to the house, one of them in a Dunnock's nest in the Victorian walled kitchen garden. This Cuckoo chick, bigger by the end than the nest on which it squatted hungrily, expectantly, duly earned a kind of fame and immortality. The film cameras were trained on it and it had a leading part in the latest RSPB film, *A Place for Birds*.

Cuckoos may have seemed prominent here but, where longer-term records had been kept, the picture didn't look quite so rosy for the species. It was even then being described as one of the most obviously declining birds in Eastern England, along with the Woodlark. With the young Cuckoos safely fledged, Joyce Grenfell made up for missing the earlier 75th anniversary celebrations when she came to officially launch that summer's Open Day at The Lodge.

If they had ever been in danger of forgetting, conservationists were quickly reminded that political change was a long game. Seven years after it was first proposed to politicians by the RSPB, the Protection of Birds Bill was introduced to the House of Lords. It sought to improve the 1954 act, to close some of the loopholes and strengthen the good bits. Year-round protection of Lapwing nests was one of its aims. The bill had reached the second reading stage in the Lords but there was little optimism that the Commons would be able to look at it. Sure enough, it ran aground due to lack of Parliamentary time.

Birds, with their often transnational life cycles, had long made it easy to argue that conservation is an international endeavour. By the mid-sixties, conservationists were taking increasingly bold steps to tackle problems across borders. The International Union for the Conservation of Nature (IUCN) met in Switzerland, and Peter Conder reported afterwards on the main issues discussed. He lamented the British government's 'lack of a strong conservation policy to ensure that there is some countryside left for us to enjoy', with the added pressure on rural areas now being felt in the fast-accelerating leisure age. On the question of pressure from developers, he re-emphasised the RSPB's position that 'planners should take ecological advice on landscape development at all levels'.

And on the threat posed by introduced species, which would develop into one of the most serious threats to native ecosystems in later years, he reported the difficulties faced by the conference in agreeing a policy. 'The division of opinion was so great (the Russians and Americans being very interested in the introduction of fur-bearing and sporting animals, respectively) that ultimately the meeting could only piously hope that the effects and side effects of any proposed introduction of plants or animals should be thoroughly investigated beforehand.'

Another increasingly important player, the International Council for Bird Preservation (ICBP), held its world conference in Cambridge. Delegates arrived from 28 nations, and agreed on the collective need to support conservation in developing countries, most of which did not yet have the wherewithal even to be represented at this gathering. Speakers described the often demoralising task of compiling the *Red Data Book* of the world's most endangered species, steadily increasing.

1967

There is something particularly hellish about the image of a bird coated in oil, wings spread but useless, eyes wide and desperate, accusing, full of fear, brought to earth, weighed down, drowning, choking, dying in our economic lifeblood. So too the image of bird corpses littering shorelines. It arouses something of the legacy of warfare on beaches, victims exposed, against an unseen but very real threat from somewhere out there.

A short clip of footage was posted recently on the internet showing a bird coated in oily sludge, like a figure dipped in thick, molten chocolate. It is unrecognisable – pathetic, even – as it feebly flicks its drooping wings, attempting escape. It is succumbing, falling, lying flat on the surface of the clinging goo; spread-eagled, almost cruciform. It is a powerful, sickening, emotive image – and it caused a minor outcry.

The incident was filmed on the Channel Island of Guernsey, closer to France than to England, in a disused quarry on a remote headland, surrounded by high fences with a padlocked gate. The quarry has a lake within its high walls: a lake of crude oil. It is the very same crude oil that spewed out of an oil tanker 45 years ago. It is a faintly surreal and eerie monument to an infamous disaster, a symbol of the lastingness of the damage it did, and of the collective feebleness of efforts to clear up.

Tragically, this nominal proportion of the total amount of oil spilled back then is still, to this day, killing birds and other life forms. They mistake the mirror-like, reflective surface for water, or a solid platform. Why, in the end, would they not? It snares them in an instant, killing them in minutes, leaving them preserved where they fall, ghostly outlines on the surface. The response to the footage has meant that the local authorities are now trying – again, they have tried before – to do something about this grisly death trap. They didn't create the mess, it just happened to them, and they were left to live with it. You can only wonder if the ship's owners, and the oil company that chartered it, still have this on their conscience, or ever did.

We can trace the origin of this contemporary scene to the spring of 1967, which began with what would become perhaps the iconic environmental disaster. The *Torrey Canyon* supertanker ran aground on Pollard's Rock, a reef that lies off the toe of south-west England, or Land's End as it is known. Its side badly gashed, the wounded ship began to bleed oil. Overnight, the spill created a 20-mile slick along the coastline of Devon and Cornwall as the first of the ship's 120,000 tons of crude oil cargo spewed into the churning sea. Acting quickly, the RSPB set up two teams to work with the RSPCA in both affected counties. The partner bodies set up rehabilitation centres for oiled birds at Dungeness nature reserve in Kent and at Minsmere in Suffolk.

A week later, on Easter Sunday, the ship split in two, and a further 30,000 tons of crude oil were discharged from the shattered hull. I wish I could say I shared my birth date with some more auspicious moment in the history of human endeavour, but I am sad to record that it is this one. The Royal Navy attended the stricken vessel, pumping huge quantities of solvents and emulsifying agents over the slick in an attempt to disperse it. With bank holiday crowds looking on from the normally scenic and always popular tourist headlands of Cornwall, the RAF then performed what must have looked like the re-enactment of a scene from the war at that time raging in Vietnam. Planes attempted to sink the floundering ship with bombs, a quarter of which missed. They then tried to set fire to the sheet of oil, first with kerosene, which didn't work, and then with napalm. That did. The sea caught fire and sent flames and black smoke heavenward in what must have seemed to onlookers like a vision of the apocalypse. The stink can only now be imagined. Even before the fires, the stench of the crude oil was said to be overpowering, and induced nausea in anyone venturing close.

As fate would have it our avuncular, pipe-sucking Prime Minister Harold Wilson was on holiday in the region, taking a train to Cornwall en route to the Scilly Isles. He had a ringside seat for the nightmarish events unfolding around the disaster. Ornithologists calculated that a minimum of 10,000 birds had been oiled. The real death toll was probably much higher. Just over half were treated, with a mere 500 surviving in the short term, and the rest perishing despite the desperate efforts of rescue volunteers.

At the final count, of 8,000 birds rounded up, little more than a hundred were released to the sea again. Sixty of these were fitted with leg rings, and 16 of these were later recovered, dead. It would cause much subsequent agonising over the value of attempting to rehabilitate oiled birds. Was it in fact more humane to put these stricken creatures out of their misery rather than prolong it in a well-intentioned but perhaps misguided attempt to retrieve them? It was clear that oiled birds soon chill and go into shock. They also swallow oil rapidly in their frantic efforts to clean their plumage. From these effects there is seldom any chance of recovery out at sea.

Silent Spring may have been the spark, but the *Torrey Canyon* oil spill changed the landscape of conservation in Britain. The images of the wreck dominated the front pages and the television news bulletins for days as the drama was played out to a shocked public. Shocking as the *Torrey Canyon* disaster may have been, and enduring in the collective memory, there was worse to come, and not long after. It wasn't the worst, but it was the most vivid. Greenpeace and Friends of the Earth were established in the UK not long after the *Torrey Canyon* debacle.

Interest in birds was now thought to be the country's fastest-growing hobby. Adverts for a new bird food called Swoop were starting to appear, as feeding garden birds grew in popularity. The new wave of enthusiasm for birds brought its own pressures, and guidance was by now being issued on how to avoid disturbing them. The RSPB launched an appeal to raise what in 1967 seemed the astronomical sum of £100,000, for nature reserve creation. It was the first such fundraising drive since 1953, following the great floods that had done so much damage in Eastern England that year.

RSPB chief Peter Conder warned of the prospect of a 'birdless world, too dreary a place to contemplate'. A man on trial for illegally trapping wild finches in the north of England pleaded that he was trying to save them. He told the bench: 'Wild birds are becoming so rare, dying from the use of insecticides, that it will soon be up to individual breeders to make the stocks up.' His plea seems to have been effective. Summing up, the magistrate told him: 'You are a bird lover and this was obviously not cruelty as in the majority of RSPCA cases. You did know you were doing wrong, but we are going to be lenient.' The man was fined £5 and about the same again in costs.

Fears about the world's 'population explosion' were by now starting to figure prominently in articles and the letters pages of Sunday newspapers. England was said to be at this time the most densely populated country in the world, with Britain's population increasing at the rate of 250,000 people per year. Author Paul Ehrlich was preparing his influential book *The Population Bomb*, published the following year. The mood of pessimism was hardly likely to be lightened by the economic woes of the country, and the ignominy of devaluation of the pound.

The loss of hedgerows from the countryside was being calculated. Half the hedges of Huntingdonshire alone had been ripped out. Voluntary safeguards to protect the best hedgerows were at best ineffectual. 'A threatened creature faces a serious risk of extinction during the course of investigations if it is insisted that any damage has to be proven with absolute certainty,' RSPB Chairman Stanley Cramp pointed out.

Something else happened at or around this year that would change the face of the British landscape. A new, unusually aggressive strain of Dutch elm disease arrived. It was traced to a delivery of Rock Elm logs from North America. It passed rapidly into living European Elm trees and began its silent spread, borne on beetles, through the widespread English Elm population that was once so tightly woven into the fabric of these islands. The fungus is still out there today, clinging to its beetle vectors, moving north.

There were some crumbs of comfort against the bleak backdrop. Protection had been secured for Lapwing nests. There would also be wider restrictions on the chemicals dieldrin and aldrin. The RSPB put the word out to the public that no more bodies of dead birds should be sent to The Lodge. Instead, these should be addressed to Ian Prestt (remember the name) at the Institute for Terrestrial Ecology (ITE), the government-funded Monks Wood research station near Huntingdon.

Members of the public were also asked to contact Dr Snow of the Bird Room at the British Museum (Natural History), also in need of freshly dead, undamaged specimens of birds. Not to put any pressure on the reader, of course, but they did add that 'this request is made to avoid the necessity of shooting birds'.

Despite its eco-tribulations, 1967 is fondly remembered for the first summer of love. 'All You Need is Love', the Beatles advised, and Procul Harum described somewhat more opaquely 'A Whiter Shade of Pale'. 'Are You Going to San Francisco?' was the question posed by Scott McKenzie, while it remained more likely that UK beatniks would be attending the Festival of the Flower Children at Woburn Abbey in August. As well as biocides, experimentation by the pharmaceutical industry also produced some of the products fuelling the turn on, tune in, drop out culture of the times – the amphetamines and barbiturates that arrived and became widely available to bohemian types from the early sixties.

In the autumn, an historic project was launched that would attempt to map all the breeding birds of Britain and Ireland. It followed a long period of debate among ornithologists about the feasibility of such an undertaking. Many influential voices considered it futile, and no one underestimated the scale of what was proposed. It would require the mobilisation of observers in all parts of the British Isles, and it would take around five years to build a reasonable picture of bird numbers and distribution. The structure of the project was formalised by the BTO, with the Irish Wildbird Conservancy leading for Ireland. It would take almost a decade for the results to be compiled and analysed, and the resulting maps to be published. But it would be worth it, for this systematic and painstaking process would provide the first comprehensive baseline data for all species across the countries. It would provide a yardstick against which bird numbers – and therefore the fate of the environment as a whole – could be reliably measured in years to come. What it wouldn't yet be able comprehensively to do would be reflect on how much had changed for each species – whether increases or declines had been experienced – but it would allow that to happen in future.

It was the biggest project of its kind ever attempted and would set an example that could be followed soon after in many other countries. Up to 15,000 observers provided the data, through 150 regional organisers, over five years starting in 1968 and ending in 1972. Books with maps showing distribution of birds in Europe had been produced before, but not with this level of detail underpinning them. This story resumes in 1976, when the task of amassing and compiling the data was due to be completed, and the atlas finally published.

The RSPB had 36,000 members by the end of the year, among them by now my own family. My mother was among the thousands of concerned citizens caught by the mood, and signed us up. The family had returned from Uganda in the spring, shortly after I was born. There were early signs of political instability there. My parents chose to relocate to Scotland, rather than return to Ireland, where the 'Troubles' were brewing. We set up home in Dunblane after a short spell in a caravan on the edge of Cornton, on the wide floodplain of the River Forth, Stirling, where my father had found a job teaching geography and maths. In one of a sequence of uncanny coincidences that would punctuate my life, I would one day return to live almost within sight of this field, as a student at the nearby university that was due to open its doors in the autumn. The capture and execution of revolutionary Che

Guevara in Bolivia gave students a new martyr and poster-boy with which to decorate the freshly painted walls of the new campus study bedrooms, modelled, they say, on a Swedish women's prison.

1968

In spring 2010 I was passing through Dunblane, a small but growing town (or a tiny city, if you consider its cathedral, where incidentally in spring 1968 I was christened) that guards a gap in the hills where the motorway ploughs north from central Scotland towards the Highlands. I had a notion to try to find our old family home there, although I could remember only the name of the street. I had a vague idea of it, from photographs. Not of the house itself, but of us kids in the garden, with maybe a hint of front door and garden as the backdrop. One photograph in particular lodged in my mind's eye – me as a toddler in the garden of this house, in a nappy, emerging from a tea chest marked 'Produce of Uganda', in a baby-blue home-knit jumper. I'd taken this one to primary school when the teacher asked the class to bring in photos of ourselves as babies. I had no conscious or coherent memory of the house, as we'd left there in 1970, when I was three years old. I remembered my dad talking about the nearby farm where we used to walk to pick up fresh milk.

So here I was again on a spring Sunday morning. All was quiet in the human world, but it was rowdy with birds. This is the time of day when birds are active, commuting between places of business. And the time of the week when there are even fewer people around than normal to disrupt them. I inched the car forward, peering at the row of century-old sandstone villas. None was obviously the one. Someone else was up; a man in a garden, watching me. He was tall and elderly, and supervising two small children, who were playing with a hose. I guess I may have looked a little suspicious, although he seemed friendly enough to stop and chat to.

I explained to him my mission. 'We used to live in this road, but I'm not sure which house,' I told him. 'What was the name?' he asked me. 'Oh, you wouldn't remember,' I replied. 'This was 40 or more years ago.' He looked undaunted. 'Jameson,' I offered. There was a broad smile, and instant recognition. 'Oh yes, I remember Kay!' he chuckled. 'I remember well!'

He proceeded to reel off the names of my brother and sisters, Kevin, Clare and Brigid. We used to play with his two children, whose own children were now right here, playing. As it turned out I remembered his name too. I remember my sisters talking about his daughter. Dr Crowther, family GP, now retired. He took me in to meet his wife. She had been best of pals with my mum. They insisted on taking me down to the old house. I was introduced to a slightly bewildered occupant, another face that looked familiar – who'd been in the house ever since we left, and who looked like he might be a little worried I'd found some loophole in the paperwork and come back to repossess it.

I had a cup of tea with the Crowthers, and a shoebox of photographs was produced. Sure enough there was a small, square, white-framed black and white picture of Kevin and Clare with the Crowther kids, at the farm, collecting the milk. It seems the farmer is still farming, I was pleased to hear, but he'd sold up this farm and moved on. The town/city had long since spread itself out across the sloping pastures. The photograph had been taken in 1968. Forty years at that moment didn't feel like such a long time.

It was a wrench for my family to leave this quiet corner of rural Perthshire, on the edge of the hills, when the time came. My dad found another job at a school on the fringes of greater Glasgow. I know Kevin was distraught to leave the woods behind. But one day both he and I would return to live nearby, first as students.

Back in 1968 there was an oil disaster close to our new home, released by a damaged oil tanker in the nearby Tay Estuary. There was thought to be a silver lining to this one, as the clean-up operation resulted in the discovery of some new treatment techniques. These just might improve the survival rate of oiled birds. Rescue workers experimented with using lard and sawdust rather than detergent. They tried other ways to minimise the stress to the birds, as handling and washing might compound the victims' shock, which would often be enough in itself to kill them. This would also be remembered as the year that huge reserves of oil were discovered in Arctic Alaska. Plans were made to lay an 800-mile pipeline linking the supplies of oil to the south.

Participants in Britain's oil pollution survey, which was soon to include the Jameson clan, were urged by the RSPB to keep up the good work. They were also asked, in addition to filling in the forms, to supply where possible the wing of any oiled birds found on the shore. We'd have to start wielding secateurs at the beach.

* * *

The new Protection of Birds Act was law from mid-January. It would give added protection to nesting Lapwings, restrict the sale of dead geese, and make it an offence to disturb some more of the less common birds when they were nesting. But the RSPB didn't get everything it wanted from the new revised act. It couldn't hope to. To have had any prospect of getting the thing through Parliament, compromises had to be made. On the downside, licences could still be issued to persons (considered responsible) for such activities as the taking of eggs for falconry and certain birds for captivity. The RSPB would now have to employ a specialist to help enforce the provisions of the act. This person would work with falconers and other bird keepers to try to stamp out illegal activities among their numbers. Richard Porter was appointed to this post of Technical Officer the following year.

A Wild Plant Protection Bill was also introduced in Parliament to protect rarer flora from being removed from the wild, reflecting mounting pressure on the survival of native wildflowers, and widespread plundering of uncommon species.

Spring brought little respite from the gloomy headlines of the year before. The so-called Prague Spring took place in the Czech capital, when Russian tanks rolled in to crush leader Dubček's attempts to create a more liberal brand of communism. The year is also synonymous with protest movements coming to a head. Martin Luther King was assassinated in April. The acrid smoke of revolution was in the air, with riots involving students and workers from Eastern Europe to Paris to Mexico. Civil rights and anti-war protests took place in the USA, and protestors took to the streets in England, Poland, Germany and Spain. Against this backdrop Louis Armstrong sang with unintended irony 'What a Wonderful World', and Ken Kesey's powerful satire on power and what passes for sanity, *One Flew Over the Cuckoo's Nest*, was published.

Dieldrin was banned from sheep dips after studies of its effect on Golden Eagles scavenging sheep carrion. It was replaced by a less harmful substance produced in New Zealand, where dieldrin had been banned earlier. It was also no longer permissible to put dieldrin and aldrin in fertilisers, although they could still be used for treating potatoes for wireworm, and other specific insects. The Ministry of Agriculture issued proposals for legislation that would replace the voluntary code for safe use of pesticides, several years hence.

There was increasing media coverage of the threat posed even to commoner birds by industrialised agriculture and other pressures.

Perhaps inevitably, given the circumstances and the newspapers' appetite for conflict, there were signs of mounting tension between farmers and conservationists, even where none was necessary. *Birds* magazine ran what was billed as a 'rather controversial article' on the subject, although today it seems measured and restrained. 'Rachel Carson's *Silent Spring* and the wide publicity given to the effects of pesticides on wildlife had a more profound effect on the farming community than may have been acknowledged,' it said. A monoculture of barley had been reported to be sweeping across the arable landscape. 'The prospect of much of this becoming prairie by 2000 AD is not a pleasant one to the conservationist.' Hill farming, always a much less lucrative and tougher business than lowland cereal growing, was by this time largely dependent on subsidies to survive in many areas.

It was forecast that an area the size of Warwickshire would be lost to urban development by 2000, adding to the deterioration in the countryside's overall beauty and quality. The RSPB spoke of its 'increased responsibility in giving advice to the appropriate authority as to the wise use of the countryside', adding, with a neat touch of intrigue, that 'some novel approaches need to be developed, and plans which the RSPB have in mind may break fresh ground here'.

Nature reserves made up 0.5% of the land area of Britain by this time; 1% was thought to be a realistic upper limit. With the RSPB only a few thousand short of its target for the nature reserve fund, an ICBP appeal was promoted to raise half that amount to buy a tarnished tropical paradise called Cousin Island, in Seychelles. If it could be restored to its native glory, then bird species teetering on the brink of extinction there might yet be saved.

The year ended and someone pointed out that it had been the RSPB's eightieth. 'We were too busy to notice it,' said Peter Conder. The strong impression left by all accounts of the period is that Conder and his team preferred to look forward rather than back. There were many challenges ahead.

A now time-honoured tradition of people with bird names working for the RSPB was already well established. It's a phenomenon nowadays known as nominative determinism. A Robin replaced the Swan at The Lodge – Robin Bovey succeeding Jack Swan as reserve Warden. He would now become a colleague of Dorothy Rook the Librarian. Even a cursory glance through the history of RSPB personnel would lend strong support to the theory that your name can influence your choices in life.

1969

A curious and disconcerting absence was noted across the country in spring: the Whitethroats were missing. At the final count, three-quarters of them had failed to return from winter in Africa. Places with 20 pairs the year before suddenly had none. The Whitethroat is a warbler: widespread, unfussy, familiar, to those who notice these things. It is modest of plumage, basic in needs, inhabiting our edgelands, liking brambles and scattered thorns. It is a rewarding acquaintance to make; an easy bird to warm to, with its fiery personality and effervescent song, often performed in a faintly manic song-flight. The apparent and mysterious tragedy of the vanished Whitethroats was enough to bring an 'avalanche' of people volunteering to help with the Common Birds Census. The cause of the disappearance was under investigation. I would later grow to love this bird.

Conservationists were still awaiting the report of the government advisory committee on pesticides. Two years had passed since the RSPB, BTO and GRA had provided evidence, when the Committee first acknowledged that DDT must be reviewed.

It had by now been conclusively shown how organochlorines affected birds of prey like the Peregrine Falcon, Osprey and Bald Eagle: they disrupt hormones involved in the production of calcium for eggshells. 'The impact of these new components on the ecosystems appears as death, reproductive impairment, disruption of species balance and behavioural alteration,' wrote Lucille F. Stickel in her book *Organochlorine Pesticides in the Environment*. 'How much longer can we afford to wait before taking further action?' pleaded RSPB Chairman Stanley Cramp.

That other US eagle landed, with millions glued to their televisions to witness images, by now with the possibility of colour, of the lunar module touching down on the moon in late July. Less publicly, concern was continuing to mount in the USA over what DDT was doing to the environment. Figures were released showing that in 1964–65 the USA had produced around 141 million lbs of DDT and 119 million lbs of chemicals in the aldrin–dieldrin group, much of it exported. Residues of these enduring substances had by now been found in most living creatures, from Antarctica to northern Canada. Britain's government, meanwhile, wouldn't release figures, despite repeated requests by the RSPB for this information.

Conservation on farmland was at last being 'seriously considered'.

The newly identified need for cooperation between conservationists and farmers brought the two sides together for a two-day conference. Melodramatic reports in *New Scientist* magazine called it 'The Battle of Pendley Grove'. A hundred delegates were split into groups and given a 'war game' to play. Farmers present were asked to come up with a plan for 400 acres of local land, with maximum profit the aim. The naturalists meanwhile were to come up with a plan to maintain a rich and diverse wildlife within a farming context. The two groups then worked on ways of marrying the two. Delegates expressed hope that similar gatherings might follow, and that the national organisation that advises four out of five farmers on how to farm might also start to take wildlife into account. This, it was felt, would be a 'great step forward'. 'We have a common theme,' the RSPB noted, 'to conserve our heritage of wildlife in an ever-shrinking countryside.'

The major oil companies were working hard at their public relations. BP sponsored a competition called 'Birds and Man', offering cash prizes for photography, cine-photography, painting or graphic design, and writing. The letters page opposite an advert for this carried a more scathing view: 'The pollution of our beaches and the extermination of our seabirds only occurs because of the thoughtlessness and greed of our rich oil companies.' Shell soon afterwards launched its 'Conservation 1970' competition, inviting every secondary school in Britain to survey a piece of land and make suggestions for improving it for wildlife. The prize was a tour of conservation projects throughout Europe.

Reports were rife of seabird mortality in the Irish Sea, apparently involving even more birds than the *Torrey Canyon* disaster. Over 10,000 dead birds washed up on the Irish coast alone. The casualties were mainly guillemots and, mysteriously, many of the affected birds appeared not to be oiled. Was the cause of death some other form of toxin?

Government was accused by some of showing a lack of interest and action in responding. Corpses were analysed at the ITE and found to contain very high levels of polychlorinated biphenyls – PCBs as they would later become better known. These are close relatives of the other organochlorines – dieldrin and DDT. They had been found in birds analysed in the last couple of years at the level of 10 or 20 parts per million. The latest dead guillemots were bearing traces of PCBs at the level of *hundreds* of parts per million.

PCBs were widely used in the plastics, lubrication and cosmetics industries. Urgent further investigations were launched. The RSPB called on government to make sure this wasn't hampered by lack of funding. Over at the ITE, work was under way to assess the toxicity of PCBs. It still wasn't known how these chemicals got into the sea and what other toxic substances might have been dumped there.

Yet another, more conventional oil spill in the North Sea killed 20,000 birds, mainly rare sea ducks, which washed up on the coast of the Netherlands, and in north-east England. Not far short of a thousand bird wings were sent in by the public, four times more than the year before. The International Beached Bird Survey was formally launched.

In September, Britain discovered an oil source of its own, 150 miles off the north-east coast of Scotland. It was struck by a British Petroleum vessel chartered by US company Amoco. Britain's own oil rush could now begin. Later in the year another 8,000 birds died in an oil pollution incident affecting most of Scotland's east coast. Rare sea ducks were reported coming ashore dead and bedraggled. The source was not known.

A week or so before Christmas, government advisers on pesticides at last announced their conclusions. Government recommended some more limits on the use of aldrin, dieldrin, endrin and TDE, and some limits for the first time on DDT. While welcome, these measures fell well short of those in place in many other countries, including the USA, where by this time in the eastern states the Peregrine Falcon was extinct.

The British government report included this clause: 'Other causes of eggshell thinning are known and there is no certainty that DDT was responsible.' The 'other causes' were neither named nor evaluated. *New Scientist* magazine begged to differ, citing 'a vast body of field evidence, a known biochemical pathway and it can be validated by laboratory experiments'.

The report did express concern at the level of pesticides found in coastal marine life, but despite the presence of persistent toxins in the environment, no evidence of adverse effects on people had been found. There were economic considerations. It was estimated that a complete ban on organochlorines would have cost each member of the public six pence. Government conceded that the recommendations were a compromise. The RSPB noted that the delay and the tortuous language of the overdue report suggested that the compromise had not been easily reached.

The RSPB had opened a nature centre at The Lodge. It welcomed 18,000 visitors in its first year. Volunteers were urgently requested to help the warden cope. Nine thousand new RSPB members were recruited in five months. As the year drew to a close, these supporters were urged to make membership a gift for friends or relatives that Christmas, and for a difficult decade ahead. 'Do they feed birds in winter?' Peter Conder asked. 'It is from these small beginnings ... from that knowledge comes a feeling for the conservation, or the wise use of the environment ...'

1970

President Nixon set the tone for the coming decade when he announced on New Year's Day: 'The 1970s absolutely must be the years when America pays its debt to the past by reclaiming the purity of the air, its waters and our living environment.' The National Environmental Policy Act had been brought in and prepared the ground for a succession of further laws. The Environmental Protection Agency was set up to monitor things. Air, water, species, chemicals, waste and mining issues were all addressed, and around 35 statutes were passed.

It was designated European Year of Conservation, or ECY '70, 'the greatest international effort which the world has seen to get people to care more for their environment and to do something about it'. This included the 18 countries of the Council of Europe that met in Strasbourg in February. The Royal Commission on Environmental Pollution was set up to report each year and advise government, Parliament, the Queen and the public on the issues of the day.

When you read prime-time BBC News to tens of millions of viewers every evening, you become one of the most famous faces in the land. And so it can have done the Society's profile no harm at all when the bird-loving Robert Dougall became RSPB President. His first official duty came when he was part of the delegation that greeted the Prince of Wales, whose helicopter landed at The Lodge after a morning visit to the ITE's Monks Wood station. It was part of what was billed as his 'Look and Learn' tour to find out more about conservation.

Britain's Minister for Agriculture said he 'expected' a partial withdrawal of organochlorines for certain uses. He opened another conference discussing agriculture and the environment. 'If farmers are to increase their contribution to the national larder ... more hedgerows and banks will need to go. Scrublands and wetlands are other problem areas,' sums up neatly the official licence that farm owners had been given to transform the landscape in the perceived national interest.

The transformation was already well under way. Dr Max Hooper calculated that something like 11,200 kilometres of hedgerow had been bulldozed out of the British countryside every year since 1945. He hoped that foresters would 'continue to recognise the importance of good landscaping and the value of introducing a few oak, beech and other hardwoods here and there'. He welcomed the fact that the Forestry Commission had published guidelines on scenic planning. Conservationists were asked to understand farmers better, and to provide the practical advice needed to help them to help wildlife.

The RSPB issued its own plea. 'Farmers, please think before removing hedges or trees. We know that the rationalisation of field sizes is important, but must every hedge or tree go? Is it possible for farmers to plant some trees? ... think also before using chemicals and try to use those that are not too harmful to wildlife.'

The twenty-second of April was declared Earth Day. Spring had begun with 4,000 more seabirds dying on the Cornish coast, half of them already dead on the beaches and many more in such a pitiful state that they had to be humanely despatched. Crude oil matted the shoreline, suggesting a tanker had washed out its tanks at sea, illegally.

The RSPB now had 50,000 members and hit the £100,000 target for funding nature reserves. The World Wildlife Fund launched an appeal for £1 million. An LP record was produced to raise funds for this, led by comedian Spike Milligan, with contributions from The Hollies, Bee Gees, Lulu, Cilla Black, Bruce Forsyth, Harry Secombe, Rolf Harris (my first pop idol), The Beatles (who would split this year, over matters unrelated), Cliff Richard and Dave Dee, Dozy, Beaky, Mick and Tich.

Government now proposed another airport for London, on a place with the unprepossessing name of Foulness, a vital wintering and feeding ground for migrant birds. It should really be called Fowlness. Peter Conder set out the RSPB's case against the likely obliteration of the site. For a start, the risk of bird-strike could be nine times greater than at an inland site. If the scheme were given the go-ahead, conservationists believed that it would give carte blanche to develop every major estuary in the country. The headline threat was to a species called the Dark-bellied Brent Goose, which breeds in the Arctic. A fifth of the entire world population of this species was using the site, its only resting and feeding place in the British Isles.

This small goose has evolved a specialised lifestyle, of breeding in the remote and harsh coastal plains of Siberia, and wintering in the coastal wetlands of north-west Europe, including Foulness. A third of the world population had been known to winter in Essex as a whole. The species had already experienced an unusual population crash. In the early thirties a mysterious disease attacked its preferred food plant in these wintering grounds. Its population was decimated. It is thought that as many as nine out of every ten geese vanished. A number of countries, including the UK, banned the shooting of the species. Government could hardly have chosen a more vulnerable and less deserving bird species on which to impose another huge pressure. 'The Brent represents a major collision risk to aircraft and it is declared policy that they would be removed from the proximity of the airport,' the RSPB reported.

Other countries had moved to address their pesticide problems. Sweden outlawed aldrin and dieldrin and banned DDT and lindane from domestic use. There were wider bans on DDT for a trial period of two years. Hungary had banned organochlorines completely, the only country to have done so. Russia, meanwhile, had never permitted the use of aldrin and dieldrin.

Anxious to salvage something of the tarnished image of their industry, BP produced a film called *The Shadow of Progress*, which wasn't about oil, but which highlighted the pollutant effect of fertilisers washing into lakes and rivers.

European Conservation Year looked as though it would coincide with the worst ever for seabird mortality. In the first three months alone at least 22,000 dead birds were known to have washed up on these shores. Half the Guillemots and a quarter of the Razorbills failed to return to the sea cliffs on which they normally bred in and around the Irish Sea. At the final count, 15,000 birds were found dead. This was thought to be about a quarter to a fifth of the total killed in this part of our coastal waters alone. The total figure might even be as high as 200,000.

A new bill was announced that would be introduced to Parliament by the newly installed government following the general election. It would impose an absolute ban on oil tankers discharging any oil – not completely, but within 92.6 kilometres of land. The RSPB wanted to know what plans were to be put in place for detecting and dealing with slicks. The existing measures were largely ineffectual. As things stood, the Board of Trade was responsible for slicks more than a mile offshore. Any closer, and it became the responsibility of local government, but they were only obliged to act if an 'amenity' beach was threatened.

Environmentalists felt that the Labour government was just getting to grips with the urgency of the environmental issues. Harold

Wilson had shown himself to be interested in wildlife protection for more than just political reasons. As well as the Royal Commission on Environmental Pollution, Labour had set up a research unit to coordinate different bits of pollution study carried out by various parts of government. Prominent ministers had shown that they cared about environmental issues, and the Minister for Agriculture had increased that department's input to wildlife conservation matters.

So, when summer brought a change of government, with the Conservatives returning to power and Ted Heath to Downing Street, it was in a sense back to square one. Such is the short-term nature of party politics. Peter Conder was philosophical, and vowed to 'keep on prodding whatever Government is in power'. The Tory manifesto had made some encouraging statements, but the first list of ministers set out by Heath gave no real indication of where particular responsibility would lie for these matters. Nor had any statement been issued on their environmental policy. The RSPB continued to prompt, or rather prod. 'It will not be easy to control the dumping of industry's rubbish,' warned Conder.

It was much later in the year when new Minister of Agriculture Jim Prior made his first statement mentioning conservation. The hope and belief of the RSPB and others was that increased public awareness and knowledge would make people expect more of government and be more willing to pay for a healthy environment. This hope wasn't helped when unemployment in the UK rose above a million.

Peregrine Falcons were being monitored round the clock in the Lake District and there were some signs of recovery. Golden Eagles also reared chicks there, the first in England for at least 250 years. More species were given extra protection when they were added to Schedule 1 of the Protection of Birds Act.

Max Nicholson, Director General of the Nature Conservancy from its launch in 1952 until 1966, wrote a book called *The Environmental Revolution*. It pulled no punches. 'The renewal and the healing of a sick society through creative intimacy with the natural environment could bring a transformation of the kind and scale which our degenerate and self-disgusted, materialist, power-drunk and sex-crazed civilisation needs,' he wrote. He went on:

The brief authority, prestige and dominance of the man-made wilderness of the great cities is collapsing. It may be that the rot has already gone too far. Human numbers and material demands may be destined hopelessly to outrun the most that ingenuity can now achieve towards restoring the equilibrium through the sensitive and healing use of the natural environment.

Another environmental critique – *Since Silent Spring*, by Frank Graham Junior – was published. 'Rachel Carson's vindication has come, alas posthumously, with the banning of DDT by the Canadian Government,' he wrote. These were among a rash of books warning of the likely consequences of our impact on the planet, including *Before Nature Dies*, now published in the UK. This was a powerful critique of environmental degradation written by Professor Jean Dorst of the Museum of Natural History in Paris and first published in French in 1965. In it he argues that 'pesticides are like drugs. Most of them are dangerous poisons, fatal if you take an overdose. No one would dream of taking ten to a hundred times the amount of medicine prescribed by a doctor, yet pesticides are sprayed regardless of the consequences.'

Conservation of the environment had gone from being a minority interest to a matter of growing public concern. The US Environmental Protection Agency was founded, and a Department of Environment for Britain. Rachel Carson was cited as having influenced these changes.

The Ecologist magazine was launched by Teddy Goldsmith. In its first issue, Assistant Editor Robert Allen looked ahead, and the overall approach adopted by the title was summed up quite neatly in these lines: 'Interplanetary archaeologists of the future will classify our planet as one in which a very long and stable period of small-scale hunting and gathering was followed by … technology and society leading to rapid extinction.'

The decade of flower power was ending. Environmental pollution was causing mounting public concern, not just toxic chemicals on farmland, but sewage pollution of river and sea, fertiliser leakage from farmland into the water table, and the apparent dumping of chemicals into water bodies and the oceans. There were disturbing stories of increased contamination by lead and other heavy metals.

As ECY'70 drew to a close, some high-profile commentators on matters scientific concluded that the initiative had been counter-productive. The RSPB took a more optimistic view, eager to make sure any impetus from the year was not lost. The message to government was that they would be expected to maintain their concern and interest in what would undoubtedly be a challenging decade to come.

The Seventies

1971

As the new decade began, a mild winter was recorded at The Lodge. The first Chiffchaffs returned and were singing from The Lodge treetops on 19 March. One seen at Dungeness in Kent in early February was even thought to have spent the winter here.

Early in the year, in the Iranian city of Ramsar, representatives from two dozen countries gathered to make an agreement on conserving the most important wetlands in the world. Each country agreed to produce a list of its best wetlands, many of their estuaries, and to commit to protecting them. The Ramsar Convention was now in place, with immediate implications. The government's own Nature Conservancy had already classified Foulness Marshes as a Grade 1 site – one of the finest in the country, and internationally important. For an airport to be built there the site would have to be removed from the British list before the country signed up to the Ramsar Convention.

The third International Beached Bird Survey took place over the first weekend in March. One of the conclusions being drawn was that continuous smaller oiling incidents were adding up to as serious a threat to bird populations as the more spectacular and widely publicised disaster events. 'When do we have to accept that the sea is not a bottomless garbage tip and when must we stop using it as one?' wondered Peter Conder.

Spring also brought the latest census of the UK population, a 'particularly inquisitive' one, according to *The Times*. Whatever bird populations had done in the decade since the last census, *Homo sapiens* had increased by more than 2.5 million. There were now more than 55 million people living here. Major cities like London and Glasgow, however, were losing people. A large part of Glasgow's population was being 'over-spilled' to new towns, as tenement blocks were emptied and flattened. My family moved again, to a slightly dilapidated cottage in an older corner of one of these burgeoning new towns. We arrived even as the fields around us were being smothered in building sites.

Conder spoke of the continuing struggle on pesticides, and the 'considerable foot-dragging'. The garden use of DDT had still not been withdrawn. Conder suspected it was because industry had a lot of branded containers still to fill (with DDT) and shift. 'What happens if manufacturers overestimate their DDT requirements?' Conder asked. 'Will they then make more containers?' The ministry was also continuing to sell a booklet called *Chemicals for the Gardener*, which recommended the use of DDT. 'Does the Ministry find it easier to misguide people than to rewrite the booklet?' he wondered. This guide lists no fewer than 26 DDT products, of which half were based on DDT only. Recognising the increasing importance of gardens, the RSPB began to issue guidance on the use of domestic pesticides.

In the face of government prevarication, the RSPB's tone got stronger. 'It is perhaps part of a government minister's job to reassure people that all is well when it is not ... The evidence all suggests that the Minister hopes to quietly shelve the plans for withdrawal of organochlorines. We will fight this. His job is not to protect short-term minority profits but to consider the well-being and wishes of the public. A clear date for the implementation of these recommendations must be given.'

The newly created Department of Environment was an important milestone. It may also have inspired a BBC fiction series called *Doomwatch*, about a government agency tackling environmental crises. Gordon Rattray Taylor wrote *The Doomsday Book*, which predicted both another ice age, and global warming.

The struggle against DDT and other organochlorines was now a decade old. The chemical was finally banned in the USA after studies on laboratory mice showed links to cancer. The PCB issue was resolving itself rather more quickly. Intriguingly, one major chemical company withdrew PCBs 'where there is no reasonable control of their possible release into the environment'.

It remained unclear how these substances had come to be in the Irish Sea, or the process by which they were killing fish and birds over a period of years. It seems extraordinary that these pollutants could have been so lethal to wildlife in the context of the vast marine environment. Understanding how being doused in chemicals or eating contaminated food might kill birds is one thing, but this looked like a whole other level of toxicity. The company called it a 'fair commercial sacrifice', adding that 'there is no firm evidence that the present levels in the environment are harmful'. It was hoped that the handful of manufacturers in other countries would follow suit.

The length of beach being surveyed by volunteers had doubled and the number of dead birds reported had quadrupled since 1969. A thousand miles of coast were now being covered, with 250 people providing 100 reports on the Irish Sea incident alone, and 500 bird wings submitted.

The Secretary of State for Education and Science was asked in the summer whether she would give instruction for the dispersal of oil slicks threatening seabirds, as well as beaches. In a written reply, a certain Margaret Thatcher assured all that urgent attention was being given to the problem and that she hoped to be able to make arrangements shortly.

Oil pollution incidents were by now being reported from all the world's oceans. In early March the international survey took place over a weekend. The full impact of the north-east coast oil spill had now been calculated: it had killed a total of 14,500 birds. The Dutch spill had claimed a staggering 41,000 birds. A grant was received to pay for a report on all the information gathered in the last five years. The first studies were done to build a picture of the proportion of birds killed actually being found. Only one in five of the bird corpses dropped at sea again were recovered from beaches. Many sank.

It was thought that the increased drilling operations for oil would be another likely source of oil slicks, both from leaks and from the fuel-oil mixes used to lubricate drills and hydraulic jacks. Cargo ships were also known to routinely dispose of spent fuel-oil residues when cleaning out tanks to prepare for safety inspections.

Supersonic technology brought fears that test flights of the new Concorde might affect seabird colonies on the west coast. Witnesses were asked to share any observations of the behaviour of birds at the time of these test flights, the dates for which were not yet known. They were asked to look out for 'signs of panic', and whether 'mass dread flights' took place. Would nests become vulnerable to attack by other birds? Did birds show signs of getting used to the noise, or were eggs failing to hatch? Did chicks suffer from shock, or were chicks and eggs displaced or scattered?

The RSPB duly received 15 reports on the effects of sonic booms on birds and mammals, and government's Nature Conservancy a further 11. Flocks of gulls, waders, Rooks and Jackdaws were said to have been particularly disturbed, albeit briefly, and signs of alarm had been noted in sheep, goats and deer. Test flights were set to continue over the Irish Sea and Cornwall. In September, a team of activists launched a small fishing boat from Canada, to protest about nuclear testing. Since then, the Greenpeace movement has grown to a membership of 2.8 million around the world.

Specimens of some of the food chain end-users were still welcomed: Great Crested Grebe, Heron, Sparrowhawk, Golden Eagle, Peregrine, Kestrel, Guillemot and Kingfisher, as well as rarer birds of prey and one mammal, the Otter. Analyses had begun to test for other pollutants such as toxic metals, mercury, lead and cadmium, and industrial effluents like the PCBs.

The prestigious BBC series *Horizon* broadcast a programme called 'Due to Lack of Interest, Tomorrow Has Been Cancelled'. It prompted one alarmed viewer to write: 'The idea that this planet will be unable to support life beyond the 21st century is surely the most terrifying prospect man has ever tried to face.'

Peter Conder had a response for those who accused environmentalists of exaggerating the threats we faced, and doom-saying. 'If we are the prophets of doom, you can see who the doom-makers are.' He described a pile of paperwork almost two feet high on his desk relating to the third London airport enquiry. 'I wonder how many people, MPs included, made up their minds and opened their mouths without reading any of it?'

'Admittedly,' he went on, 'you don't need to do more than visit the area to realise that to plonk an airport down at Cublington is stark lunacy.' But the main concern was to continue to protest at the move to put the airport at the alternative, Foulness, which would, said the RSPB, be 'much more expensive, in the wrong place, and an environmental disaster'. The Roskill Commission was set up by government to gather views and evidence. It advised against the Foulness option. The government promptly ignored its own commission, on 'environmental grounds'.

J. A. Baker lent his support to the chorus of voices raised against the government's decision. It took someone with his powers of description to do full justice to such a setting as Foulness, and to the philistinism of the plan to transform it. 'An austere place, perhaps, withdrawn, some might say desolate. But the silence compels. It is a very old silence ... The wilderness is here.'

Conservationists were working hard to increase public (and political) awareness of the value of estuaries – an acquired taste, not everyone's first idea of scenery. *Wilderness is not a Place* was chosen as the name for a film about estuaries, taken from J. A. Baker's article in *Birds* magazine, in which he wrote 'man is killing wilderness, hunting it down'.

He ended, in a way, on a note of hope for the birds, with what may be the last lines the chronically unwell writer ever penned for public consumption. 'They were here before the coming of man, they will endure the shadow of our tyranny, they will fly out into the sun again when we have gone.'

1972

Ugandan President Obote was unseated in a military coup, and Idi Amin took control of the country. Europeans and Asians were by this time leaving in droves, and in a hurry, as that tragic episode in the country's history began to unfold, distressing for my parents and their many friends to witness and experience, as they left others behind. Amin would later declare himself the 'uncrowned king of Scotland' as Uganda descended into chaos and bloodshed.

My mother Kay Moorhead developed her love of wildflowers, butterflies and birds in the garden and environs of her father's manse in Claudy, near Derry. Like many people his was a farming family, but he had left home to study theology at Edinburgh. Mum always spoke very fondly of the late thirties and forties world of her childhood in rural Ireland, a world greatly changed by the time it was knowable to me and my siblings on family holidays there. She enrolled all four of us in the Young Ornithologists' Club, as it was then, and we were brought up on RSPB/YOC literature of one kind or another. We had a butterfly poster on the toilet wall, I remember, and images from it are still imprinted on my mind, scientific names and all. Ugandan souvenirs decorated the place too, and Swahili phrases still punctuated my parents' conversation, Irish accents notwithstanding.

I had a squabble with older sisters Brigid and Clare over ownership of a back issue, not of the YOC magazine, but of *Birds* magazine itself. It always had a painting on its cover in those days, and this particular issue had an unusually melodramatic scene: a male Sparrowhawk with a Blackbird pinned to a plucking post. Sparrowhawks at this time were virtually extinct in large parts of lowland Britain. Mum had to intervene in the dispute and, to soothe my tantrum, I got to put the picture on my bedroom wall. I was already in the grip of a serious birds of prey fixation. My sisters were not, in the end, *exclusively* interested in birds of prey, what with their other interests in life like David Cassidy and Sasha dolls.

The old soldier George Waterston retired as leader of the RSPB in Scotland, and as summer ended a migrating Osprey – that iconic species of conservation and life retrieved, and for which so many hours of conservation volunteer time had been expended – was seen by excited staff as it flew over The Lodge on its southward migration. 'Justice demanded that an osprey should one day return the compliment.' reported *Birds* magazine.

Buried in the archive, I was pleased to discover that the volunteers who guarded the famous Osprey nest at Loch Garten in the Scottish Highlands operated out of a Bedford Dormobile, just like the one my family had. That year, we piled into our own version of this no-frills van with its pop-up roof bunks, Formica table and sink, and rolled south for our first visit to London, for cousin Alwyn's wedding. Her dad (my dad's older brother) and mum had left Ireland in the fifties for better economic prospects and a quieter life in southern England. He was by now Pensions Manager for a small but growing retail business called Tesco, with its office in Reading. We camped in north London, in a suburban field called Theobald's Park. As part of the big city trip we were taken to the zoo, at that time constantly in the headlines because of Chi-chi, the Giant Panda that had tragically died in April, to the dismay of the nation. My abiding memory of the zoo is not a happy one. It is of vultures spread-eagled on the concrete floor of cages that seemed barely wider than their wingspans, with the final indignity of mice running rings around them. It was a confusing and enduring image for an impressionable young mind, but left me with a sympathy for vultures that would resurface in later life. The Buffalo on a rope, glaring at us, just upset me. I think I was happier at the campsite, kicking a ball, exploring the spinney at its edges in this pleasantly mild, ambient new land they called England.

Zoos at that time still had a long way to go to improve standards and conditions and distance themselves from animal circuses. Peter

Conder was critical, at the time: 'The growing rash of zoos of various sizes and conditions is a symptom of badly misdirected enthusiasm for nature.' There was as yet very little legislation to prevent anyone from setting up a private wildlife collection in a backyard, fuelling the wild bird trade, of which Conder was a vocal critic. 'When you see them in a cage in this country they look bedraggled, bored, scruffy and quite ignoble.'

The RSPB continued to prod government to invest more in its Nature Conservancy. The state's network of research bases and nature reserves was also in need of a funding boost. While the Nature Conservancy was acknowledged as one of the best organisations of its kind in the world, 'to say that,' Peter Conder pointed out, 'is really only to say that most other countries' efforts are truly pathetic.' But amid the generally bleak outlook, some other countries were giving a lead. The West German government was promising to spend £4.5m by 1975 on cleaning up the environment, which included an outright ban on DDT by that time.

The Lodge was by now so popular at weekends that it might soon be necessary to close the gates if the warden thought that its birds and habitat might face intolerable pressure. The nature discovery room was swallowed up by the increasing demand for staff workspace. The growing Society had begun to think in terms of five-year plans. The headline points of the next plan were: to average five new nature reserves every year, to appoint new members of staff to work on bird importation, planning and Puffin biology, and to renew the post of Farming and Wildlife Adviser. The publications staff would increase from five to nine, education staff from three to eleven, local reps from 100 to 300, local groups from 20 to 100, three new nature centres were to be built, three English regional offices would be opened, the first in 'the north', and the film show season would expand from six to ten months of the year. There was more talk of continuing to 'prod' government and its relevant departments. If the Society could demonstrate that it was 'active, useful, sensible and economical', success would surely follow.

The RSPB praised the growth in biological recording, aided by the latest technology: 'Thousands of amateur naturalists are listing the animals and plants all over Britain ... The information they collect is being turned into maps by a team of professional biologists using a computer.'

Christine Bradley of Derby became the RSPB's 100,000th member. Society President Robert Dougall presented her with a Robert

Gillmor painting of Avocets. Not everyone, it seems, had grasped the administrative challenges involved in managing the spiralling number of membership record cards. To help with the burden, members writing in to notify the Society of a change of address were asked to provide details of their old address, as well as the new. Perhaps, they may have been thinking, one of those new computers would help ...

The by now annual gathering of RSPB reserve wardens convened at The Lodge. The growing force of 27 staff present included the first woman – Bridget Moore of Vane Farm. The Society's second members' gathering was held in Malvern. Over 400 people attended, to hear Environment Secretary Peter Walker describe the challenges faced by the nation in the next five years. Pollution was the watchword. A survey of air quality was soon to be published, following one already completed for fresh water. 'Year by year the rivers of Britain will become cleaner,' he promised. He said there would be new regulations on vehicles, and that a lot of money would be spent to minimise the effect on birds of the proposed airport at Foulness.

In the wider countryside, it was illegal to destroy a nest or take an egg of a protected bird, but there were no constraints on landowners or local authorities bulldozing and burning hedges and trees in the breeding season, when scores of nests would likely be destroyed. Two local councils tried to take a lead by offering farmers £3 per tree to leave them unmolested in hedgerows. It was hoped that other councils would follow suit.

Stubble burning was still legal. One such fire raged out of control and destroyed a nature reserve in Essex, just one example of the collateral damage being caused to trees, hedges and other habitats by these fires, as well as the hazard to traffic and asthmatics often caused by the drifting smoke. Another blaze got out of control and swept through a huge area of rare Dorset heathland, incinerating dozens of pairs of Dartford Warblers, rare Sand Lizards and Smooth Snakes, and threatening homes.

The issue of population growth continued to exercise minds. World population had reached 3.7 billion and was growing at the rate of 74 million a year. The environmental cost of motoring was also now being apprehended, and an irate letter-writer set out three of the issues: 'Driving a car is environmentally negligent, parking one is a form of littering, and a new motorway merely gets the driver from one oiled beach to another with unprecedented convenience and speed.'

Sweden hosted the first world conference on the human environment. 'We hope that the conference will help create a new sense of direction for mankind, based on man's interdependence on nature,' the RSPB urged. 'Perhaps new international standards of economic behaviour will be required.' The Swedes had a particular axe to grind: acid rain.

1973

Britain became a member of the European Economic Community (EEC) from the turn of the year. Ted Heath's Conservative government had signed up the previous January, although polls showed public opinion was against the move, and both main political parties were split. Conservationists here began to take more interest in matters continental.

Another Bedford Dormobile was pressed into action as a vanload of intrepid RSPB staff crossed the Channel and headed south to Bordeaux to lend support to the annual protest against the shooting and netting of around 5 million migrant birds in south-west France. The hunting had been illegal there since 1905 but the authorities had done little to impede it.

The rapid growth of package tourism in the past decade was impacting on the natural environment in Mediterranean destinations, of which Majorca was especially popular, and appealing to nature lovers: 'Where in 1962 only a few local fishermen were on the marsh there are now strips of hotels and the reserve behind them is busy with naturalists.'

Cyprus was also in the news. The BBC broadcast a programme called *Down to Earth*, discussing the importation of pickled songbirds from Cyprus, where migrant birds were being trapped on glue sticks. Viewers were invited to contact the RSPB with their views, as a result of which 900 letters and several petitions were received, all calling for a ban on this trade. In the summer months the RSPB and the ICBP sent a report to the relevant government departments calling on them to exercise their powers to ban the import of these pickled birds, pointing out that 'it is absurd that these birds run the risk of returning to their breeding areas in a jar of pickle'.

A million signatures were gathered on a Europe-wide petition presented to the Italian government along with a threat to boycott Italy as a holiday destination until it outlawed the trapping of songbirds. An estimated 150 million wild birds were being killed in Italy each year. Public opinion was turning. The League Against the Destruction of Birds there was increasing its membership spectacularly, from 800 to 10,000 since 1970.

Meanwhile in Belgium, government relaxed its total ban on the netting of wild birds, just a year after imposing it. It set a limit of 120,000 on the number of birds caught. Conservationists knew that this move would make enforcement difficult. Additional bird protection laws were also introduced in Spain to curb excessive hunting of species increasingly ill-equipped to endure it.

This was declared tree-planting year by the Department of Environment. Plant A Tree In '73 was the slogan. 'But don't just plant for ornament,' urged the RSPB, ever determined to add value: 'Plant with wildlife in mind!' A committee was set up under Lord Sandford, and the public was invited to write in with suggestions as to 'where trees could usefully be planted'. Dutch elm disease was tightening its grip, having first been identified in Britain in the late sixties. Scientists from the Forestry Commission tried injecting fungicide into an elm in London's St James's Park, in a desperate search for a way of combating the deadly fungus.

'My problem is that I personally dislike a perfectly legitimate activity: aviculture, which is defined as the art of breeding birds in some form of captivity,' Conder wrote. Perhaps five years in a prisoner of war camp had something do with it, although plenty of people would share his sentiment without having endured a prolonged deprivation of freedom. Conservationists were working with the British Bird Fancy Council to try to make sure that keepers respected the law and didn't augment their collections with birds stolen from the wild. One captive breeder of finches reported someone netting Goldfinches within 20 miles of The Lodge, and boasting a profit of £100 a week from the practice.

Conder also had twitchers in his sights. 'Today too many birdwatchers are concerned only with noticing birds and ticking lists,' he commented. A frank exchange of views promptly ensued on the letters pages.

At long last the withdrawal of aldrin and dieldrin was announced in the UK. When the year ended, they could no longer be marketed. They were replaced by organophosphorus compounds, also highly toxic, but at least able to break down rather than persisting and accumulating in the food chain.

A public hearing began in the USA, where it was reported that most humans now carried dieldrin residues in fatty tissue. Breast-fed babies were receiving between five and nine times the daily volume deemed acceptable by the World Health Organization. Some claimed that it caused cancer. Experiments on mice had indicated that high doses of dieldrin increased the incidence of malignant tumours.

Duryea Morton, a director of the USA's Audubon Society, crossed the Atlantic to address the RSPB's members' conference and impart some wisdom. He gave the illustrated lecture he had devised for the US market to help recruit supporters. 'It was interesting to compare the American philosophical approach with the more didactic effects of English lectures,' conference noted. Another speaker urged the RSPB and the county Wildlife Trusts to work closely together as a unified force against the growing threats. Since 1966 there had been three attempts to find a way of actually merging the two organisations, each of which failed to satisfy the councils of both.

New Scientist journalist Jon Tinker called for members of conservation organisations to be 'politically activated'. 'It was,' Tinker argued, 'no good to claim that conservation ought to be kept out of party politics because to do so would relegate it to the level of decimalisation and the colour of London buses.'

'Both speakers,' it was recorded, 'gave examples of the current ineptitude of the conservation movement and the reaction from both the floor and the platform showed that there was a consciousness, if not a complete acceptance, of the truth of some of their criticisms.'

The Washington Convention on the International Trade in Endangered Species (CITES) was created. The RSPB called for a wildlife police force, to tackle widespread problems of criminality: 800 possible infringements of bird protection law were reported to the Society in just one year. In 1963, a third of the RSPB's annual report had been taken up with discussion of the issue of toxic chemicals. Ten years later it was difficult to isolate the most pressing of the threats facing birds and being tackled by conservationists.

1974

Our family of six would make regular Sunday trips the short distance to the Ayrshire coast; not, as in most families, to make sandcastles or lie on a towel (although to be honest the scope for sunbathing at Ardrossan was always a bit limited), but to gather seaweed from the shoreline. We collected this in fertiliser bags and took it home for the veg patch, after letting it rinse clean of salt in the rain that was always plentiful in west-central Scotland. Sometimes, we would also walk the tideline looking for dead birds, as part of the Beached Bird Survey that was a minority pastime of the period. There were still a lot of oiled Guillemots, Puffins and Gannets to record.

We were never in doubt that the data we provided were useful. It was only recently I learned that opinions have differed on this point. Dead bird records are all very well, but some scientists made the case that the most important thing is to know where a bird has been oiled, not where it washes ashore, which seems completely reasonable. Subsequent studies – the so-called 'corpse drift experiments' – showed that dead birds could travel hundreds of miles before making landfall; further even than some of them travel when alive. We know this because some diehards took the trouble to board fishing boats with bags of dead birds. These were carefully tagged, thrown overboard, and then recovered by beachcombers like us wherever they happened to turn up. I don't remember if we ever found any of these tagged ones. But I never cease to be inspired by the lengths some of my colleagues will go to in the name of conservation science. Well, someone had to. And we were usually home in time to watch *Cartoon Cavalcade*.

Six hundred oiled birds were recorded on the beaches of Ayrshire in January and February, some of them ours. The RSPB had recently appointed a specialist in Scotland to cope with the challenge of a rapidly expanding oil industry. 'By all means extract oil but don't spoil everything else in the process,' summed up the conservationists' position.

Labour won the spring general election called by Edward Heath to answer the question: 'Who runs the country?' A series of strikes had prompted government to impose a limit on businesses using electricity – the so-called 'three-day week'. This meant no television after 10.30 in the evening. It was designed to inconvenience the public and bring pressure on the unions. Harold Wilson won the election narrowly. His new government quickly called a referendum on membership of the EEC, in response to public demand.

It was World Population Year, and government even appointed a minister for population, the job going to Leader of the House Jim Prior. With minds turning to the possible exponential growth of human population in a rapidly developing world, conservationists began thinking and talking more in terms of our responsibility for future generations. What sort of world would our children, and children's children, inherit from us?

In the face of this increasing pressure, the Council of Europe began to devise a network of protected areas for wildlife across Europe. Demands were also being made of member states to strengthen protection measures, and to sign up to the Ramsar deal that was on the table to protect the most important wetlands.

RSPB membership broke the 150,000 mark, subs went up from £2 to £3 and an appeals organiser was brought in. A donation of £70 was received from the North Kent Sun Club, a group of naturists. They had held their annual open day in a wooded setting in May, with the local members group represented by a man called Jack Pink, who accepted the donation.

Comedian and national treasure Eric Morecambe had been much in the news after a heart scare. He described his fondness for birds in an interview in *Radio Times*. 'I started when I had the heart attack,' he said. 'I had to go out walking a lot and I got bored. So I bought a book. You don't just go and wander about. You give yourself say a week to find a particular bird. I saw a bird on the golf course. I thought it was a Parrot. I thought hello, it's escaped. I rang up Gordon [Benningfield, artist] and described it and it was a Green Woodpecker. Marvellous, marvellous feeling. Most of the best birds you see by accident, you know. I met my wife like that. The three Fs are my other hobbies – football, fishing and photography. You might go fishing, you see. Slip a pair of small binoculars into your big poacher's pocket …'

Our family summer holiday, complete with cousins, was in a farm cottage on the Sky Road in Connemara, County Mayo. The songs that transport me right back there are 'Pinball' and 'Band on the Run' by Wings. There were Golden Plovers on the hill above the house and the rocky cove where we went rock-pooling and caught eels. But if there is a defining soundtrack for this year it would be Mike Oldfield's techno-hippy instrumental album *Tubular Bells*, the must-have record of the time, which managed to combine new-tech keyboard effects with a folksy vibe. My brother had a copy, and we would listen to it enraptured, when it wasn't Steely Dan, or The Sound of Philadelphia.

There was a curiously low-key reaction to the announcement that the plan to put London's third airport at Foulness had finally been shelved. Perhaps it didn't do to gloat, or perhaps the real reasons underlying the decision were less to do with any genuine concern for conservation of important places than other economic reasons. Conservationists produced a bold blueprint to create instead a National Park.

1975

Sir Julian Huxley died on Valentine's Day. In an interview the previous year he had reflected on the changes in birds he had noticed. 'It seemed from his and my memories of Surrey that we have lost more in the last 20 years than in the previous 50,' interviewer Jon Tinker said of his conversation with the great pioneer of natural history. 'Yes, there have been enormous changes,' Huxley had told him. 'DDT has killed off so many insects, and in doing so has poisoned the birds.'

He had spoken of his fondness for Nightjars. 'That's one of the birds I sadly miss in Surrey now,' Huxley reflected. 'Till about five years ago you could still hear the natterjacks. Nobody knows why they've all gone. Just a mystery.' As fate would have it, the Nightjars didn't come back to The Lodge from their African migration later that spring.

There was change at the top of the RSPB. Peter Conder stepped down after 12 years in the Director's chair. 'On the international scale we must make our expertise more readily available,' he declared in a parting message, at a time when the ruling Labour Party was still deeply divided on whether the country should even remain in Europe. A growing stream of representatives from organisations abroad had been passing through The Lodge, eager to emulate the RSPB growth model, if that were possible in their national contexts. Many of these discussions and deliberations, as they have been since, must have centred on the intriguing question, 'Why does the British public care so much about birds?'

The terminology was changing. 'The word conservationist has become fashionable, the word naturalist has become rather dowdy,' Conder reflected. 'We should refurbish it, by exerting ourselves to become experts in managing wildlife positively and defending nature.'

It was also a year of major political changes. It had been designated International Women's Year. The Sex Discrimination Act and the Equal Pay Act were brought in. Margaret Thatcher ousted Edward Heath to become leader of the Conservative opposition. It had also been designated Wetlands Year. To mark the event government finally signed up to the Ramsar Convention, the international agreement on conserving wetlands drawn up in 1972.

Richard Mabey's *Pollution Handbook* was published, based on a survey of clean air and water by *The Sunday Times*. At the time it was thought that sulphur dioxide in the atmosphere was the reason why Scots pine trees were unable to grow in the industrial Pennines, while stunting tree and grass growth more generally.

There was an outcry when more than 2,000 birds were found dead on arrival at Heathrow in a consignment from Calcutta. The wretched birds were packed into boxes, and their water supply and food had run out. Another incident involved 500 birds crammed into cages at nearly 20 times the density permitted. 'It is a standing source of astonishment to some of us that when other countries, particularly Australia and the USA, take such drastic measures to prevent the importation of pests and infections, our own authorities seem so casual about it,' wrote W. R. P. Bourne of Aberdeen University.

A damning report called *All Heaven in a Rage* was published, revealing the horrifying facts and figures compiled in the course of the RSPB's two-year investigation into the importation of wild birds to the UK. It found that more than a million wild birds were being brought to or through UK airports each year, a fifth of the global total. Until it was published, few people had any idea of the sheer scale of the trade. The combination of the report and the grotesque images of dead birds at airports had an immediate influence on government, which pledged to ratify the Washington CITES Convention by year-end. This would require dealers to seek permits, and would put other safeguards in place to prevent the worst of the carnage and suffering.

An RSPB appeal brochure was mass mailed, aiming to raise £1 million for nature reserves. The last major appeal had been in 1967, with its target set at one-tenth of that amount. The latest appeal was sponsored by Lloyds Bank, and took place with inflation rampant, running at 20 to 30% annually. The price of oil had rocketed, and wages were escalating. Government was forced to slash spending, and to borrow £2 billion from the International Monetary Fund. It was against this backcloth that the country rushed headlong into exploiting North Sea oil resources. These were seen by some as the best hope of salvation for the balance of payments. The first commercial North Sea oil was piped ashore in June – a transfusion for the ailing economy. Oil companies were naming their drilling platforms after birds. A new proposal emerged for an oil refinery at Cliffe Marshes in Kent. Meanwhile, PCBs contributed to the deaths of 17,000 seabirds in the North Sea.

The spiralling costs of petrol, paper and postage were being sorely felt by the RSPB, along with everyone else. The costs of establishing a new warehouse and paying for the new Morecambe Bay reserve had left the organisation with a six-figure budget deficit. The five-year plan was reviewed in light of the recession. There is a gap in the archive – no *Birds* magazine for July/August 1975. I find instead a little postcard, neatly addressed in typescript to a Mr Cressey of Kent. 'Thank you for your enquiry about the July/August issue of *Birds*. Due to a financial crisis at the time this issue was not printed. Yours sincerely ... Publications Department.' These were trying times.

Fifty thousand acres of the British Isles were said to be being lost to birds forever, every year. The RSPB led in founding the Farming and Wildlife Advisory Group (FWAG). 'Quietly and steadily farmers, once wholly against the idea, are accepting the concept of farming with wildlife. It is filtering into agricultural education and the advisory services. It is being linked to landscape by planners, and there are encouraging signs of interest from the agricultural press, hitherto sceptical of the value of wildlife conservation and sometimes positively hostile to it.'

In early summer the Jamesons set off on a family camping trip to the Isle of Skye. What has stayed with me is an impression of unusually warm, dry weather; even the sea was bathe-able. The evening air was thick with midges, and my brother Kevin discovered he was allergic to crustaceans after a near-death allergic reaction to a packet of savoury rice with prawn. It was good to know there's real prawn in those. Best of all, there was a Corncrake calling in the hayfield next to the campsite. *Crek-crek ... crek-crek ... crek-crek ...* Intrigued by this siren-sound in the herbage, I set my heart on catching a glimpse of the mysterious vocalist, and so I waded stealthily through the tall grass on that summer evening, approaching the source of the seductive rasping. As I got closer, it would stop ... and then start up again somewhere else. I repeated this futile endeavour for quite a while, a picture of concentration. It was only when I finally called it a night that I realised how much amusement I'd been providing for my family and other, by now assembled, campsite users. Little would we have known then what the future held for the Corncrake, although my mum could remember their call as a common feature of life in rural Ireland before the war.

Later that summer we camped in the foothills of Snowdonia. An evening family ramble descended into chaos when a bullock took a dislike to us, and it was with a delicious mix of terror and hilarity that we scattered, Dad taking to the nettles in his shorts as we bolted for the 'squeezy' gate from whence we had come, which of course could only admit us one at a time. It was long afterward suspected that Kevin must have provoked the bullock in some way, as was his wont, but the inquest back at camp, as nettlerashes were rubbed, proved inconclusive.

It wasn't connected, but we were soon putting Kevin on a ferry at Anglesey and he went off to work in Ireland for the rest of the summer holidays. At 16, his last family holiday was over. He wasn't with us when Brigid and I found a Red Kite in the hills. We could hardly believe our eyes, as it drifted along a ridge, slowly, gently, tilting one way and then the other as it scanned the hillside below. Mum took some convincing that we could really have seen a Kite, so scarce were they at this time. We crossed the Severn to camp in Devon. I think as we splashed about in the shallows we may have regretted the family outing to see *Jaws* the movie, released that year.

1976

In a year that would be remembered for the drought of another parched summer, the new year began with 100mph winds that left a trail of havoc across the country. Sea walls were breached by pounding waves at East Anglian and Welsh coastal nature reserves. Trees and viewing hides were bowled over at reserves inland, including The Lodge. Bearing the costs of salvaging the situation could hardly have come at a more painful time economically.

The trade in endangered species had taken centre stage. Campaigning since the previous spring paid dividends when government introduced new measures from 1 January, based on eight key recommendations proposed by the RSPB. As a result, from March it was illegal to import any wild bird without a licence. Repugnant images of swans, cranes and storks in crates, pelicans with fractured necks and piles of bird corpses in aircraft hangars played a prominent part in provoking public outrage.

The country was taken aback in March when Prime Minister Harold Wilson dramatically resigned. His government was under mounting pressure, with unemployment soaring, wrangles with the unions and terrorism linked to Northern Ireland. Jim Callaghan took over. The Liberal Party also had a change of leadership after a scandal led to Jeremy Thorpe's resignation. David Steel replaced him. There was even greater political turmoil in the USA where the Watergate scandal was being played out, with the resultant resignation of Richard Nixon, and the ensuing election campaign in which Jimmy Carter triumphed over Gerald Ford.

The Young Ornithologists' Club launched a phone line for the public to call in on Monday afternoons with their observations of spring migrants, so that a weekly picture could be built up. A special survey of Nightingales was also organised that spring, to count the birds in the southern English counties and two Welsh in which they could be heard.

It's often remarked by my contemporaries that the world was a sunnier place in childhood, and I wonder how much the year 1976 influences this. Following the unusually dry preceding year, this was the sunniest in Britain for 500 years. My own recollections of its warmth are heightened by the fact that we chose this summer to have our family holiday in southern England. How singed the landscape seemed. Here was now a land of ladybird plagues, yellowing fields, hot sand and convoys of ice cream vans. We started our tour in Norfolk where my dad was on a training course for head teachers.

The extent of the drought is captured in a photograph from the time of an Anglian Water official squatting in the middle of a vast mosaic of cracked mud. It could be Grafham Water, the reservoir just up the road from where I now live. It captures starkly the extent of what became a drought crisis. It was so dry they had to legislate. The Drought Act was introduced in August as an emergency measure, to help coordinate a national response to the problems of water shortage. Families were encouraged to cut water use by half, by doing things like sharing bath water and using the water for the garden. I think we were already doing this in our household. I had always thought it the norm. With the tinder-dry conditions came the terrifying prospect of forest fires: 200,000 trees were reduced to charred skeletons after one Welsh woodland blaze alone.

Reports began to come in of major climate incidents elsewhere, like the worsening drought situation on a huge scale in sub-Saharan Africa. The sudden population crash of the Whitethroat in the late sixties seems to have been an early warning of this creeping change. Happily, the Whitethroat bounced back. Practically all RSPB wardens from a growing network of reserves were reporting again on its renewed abundance.

Ironically, but perhaps helping to underline the importance of fresh-water habitats, these unexpectedly warm and parched years coincided with Wetlands Year and its immediate aftermath. A year on from signing up to the Ramsar Convention, government had done little to spread the word to water boards and local authorities, which would have been the first and most obvious step in making the agreement work. As the RSPB noted, this meant that throughout Wetlands Year, 'the destruction of British wetlands had continued unabated'.

Film director Nicolas Roeg could hardly have timed the making of *The Man Who Fell to Earth* any better, or made a shrewder choice of male lead in rock star David Bowie, in his first movie role. Bowie plays an alien sent here to find water for his own distant and drought-stricken planet. With the ending of summer, the golden years ended, and normal service was soon resumed in Britain. It rained so hard in early autumn that reservoirs were full again by the third week in September.

A campaign was launched as part of European Wetlands Year to increase public and political awareness of the value of watery habitats. Whatever its impact, it wasn't enough to deter the Environment Minister from approving plans for an oil refinery at Cliffe Marshes in north Kent. The RSPB called this a 'bitter blow', after four years of resistance to the proposal. Cliffe was recognised as being of international importance for wading birds coming here in winter to feed, and of national importance for the ducks and geese nesting in spring and summer.

Fittingly, the RSPB's latest film was *Big Bill – The Story of a Heron*. I recall seeing this and other RSPB movies at busy public screenings in Paisley and Glasgow, of the kind that were a central feature of the organisation's outreach work at that time. There was a healthy public appetite for nature films on big screens in makeshift civic spaces, with speakers before and after.

A mere decade, meanwhile, after the project was first conceived, *The Atlas of Breeding Birds in Britain and Ireland* was finally published. 'It is obviously difficult to forecast what major new factors will affect British and Irish birds in the next 25 years, as pesticides have in the last,' wrote project chairman James Ferguson-Lees, 'but climatic recession is a palpable example and the pressures from oil, both as a direct contaminant of the sea and in its associated land-based developments, are likely to grow; so, too, is human disturbance of remoter areas.'

He picked out a few of the bird species most at risk. Of our marine birds he mentioned terns and auks, vulnerable to disturbance and to oil pollution. The continued decline of the Corncrake was noted, and he wondered what would become of the Red-backed Shrike and the Stone-curlew. Interestingly, of the birds vulnerable to unsympathetic agriculture he picked out the Little Owl and the Barn Owl. And he speculated that by the year 2000 we might have all but lost the Nightjar, the Woodlark and the Cirl Bunting. Of the established native birds that might spread he picked out Siskin and Redpoll, and he wondered if the Dotterel might begin nesting in East Anglia. And he listed 20 or more species that might colonise or recolonise these islands.

Ian Prestt became the new RSPB chief, having been identified for the role. His work as a government natural scientist had helped to devise the methods for recording breeding birds used for the new population atlas. He took office re-emphasising the importance of the RSPB's watchdog role and of securing as nature reserves the most important places for birds. His love of birds was long-standing. As a schoolboy he had won awards for studies of the Sparrowhawk and the Grey Heron, two species he would later study professionally in connection with pesticide poisoning. He had been in the thick of it at the time of *Silent Spring*'s publication, and helped to work out the link between organochlorines and the thinning of eggshells. He now found himself in charge of an organisation with more than 200 staff and 200,000 members.

'The greatest threat to birds is loss of habitat resulting from increasing human population,' he declared in his introductory message. He mentioned 'increasing public pressures of all kinds', and the increasing skills needed to shape 'what remains' for the maximum benefit for wildlife.

Despite measures to control pesticides in the USA, Peregrine Falcons in Arctic North America were still declining because of contamination by organochlorines they were ingesting while wintering in South America. That continent was also beginning to make headlines with alarming coverage and images of the extent to which rainforest was now being cleared.

A letter was received from an RSPB member who had noted that a man accused of selling Osprey and Red-backed Shrike eggs for £100 had been fined £20, with £40 costs, besides asking that 46 other offences be taken into account. 'He is still £40 to the good. I don't see that justice has been done.' The letter was from Spike Milligan. Fellow Goon Harry Secombe, meanwhile, fronted a fundraising appeal.

The House Sparrow population was thought to be in rude health, so much so that tips were still being issued on how to deter flocks from dominating at bird tables and feeders. A letter-writer reported how he had stopped at a motorway service station somewhere in southern England and 'noticed groups of house sparrows ... picking dead butterflies and insects from the front of unattended cars. Hoping this may be of some interest ...'

Tests completed, Concorde was launched on its maiden transatlantic flights. Sitcoms like *The Fall and Rise of Reginald Perrin*, and the rise of punk rock, summed up a prevailing mood of suburban alienation in a troubled country. Queen's 'Bohemian Rhapsody' became the tune you couldn't avoid, staying at number one for weeks on end, including Christmas. An alternative stocking filler, a collection of Ted Hughes poetry, was published, called *Season Songs*. Author Richard Mabey chose it as one of his recommended books to give at Christmas.

And all the years of tireless, patient and persistent campaign 'prodding' finally paid off, when it was confirmed that aldrin and dieldrin were being withdrawn from use. The ministry advised companies selling seeds that remaining stocks must be disposed of safely. Perhaps the birds could now breathe, and sing, more easily.

1977

At the start of the year, government had to go to the International Monetary Fund to borrow £2.3 billion. It was against the backdrop of this kind of deficit that the struggle to prevent the destruction of the environment was being carried out by a growing but still tiny minority movement. It was Silver Jubilee year, and the Queen requested that, given the parlous state of the economy, money should not be thrown at the occasion. Whatever else happened, a lot of paint was splashed. My abiding memory is of the empty dockside buildings in the new town I grew up in. Their windows were bricked up and painted with curtains, vases of flowers and cats on the windowsills, and smiling faces peering out.

We passed those friendly occupants for years afterwards every time we walked along those often creepy, gloomy streets between the railway station and the sports centre, which I think the Queen had visited too, to officially open. One way or another, an effort was made to cheer the place up, and add a bit of colour, if not substance, to a country which, round our way at least, had a heavy mood of post-industrial decline around it. Unemployment had breached a million again. The families being over-spilled from Glasgow's tenement clearances to the promised land of new towns like this were in many cases entitled to wonder whether it had been worth the upheaval.

It was also 25 years since a new bird species immigrated under its own steam to live in Britain. The mild-mannered Collared Dove now found itself on Schedule 2 of the Protection of Birds Act, deemed by government an agricultural pest, even though no evidence was produced that it deserved this, or any proof it caused widespread damage. It was symptomatic of a wider lack of credible science at the heart of decision-making. Culls of seals and gulls were being authorised on the flimsiest of evidence and with tenuous justification. On the plus side, the newly arrived Cetti's Warbler and others were added to Schedule 1, the protected list, four years after the RSPB first asked for this to happen.

The fight for wetlands carried on, with some protracted battles over estuaries of international importance for wildlife, and government rejecting the environmental findings of a succession of enquiries. The RSPB called these enquiries a 'pointless expenditure of time and money if a Secretary of State is going to throw overboard conclusions every time they do not suit his views'.

At European level, the wheels were in motion to create better protection for birds. The European Commission produced a draft directive for all member states. It was an attempt to make laws consistent across different countries, and to standardise hunting regulations. It also set out how habitats should be maintained or recreated to enable birds and other diversity to survive. The directive was similar to existing laws in Britain, but would require some changes to the law. The most important elements were the complete banning of repeating shotguns, bird lime, traps, hooks and any other means of indiscriminate slaughter.

Only species reared for shooting could be sold. It would no longer be permissible to sell any dead bird except game. The directive also proposed to remove from the list of species that could be hunted at certain times species of larks and pipits, which were still considered fair game in some countries. At a time when food mountains were many people's impression of what the EU meant, these 'well prepared and far-sighted' moves would help the public understand some of the benefits of wider, joined-up political and cross-border cooperation.

In response to the continuing mass destruction of migrant birds in the Mediterranean, a Stop the Massacre appeal was launched in the spring. A final push was made to raise £1 million in the Save a Place for Birds appeal, with a quiz – first prize a flight to the New York or Washington Hilton with British Caledonian airways, and £200 spending money. Second prize was a set of limited edition teaspoons.

The appeal closed at the end of the year, by which time £1.2 million had been secured, a phenomenal sum for the time. In response to some raised eyebrows from the membership, the RSPB confessed in a somewhat contrite message to feeling a little self-conscious that this may have presented 'an image of the Society which was totally preoccupied with raising money', but that this was necessary to meet the target set. The bottom line is that it enabled the establishment of important nature reserves in Orkney, Loch Garten in the Highlands, several in East Anglia including Minsmere and Fowlmere, Morecambe Bay and Rathlin Island in Northern Ireland. Some of the pressure on staff from press and broadcast journalists locally and nationally was relieved when the Society appointed its first full-time Press Officer.

Another major milestone in British conservation history was reached when *A Nature Conservation Review* was published, listing the most important sites for wildlife in the country. The question now was how to protect them, since broad policies and those who owned the sites in question could not necessarily be counted on to look after them sympathetically.

One owner of marshland in Devon reflected that the money he received from government for preserving this was a fifth of that received by neighbours growing linseed, even if they didn't harvest the crop. Some were receiving 40% state support to drain other parts of the marsh. He had refused to participate in this, and instead had added extra ponds, and allowed public access.

I remember the televised play *Abigail's Party* causing a stir, and being glued to the serialisation of Alex Haley's epic novel *Roots*. Red Rum cantered to his third Grand National win. Edith Wharton's *Country Diary of an Edwardian Lady* topped the bestseller lists. Something about the formula – nostalgia for lost nature – struck a chord with tens of thousands of readers.

Freddie Laker launched his ill-fated Skytrain, promising cheap long-distance air travel, opening up the world beyond the Mediterranean resorts for the mass market. Some years behind the general trend, and in spite of Dad's previous declarations that we'd never need to go abroad (or get a colour television – that policy decision was also quietly overturned, we were pleased to note), we had our first family summer holiday overseas. We packed the car to within millimetres of the roof with camping gear, stuck a GB sticker on the rear bumper – us kids wedged in the back between suitcases and rolls of foam – and set off for the long drive south through England to a channel port and then its continental equivalent. I was impressed by the frothing fangs of mad dogs on rabies (*La Rage!*) posters, at every turn in ports on each side of the Channel. The Rabies Protection Society had been set up the year before, to keep Britain rabies-free, as it had been for half a century. We wondered if the Dettol in the first-aid margarine tub would be sufficient protection.

Six weeks of exploration around the edge of French campsites, wildlife book in hand, opened my mind, much as the Europeanisation of politics and conservation was broadening the horizons of Britons generally. I would spend hours trying to locate the source of strange calls and songs – not always traced to birds – and link them to the descriptions in the book. Here were Hoopoes and Rollers, Ortolan Buntings, redstarts and Kingfishers, sprung to life off the page. Here too were orchids galore, flurries of blue butterflies, reptiles, apparently edible frogs and formidable insects. Mum was in her element. Dad, too, imperiously pointing out the hanging valleys and the glacial erratics of these torrid, *sauvage* landscapes. Would the soggy pastures and close-cropped hedgerows of Burns country ever look quite the same again?

Not wanting to seem too swanky, I had told my young pals that I was going to Ireland, as usual. This wasn't a complete fib, as we did also visit relatives there earlier in the summer. One of my first and most abiding impressions of Ireland, besides the image of my great-uncle George in his braces cutting the hay meadow with a scythe, and the smell of peat smoke in his cottage kitchen where he played practical jokes on us, was the number of hedgerows there, the small fields enclosed by them, and the conspicuous Magpie nests in the hawthorns.

But it wasn't much of a summer that year. In fact I think it rained pretty much every day in Ayrshire. A good year for silage production. So I was suspiciously tanned when I came back from France that August. My mates must have thought Ireland was further south than they'd been told. We had returned home to find the garden halfway to fully restored temperate rainforest, like so much of the familiar yet suddenly unfamiliar country around it; so lush, so green, compared to the sometimes arid, often craggy wildernesses we'd just inhabited.

There was a lot of readjusting to do. The old certainties had gone. I discovered that 'king' Kenny Dalglish had left Celtic for Liverpool. My brother also left home for university at Stirling soon after. The prog-rock record collection went too, including *Time and Tide* by Greenslade, a soundtrack to these inconstant times.

The album included a moody, troubling track called 'Doldrums', and something similar enshrouded me that autumn. I can trace its onset to a Sunday afternoon, after returning from a beach walk, another oiled bird survey, I think at Ardrossan, or maybe Seamill. It was like a haunting occupied me there, as though the bird-kill body count was taking its toll, the spectacle of seabird corpses finally weighing me down. If an ancient mariner could be afflicted by the slain albatross round his neck, why not me, the junior beached bird surveyor, carrying a gunge-covered Fulmar or two. It was a sunny day, windy, I recall, but the dark days of winter were looming. I was at an age where I was really starting to feel the seasons. Those west coast winters, with their constant, withering rains, rested heavily. I couldn't explain to myself what exactly was wrong but I was troubled.

The attempt to reintroduce the White-tailed Eagle to these islands, centred on Fair Isle and begun in 1968, appeared not to have worked. The birds had not been seen for some years. Another attempt had since been planned, and this year young birds from Norway were released on the Hebridean island of Rum. Paul McCartney's Wings put the nearby west coast peninsula firmly on the map and firmly lodged in the public's mind with their long-running number one single 'Mull of Kintyre' at the year's end.

1978

They tried various things with me. I even spoke to some kind of professional, in an office I am sure was behind some of those Jubilee-decorated, bricked-up windows by the harbour. He asked a lot of odd questions, which didn't help much. I eased out of the despondency in its own time, and way. The ghost was exorcised as inexplicably as it came. I'm sure it was the coming of spring, more than anything, the light and the songs, that provided the release. You feel the seasons deeply in west-central Scotland, when you are young. The short days and bitter cold of winter, the constant rain and the restless Atlantic winds can trouble a restless soul.

I was becoming attuned to the changing tones of the resident birds – the Song Thrush that spoke if not of any appreciable increase in warmth, or a cue to shed the rabbit-fur parka, then at least of longer days. And the Great Tit that cried as though to urge one last push towards spring proper. The returning Swallow was always the crowning moment, the confirmation that not only had they made it again, but that we had. Or I had, at any rate.

In fact, according to those who keep the records, we'd actually been having a run of relatively mild winters. This could explain reports of the normally migrant Blackcap now spending the winter in these isles. Records were requested by a Mr Leach of Alloway, in Ayrshire – better known as the home of the bard, Robert Burns, just down the way. We'd soon have our own winter Blackcap to report from the garden, a bird we'd only got to know on French campsites, now visiting the frosted birdtable, and looking distinctly out of place.

I spent a lot of time exploring the loch I'd adopted as my favourite bolt-hole. 'The Floating Marshes' they called it locally, and in places you did get the distinct impression you were walking on a raft of aquatic plants: a sensation not unlike trying to stand up on an airbed on a swimming pool. This was a little disconcerting, especially when you could see the murky depths of the loch's open water ahead. The marshes had Snipe 'drumming' overhead in spring, a sound they make with their tail feathers as they plummet earthward. It had Water Rails grunting and squealing unseen in the reeds. One evening, Kevin and I even heard the rasping of a Corncrake, which I can only suppose now was just passing through on its way north.

> Mourn clamiring craiks, at close of day
> 'mang fields of flowering clover gay.
>
> Robert Burns

I established a nature reserve of my own. It was about the size of a hearthrug, squeezed between the coal shed/wash-house in the back garden, and the site of occasional bonfires to burn household rubbish. It was partly on the site of a former midden, which we dug out as a project one summer, collecting the bottles and fragments of pottery within it: the clay pipes, and other historical artefacts. This included coins – a large old penny and a Gordon Banks World Cup 1970 Esso souvenir. I also turned up a plastic bust of Tommy Gemmell – Celtic legend – to be scrubbed clean and adorn the mantelpiece. I thought it curious that the people who'd lived in this house before us were also Gemmells. They had a farm up the road too. I decided that big Tam, goal-scoring hero of two recent European Cup finals, must have been part of this farming family. Ten years later, as chance would have it, I ended up living just along the road from a hotel he was running in Bridge of Allan. I used to see him out and about, but I never summoned the nerve to stop him for a chat.

I grew Ox-eye Daisies in the 'meadow' bit, and Foxgloves in the 'woodland glade' under the plum trees. I introduced some tadpoles to the 'pond', an old butler sink, and a pile of rocks for things like Woodlice (we called them Slaters) to hide in. I nailed a cross together, and in white paint daubed the word 'nature' on the horizontal bar, and 'reserve' on the vertical, lest anyone be in any doubt about the designation (and limits on development and access) of this part of the garden. I still have a cherished photograph of this small but I like to think important contribution to the ecology of Scotland, in increasingly difficult times for special places.

A huge Sycamore tree loomed at the end of our neighbours' garden, owned by an Italo-Scots family. He was a grocer from Turin, and sold *frutta e vegetali* down the town. It seems apt to point out that Sycamores were thought to have been brought to Britannia by the Romans. But it would be an exaggeration to claim that fruit and veg were introduced to oor wee toon by Signor Biondi. The Sycamore towered over my reserve, and over the railway line that ran to Irvine and west coast destinations beyond. It was a popular roost site for Starlings. Thousands of them would descend on it towards dusk on late summer and autumn evenings, as though inhaled by its foliage, then exhaled again in a seething tumult. Encores could sometimes – I am a little sheepish to recall – be encouraged by a little clap of the hands by the watching Jameson audience – just to prolong the show, you understand. I loved how so many birds could just disappear within that canopy of leaves, and the din of their conversations as they settled for the night, like excited children on a mass sleepover. I thought of that Sycamore as our 'singing-ringing tree'. In spring the gallus Stuckies, as we called them, dispersed to find territories. One pair lingered to nest in a crack in the crumbling wall between our gardens. At that time Starlings, like House Sparrows, were so numerous, so in your face, that no one could have predicted they would ever become a species of conservation concern.

The Sycamore had one bare branch that stuck out, at eight o'clock, if you like, with a kink that provided a ready perch regularly used by the

Whitethroats that nested in the bramble-covered railway embankment below, each spring. The Whitethroat became our special, unusual bird. At that time we thought it quite rare, having read of its troubles in Africa, where years of drought had caused its population to crash. I don't recall ours ever failing to return. It was the first warbler I got to know well, with its scratchy little song and its quirky ways. It has a charmingly irritable range of noises when you get close, a throaty little growl, like a tiny car ignition not quite sparking to life.

I would encounter this on the railway bank when crawling among the savage bramble stems and Cow Parsley. One May afternoon I actually found its nest, even without trying. It had well-grown chicks in it, eyeing me closely, beadily; so crammed in they probably couldn't move much other than to gape for food at the appropriate moment, chins rested on the rim of a delicate basket woven around stems, low in the undergrowth. One of them had a green leaf stuck to its eye, and was partially blinded as a result. I carefully freed it from this unlikely snare, and slipped away, covering my tracks.

The railway bank of course was officially out of bounds, but in reality was a regular sanctuary and place for den-making. I remember retreating there in the summer, as Scotland's World Cup campaign in Argentina foundered against the challenge of Iran, and the nation was taught a bitter and well-heeded lesson in not over-estimating its status in the world. It was a lukewarm summer in 1978, a miserable one in Scotland after the come-uppance of the World Cup, for those of us young or gullible enough to have believed that our tiny nation might actually have been in with a chance of winning the thing. Besides, Iran has about 15 times the population of Scotland. Nobody mentioned that at the time but I checked. Maybe a draw wasn't such a bad result.

A stream – or burn, as we called them – flowed along one edge of the playground at our primary school. Burns smelled differently in those days, and I realise now, if not then exactly, that this was to do with the untreated sewage that formed part of the flow. I probably didn't quite get the geographical connection at the time, because the railway station and its coal-yards lay in between, but the same burn flowed along the base of the foondry wa'. This was all that remained of a former foundry works on the other side of the west coast Glasgow to Stranraer railway line that spliced the town. I think it was in part because of the barrier formed by this railway that I didn't connect the two burns as being different stretches of the same one. But in any case I used to potter along both, with my mates, finding occasional items of interest, and spending idle hours jumping off the buttressed brick wa' across this burn, to the bank on the other side, where dairy herds chomped noisily on lurid green sward.

The burn disappeared underground into a concrete tube, where the whiff was amplified, and the toilet paper waved like bleached pond weed in the gentle current of the shallows. On one occasion, crouched at the water's edge, baseball boots balanced no doubt on boulders and hoof-sculpted mud, I lifted something out of the water that had caught my eye, something floating downstream. I quickly dropped it, realising to my disgust at least – my mates were too amused to really share the horror – that I had been holding human excrement; or 'a shite', as Sammy put it more succinctly, in the Anglo-Saxon/Lallan Scots. I'm not sure when the question of using the burns of north Ayrshire as open sewers would reach the in-tray of a cabinet minister, but one day I might be old enough to find out.

The main river through the town was subject to regular pollution episodes, besides the ongoing, background contamination of sewage and fertiliser run-off from farmland. 'Ye're mad swimmin' in there,' I remember one old fella calling out to us from the bank on a rare sunny day in July, warm enough for jumping into the tea-coloured broth with its piles of foam at the edges. 'Ye'll catch cholera.' We weren't to know it but Friends of the Earth were busy producing a booklet called *Polluters Pay*, which explained how to make the 1974 Control of Pollution Act work for you, when industry or local authorities were polluting rivers, land and air. We could have done with a copy on the infamous occasion when cyanide leaked into our river. What fish there were went belly-up along its length. This would probably have been enough to discourage us from taking the waters.

The once widespread Otter was by now reported extinct in large parts of the country. Pollution, disturbance and lack of cover along rivers had forced them into retreat. Pesticides were also implicated. Otters were still being hunted, and drowning in fishing nets. From the start of January, some kind of belated milestone was reached when the Otter became a protected species in England and Wales. Until that point it had not been illegal to kill, injure or take one from the wild. Assuming that people would now stop killing them, all Otters needed was an unpolluted river system (they weren't doing so badly in Scotland, away from the industrial lowlands) and they could begin their comeback. This would take a little bit longer to arrange.

Besides the polluted state of many rivers in the seventies, there was the issue of how rivers are actually physically managed and maintained to consider. Technological advances had led to ever-bigger machinery seeking to operate in even wider spaces, free from complications that might add time and cost to dredging and scooping operations. The first moves were made by the RSPB to influence this modern-day river management, and the work of Water and Drainage Boards that maintain the flow of rivers and streams. These boards were seeking increased powers to control all vegetation within 30 feet of a channel, and to prevent planting of trees within that range; essentially seeking a clear run with their huge earth-moving machines to bulldoze anything in their path and leave riverbanks clear of any obstacle. Conservationists, for obvious reasons, have always seen the value in a more sensitive and considered approach to riverbank management. And so the RSPB objected to the proposals, and asked the Department of Environment to take it up with the Minister for Agriculture, who would have the final say.

The places where rivers meet the sea were still under constant threat, with planning battles continuing over the Cromarty Firth, Portsmouth and Morecambe Bay. But perhaps the best example of all was the Ribble Estuary. In the summer months the RSPB entered negotiations with the owner to buy the site, to protect it from the threat of development. It was independently valued at £560,000. The RSPB bid more than this, backed by grants from the Nature Conservancy Council (as it was by now known, or 'NCC') and World Wildlife Fund. Sadly, the land was sold to a developer who bought it for a rumoured £1 million.

The RSPB mobilised voluntary bodies to defend the site. The NCC also advised government to spare it, by buying it. MPs of all parties signed a motion in support, and some asked questions in the House. Nine months later the government, under pressure from MPs, the public, the media and its own advisers, bought the land from this developer for £1.725 million. The estuary had been spared. It was a milestone victory, but would it all have been necessary if special sites like this had protected status in the first place? 'Even now, speculators may be looking through the NCC's own *Nature Conservation Review*, searching for sites to threaten in order to make a quick profit from the tax-payer,' wrote Ian Prestt. If protected status were in place it might prevent these situations from arising in future. Next time, he warned, 'the tax-payer may refuse to be blackmailed again'.

A friend of mine worked for a summer picking fruit in Israel. He witnessed intensive spraying of orchards, and the aftermath. Not only were dead insects strewn below the trees in the morning, but birds as well. He vowed never to eat a peach again. It was reported in the late seventies that an insecticide called azodrin was being used in orchards and on cotton and alfalfa, primarily to kill the Levant Vole. Conservationists wrote to the Israeli government to express concern at the bird-kill – not only of small birds and other wildlife, but of birds of prey consuming the corpses of these poisoned animals. 'As in many other countries,' replied the Minister for Agriculture, 'economic necessity and professional considerations make it impossible for us to impose a ban on this insecticide'.

After an absence of 23 years, the magnificent Bonelli's Eagle returned to nest near the lake of Tiberias in Israel. Tragically, the pair was found poisoned, three weeks after they had laid a clutch of eggs. At least 600 pesticides were at that time registered in Israel, so it wasn't known which of them had killed the eagles. Incidents like this would help to raise the global profile of the wider collateral damage still being caused to wildlife by excessive pesticide use.

With membership now at more than a quarter of a million, the RSPB had embraced the technological future: manual administrative processes had been replaced by a computer system. 'This major step was not taken lightly and arose from the advice of experienced independent consultants,' they reported. There were teething troubles, and national power cuts at critical times, eventually forcing a suitably contrite 'apology to members' to be published. The YOC's spring migrant phone line meanwhile took 3,500 calls. The first birds were coming in on the crest of south and south-westerly winds in late February. Unusual reports included Wryneck, Hoopoe, Black Vulture in Wales, and one Dodo. Which walked, presumably. The cause of bird conservation found a new comedian-champion, Bill Oddie of *The Goodies*, who opened an RSPB shop – The Avocet – in Brighton.

The supertanker *Amoco Cadiz* ran aground off northern France in March. This rapidly turned into the biggest oil spill ever, from an identifiable source. There would yet be bigger ones, but no ship's name could be attached to them. What the images of the spill couldn't show, vivid though it might be, was the stench.

'I could smell the stuff a mile away,' reported RSPB Biologist Peter Hope Jones, who boarded a ferry at Plymouth to attend the disaster. Thousands of birds of 34 species were recorded among the dead, including Puffins, divers and shoreline waders. Dozens of species of fish were washed up.

I soon became accustomed to the disgusting smell of the oil, and I even grew used to being covered up to the wrists in the stuff. But, there were times when opening up a bird produced a sight and smell I would rather not write about ... The abiding feelings were of sadness, of anger, and – perhaps worst of all – of impotence in the face of man's continued abuse of the environment in his questionable progress towards some economic nirvana.

Ten years after the *Torrey Canyon*, and just like its predecessor, the *Amoco Cadiz* disaster would live long in the public memory, with images broadcast across the world. But while this was the biggest tanker disaster, an even bigger one, in bird mortality terms, had already taken place. Mysteriously, there was no ship name to attach to it. Oiled birds were washed ashore in north-east England from late January. Many of the corpses were so badly oiled they couldn't be identified. Despite pressure and criticism from the RSPB it took the Department of Trade three weeks to send a plane out to survey the slick, by which time it was too late to take any action that might have prevented further devastation.

In light of recent oil spill debacles, the RSPB lobbied Energy Minister Tony Benn with concerns about the likely impacts of near-shore oil developments. It had been calling for just a small portion of the huge revenues generated by this developing industry to be put into research and development of methods for preventing pollution, and for detecting and tackling slicks at source. Mr Benn had a tough job to reconcile the rapidly developing industry with the need for safeguards. It was clear that an agency was needed, independent of the drive to generate profits, to guide the latter of these two objectives.

The Corncrake was being silenced. Most rural people knew that. A survey was carried out, organised by Dr James Cadbury, with participants venturing out in the night in remote places where the birds clung on, including Skye. The species had been surveyed just before the war, and a population estimate had been arrived at through the BTO's late sixties survey. In the years since then, the Corncrake's range appeared to have contracted by more than three-quarters. It had long ceased to breed in England and Wales, and looked set to completely forsake the Scottish mainland for the sanctuary of the isles.

Ex-RSPB Chairman Stanley Cramp was commissioned by the European Community to produce a report on Europe's birds, to review what was known about their status and changes, and to make recommendations for the future. The proposed Birds Directive aimed to make inhumane and indiscriminate trapping of wild birds illegal across Europe. It therefore came as something of a shock to find this still going on just a few miles from the RSPB's headquarters. A man appeared at Bedford Magistrates Court charged with using bird lime – glue on perches – to catch wild birds. He was found guilty and fined £50.

As the ICBP gathered in Macedonia for its annual conference, Europe's Council of Ministers had yet to reach complete agreement on the proposed Birds Directive, which would cover all member states. The conference agreed unanimously to express its regret that small differences had been allowed to derail the proposals. This displeasure was communicated by telegram to all governments. Representatives of the major bird protection organisations later met in Florence, hosted by the Italian partner, which had mushroomed since 1966 to a membership of 16,000.

In December, ministers from nine European countries finally reached agreement on the Birds Directive. Some had been dragging their feet over restrictions on the shooting of Skylarks and Ortolan Buntings, and selling of dead birds. The agreement finally signed had inevitable compromises. The RSPB expressed itself 'disappointed that it was necessary to sacrifice the skylark'. The directive would now have to be made to work. All member states would have to amend their national laws to accommodate its requirements. They had two years. Conservationists would continue to press the authorities to understand and to honour the obligations. More research was needed to show what impact the continued hunting, eating and sale of larks and other species was having.

With a Birds Directive now in place, giving status in law across borders, attention could now turn to the places they depended on for survival: habitats. It remained to provide protection for the best and most important of these.

The chilly summer was a prelude to the ending of a run of comparatively mild winters in the seventies. Sub-zero conditions settled over the country and the rest of Western Europe late in the year. Some people speculated that another ice age was on its way. The icy grip of winter was fun for us kids, but meant more tough times for wild birds. One by one some of the newly joined-up bird-protecting countries of Europe imposed bans on the shooting of ducks and geese while the arctic conditions prevailed, rendering these quarry species cold, hungry and presumably less of a sport. Exceptional numbers of these birds arrived to seek refuge in the UK, driven out of their usual wintering areas on the continent by the bitter conditions.

To the considerable surprise and bemusement of our European neighbours, by mid-January this was the only country still to ban the shooting. With widespread reports of wildfowl and wading birds incapacitated with cold and hunger, wetlands frozen solid, impenetrable coastal mudflats, dead birds everywhere and huge bags of birds being shot, and the conditions forecast to continue, the RSPB had to insist that government put a stop to the wildfowling.

1979

They kept calling it the winter of discontent on the TV, but with west-central Scotland ice- and snow-bound and the schools closed for weeks on end due to lack of coal for the boilers, it was difficult for some of us to see it that way. We could see the birds were struggling though, stark against the wintry landscape. The loch was frozen so solid we could access all areas, and while I wince a little now to think of us standing on it, that ice really did seem to be two feet thick in the middle. 'Mr Blue Sky' by ELO was the anthem, and still speaks to me of the magically glittering landscape that had suddenly taken over where the drab and damp one had been just weeks before. We kept the backyard well scraped and scattered with crumbs.

In an eerie echo of the early sixties, large numbers of Brent Geese were found dead on the Essex coast in February, in mysterious circumstances. Fears that they had been poisoned were confirmed when laboratory tests revealed insecticide poisoning. Residues of a product called carbophenothion were found on grain that the birds had consumed, and in their organs. This was one of a new generation of organophosphate insecticides used on grain, against Wheat Bulb Fly. It is acutely toxic to animals. Brent Geese wouldn't normally have foraged for grain like this, but it seemed that someone had put this food out for them specially, unaware of the risk, perhaps to help them through the hard weather. Carbophenothion had already been withdrawn from use in Scotland when wild geese died after eating it in wheat fields.

The hard winter took weeks to release its Baltic grip. The Redwings from Scandinavia foraging in our snowy garden looked set to make the move permanent. When the full impact was later assessed, it was found that small birds had suffered huge losses, especially in the north, with almost half of all Wrens perishing in the freeze, and the other little guys – Long-tailed Tits, Goldcrests and Treecreepers – also depleted. The YOC spring migration phone-in had its first report of Swallow two weeks later than usual, the birds held up by the cold weather and nipping winds from the north. Cuckoos returning in April had to forage for food in snow at a nature reserve in Wales. Swans were reported as declining, believed to be because of discarded fishing line, lead shot and hooks. The YOC organised its members to collect evidence.

A general election was due, and the RSPB was ready to fully mobilise its membership to quiz candidates on environmental issues. After the decade just gone, it was no surprise that oil pollution should also now be considered an election issue. Since 1971, there had been almost a hundred major oil pollution incidents. To underline how much more seriously pollution was being taken, a new Marine Pollution Control Unit was set up by government. By April, the Beached Bird Survey had helped to identify 20 major pollution incidents in the preceding year alone.

A problem for migrant birds like the Redwing was identified around gas flares on oil platforms. 'Incinerated starlings fell into the water like smoke bombs, and when daylight came great numbers could be seen dead on the sea,' ran one gruesome account. The RSPB made enquiries but was met with denials. 'There may be no threat to survival of what are, in most instances, common species,' the Society reflected, 'the most disturbing aspect is the serious doubt it throws on the credibility of oil companies.' Industry had also resisted most attempts to have independent observers placed with their oil installations.

Margaret Thatcher's Conservatives won the June election. The new PM quoted St Francis when she famously declared 'there is work to be done', which may have given optimistic conservationists a slightly misleading impression of her party's priorities. Michael Heseltine was appointed Environment Minister, and he at least appeared to have a decent grasp of green issues. He rhymed some of them off in an early speech to business leaders: drainage of wetlands, ploughing permanent pastures, chemicals, loss of hardwood trees to conifer plantations, canalisation of rivers and oil pollution. He also recognised Britain's leading role internationally and pledged to maintain this.

A new conservation battle front was opened – forestry. At face value the public might have welcomed – and expected conservationists to welcome – the Forestry Commission's announcement of a plan to more than double the area of commercial forestry plantation over the next 50 years. It described this as 'a long-term goal of creating, on some of Britain's poorest land, up to a further 1.8 million hectares of plantations', saying it was 'technically feasible and appears to be a prudent investment'.

Not everyone relished the prospect of more plantations. 'We should be perfectly clear that expansion of forestry is often at the expense of different and more interesting communities,' the RSPB responded, drawing attention to the 'damage caused by modern forestry practice to wildlife in general and birds in particular'.

Attention turned to farmland issues; not just the usual suspects – hedgerow loss, drainage and agrochemicals – but farming in its totality. Its effects on wildlife were now being described as 'enormous and rarely beneficial'. The RSPB appointed a specialist to deal with farming and forestry problems. But despite the efforts of the Farming and Wildlife Advisory Group, only a 'minute proportion' of farm owners were seeking advice on wildlife conservation. A disappointing number seemed actively opposed to the idea.

'It is hardly logical to destroy, for example, a small yet valuable area of wetland in order to add to the warehouse stores of unwanted butter and skim milk powder,' pointed out Ian Prestt. 'Compensation given to a farmer to hold his land from destroying a SSSI is wholly derisory and in strange and painful contrast to the generous grants available to him to plough the shrinking acreage of heather or to drain his marsh.'

There would be much talk from here on in about these best places for nature, lumbered with the clunky and forgettable title Sites of Special Scientific Interest – shortened to the only slightly less laborious SSSIs – pronounced 'triple-ess-eyes'.

'The fact is,' Prestt went on, 'that no-one, as yet, knows anything like enough about the economics of multi-use of land, nor about the effective ways in which government funds might be re-deployed to maintain a better balance between food production and wildlife conservation. And it really is about time that someone did.'

He had laid down two of the looming environmental challenges of the coming decade, micro and macro – protecting special places and agriculture.

1980

The decade entered its final year the way it began, with oiled seabirds drifting ashore in depressingly large numbers. Survey volunteers were scrambled into action over the new-year holiday period in south-west England. At the final reckoning, it was the worst bird-kill in this part of the country since the *Torrey Canyon*. Hundreds of birds were taken into care, but every one of them had to be put down because the oil could not be removed from their plumage in any meaningful way; a heart-breaking task for the volunteers.

Rachel Carson was posthumously awarded the Presidential Medal of Freedom, the highest honour a civilian can receive in the USA. Here in the UK, pesticide problems hadn't gone away. The Royal Commission set up to investigate pollution by agriculture now produced its 300-page report, which was debated in Parliament in January. It strongly backed RSPB concern about the threat still posed by DDT and similar substances. In 15 years, successive governments had pledged to adequately restrict the use of these products. The shocking news was that if anything their use had been increasing since 1974.

Scientists were now finding Sparrowhawks suffering reproductive failure having accumulated residues of something called DDE, a derivative of DDT. The species had yet to recolonise the south and east of England since its disappearance in the sixties, under the first wave of lethal agrochemicals. Impacts on wild plants were starting to be noted in the wider farmed environment, with 23 arable wildflowers described as very restricted in distribution. Of these, 14 were endangered.

Another problem insecticide was in the RSPB's sights: mevinphos. It had widespread and legitimate uses, but was also being widely misused, in concentrated form, as a poison. It figured prominently in the report *Silent Death*, a compilation of incidents in which poisons had been used to illegally kill birds and mammals. This would prove to be the worst poisoning year on record.

The spring-migration phone line was boosted by coverage on the BBC's *Blue Peter* and *Wildtrack* children's programmes. Call centres were set up in mid-Wales, Belfast and Edinburgh, and by the Irish Wildbird Conservancy in Dublin. Six thousand calls were taken. Spring also brought much talk of the new Wildlife and Countryside Bill that had been introduced, to go through the Parliamentary mill. It was expected to be 'as vital to the future of bird protection and conservation in this country as any legislation since the RSPB was founded'. And yet it was a 'hotchpotch of proposals', wrapping up not only the previous acts protecting wild birds, but every kind of countryside issue, including bulls on public footpaths. It was feared that important details might be lost or overlooked in the melee, or stramash, in the Scots.

In the past, conservationists had been on the inside when the law-making process kicked off. Their own officials had been parliamentarians, as well as representatives of conservation bodies. This time it was different. 'Perhaps then,' said Ian Prestt, 'we should not be too surprised that the proposed revisions of the Protection of Birds Acts are good in parts but disturbingly bad in others.' There was much legal revision at a national level, and delays in the introduction of the new laws led to a spate of crime involving thefts of birds of prey.

In March, a World Conservation Strategy was launched in 32 countries. It was said to be the first time that governments, non-government organisations and experts had got together to take a serious global view on integrating conservation with development. It was a genuine attempt to create a blueprint for survival. The USA called for the establishment of an international conservation corps. The human population of the planet was now 4 billion, up by a third since the early sixties, and on course to increase by another third by the year 2000. By that time it was reckoned that 3 million of the 5 million known species on Earth would be extinct if we maintained the present rate of resource depletion. 'Ten years ago this depressing scenario would have been envisaged by the professional doomwatcher,' said the RSPB. Now, the realism was evident more widely and – crucially – within governments.

For those with a focus on birds, it was recognised that there must be a change of emphasis, away from 'fire brigade action aimed at protecting individual species and towards action to preserve critical but vulnerable habitats, thereby preserving populations'. This meant change for the RSPB, too. The 'trend has been away from purchasing reserves purely to protect rare species towards acquiring areas known for their communities and their importance to birds in general … The pattern to date has been to record the population declines first and then look for a reason.'

Migrant birds fitted with leg rings were beginning to reveal more about migration. The RSPB illustrated this by plotting some of the species on a map of Europe and Africa. The captions read like a roll call of the fallen in war:

Pied flycatcher. Ringed in South Wales in 1974.
   Caught and caged in Spain February 1975.
Wheatear. Ringed in Kent 10 September 1969.
   Found dead Mid-Sahara 18 March 1971.
Dotterel. Ringed as a nestling in the Grampians in 1975.
   Shot in Morocco January 1979.
Woodcock. Ringed as nestling in Finland, June 1974.
   Shot in Yorkshire January 1975.

Inevitably, the conservation struggle was becoming more technical. The mission to protect species moved further into the arena of international agreements signed up to by national governments. These deals obliged countries to protect the best places for wildlife. The British government, in a country with a long conservation tradition and mass support, where it would be reasonable to expect a lead to be given and a good example shown, was falling short.

The thing that stops a government protecting a special place is usually the financial interest of owners and industry, generally believed to translate as the short-term economic interest of government. These interests had been given an effective right of veto in deciding what would become a protected site and what would not. Specialists had so far identified 3,500 such places. Half of them were vulnerable to being destroyed by farming or commercial forestry. Well over a hundred were already being spoiled and in some cases severely damaged each year. There was very little to stop this happening. The RSPB called for a system of protection along the lines of those in place and accepted as normal for ancient monuments and the most valuable old or otherwise interesting (listed) buildings. Should the best bits of the natural environment be treated differently?

The hills of Wales provided a useful case study, where decades of excessive exotic conifers in the wrong place, too many sheep and too much burning of heather to create the grazing for these sheep had dramatically reduced the range of life forms these uplands could support. In response, conservationists attempted to save the best bits, and identified nine of the most important surviving sites. Government's conservation authorities agreed these were special places, but their forestry and farming counterparts had other ideas. After months of deliberation, government gave up on one of the sites and allowed its purchase by commercial forestry interests. Virtually the whole of it disappeared under spruce trees. The RSPB spoke ruefully of the 'weakness and uncertainty' being shown at this time by the government agency, which had little power to prevent such wilful vandalism.

A law change was looming that would remove some of the ambiguity from around recreational egg collecting. It would all be made illegal, at a time when the activities of eggers seemed to be on the increase. The RSPB suggested that existing egg collections should be registered, so that the difference between an old egg collection and one assembled since the law change might be readily apparent to those expected to enforce the law.

I am old enough to have grown up in a time and a place where the searching for and the taking of birds' eggs was a matter-of-fact, everyday business for the youth of the small town where I went to school. There was a growing sense of its harmfulness, and understanding of its illegality, a consensus that birds needed protection and could no longer sustain this pressure in a changing world. Many of the leading ornithologists in the long history of the discipline here started life as enthusiastic eggers, and there is much that can be learned by young people about the ways of birds and the wild by working out how and where birds nest. But this was now.

Although I spent many hours 'up the country' scouring hedgerows and ditches, and fields and woods, alert for birds' nests, I never had any desire for an egg collection, and I never robbed a nest. It might have been different had my parents been less enlightened on the subject, but I'm not sure. I never felt the need to own the eggs of any of the birds whose nests I found. On the contrary, I wanted to visit again, within reason and without risk of disturbing the birds, to see the progress of their projects, to appreciate the minor miracle of their developing contents. Knowing where a bird was nesting was a window on to its inner world, a chance to see the birds in action, close, on repeat occasions.

So it was with a mixture of remorse and curiosity that I would witness the interventions of my peers in the nesting attempts of birds in the thorn and elder bushes around the edge of the school, and beyond. Of course their own nest- and egg-finding efforts added at times to the volume of such things that I was able to see, and perhaps enhanced my own store of knowledge. But I saw too many nests 'rooked' as we called it, when the structure was cleared out, destroyed or left hanging, dashed to the ground, and I knew too well the fate of most of the eggs taken – broken and wasted by clumsy fingers, or in the act of blowing the contents out. I saw boys attempting this using thorns for needles, and often discovering that the embryo inside was too well developed to pass through the pinhole pricked in the end of the egg. The more practiced eggers would claim to have substances at home that could dissolve the more solid contents of an egg.

I saw at least one egg collection of a schoolmate, proper cabinets stored under his bed, slid out to reveal banks of eggs of some species I'd barely ever set eyes on, neatly arranged in nests of cotton wool, and labelled. Some of these had been sourced from expeditions to far-flung locations, like the moors far to the south and east that were well beyond my rambling range, and to which I am sure eggers like him were taken by the adults who supervised the hobby.

I also knew boys who would launch egging raids on islands in the Firth of Clyde, taking their lives in their hands to bob across the choppy waters using inflated lorry tyre inner tubes as rafts. These small seabird colony islands were practically paved with eggs, shore-to-shore in late spring. An egging frenzy probably gripped the collectors when they found themselves in this situation, taking entire clutches of elegantly tapered and blotched eggs of gulls, terns, waders and other species, filling a bag of some kind, and then attempting to make the return journey while keeping this fragile booty intact.

One of my contemporaries made the headlines on national TV – *John Craven's Newsround* – one evening. He had to be rescued from an islet in the Clyde, I think because his inner-tube raft was gashed by barnacles. He was airlifted by helicopter to the mainland, I assume via the local infirmary. It all sounded a bit heroic, and of course getting a mention on the BBC was unexpected celebrity for a schoolboy from round our way. Presenter John Craven never mentioned egg collecting in that bulletin, and I realise now that it would have been unwise for him to have done so, even had they known. Back home, we knew very well what the young miscreant had been up to.

Taxidermy was also in the new law's sights, to make it more difficult for unscrupulous wildlife-stuffers to work with corpses of ill-gotten protected species. New regulations would also make it more difficult for stolen wild birds to be secreted into falconry networks, where they couldn't easily be traced. There would be further constraints on the selling and exhibiting of caged birds. None of this was intended to stop people from enjoying stuffed, caged, trained or otherwise performing birds, if that is how they chose to indulge their interest, merely to make it less tempting to supplement captive populations with fresh blood stolen from the wild.

The announcement that an area of tropical forest the size of Wales was being felled each month had many people reaching for the world atlas. The National Academy of Sciences thought a little bit bigger when it now reported that an area of tropical moist forest about the size of Britain was being destroyed each year. At this rate many countries would have no lowland rainforest left by the end of the eighties. By the turn of the millennium, they said, 'virtually all accessible tropical moist forests will have been eliminated'.

A National Tree Campaign was launched, partly inspired by the widespread loss of elms in the landscape. Dead elms were being hastily cleared from the countryside, even though dead trees still provide nest holes and standing dead elms are not often especially unsafe. The Tree Council hoped to raise £1 million to plant trees for three years. I don't recall my own school engaging with this national initiative. I do remember us collecting crisp packets frenetically for some months – not that we needed too much encouragement to eat crisps or rake in bins – to earn something called 'flutter-bys', that we sent off for but that never turned up, because the crisp-maker went bust. My own lasting contribution to the cause of trees that year was to engrave an existing one.

On a gentle hill above my loch basin is a grey-barked beech tree with an ever-widening scar, in the shape of CJ, and below that the number 80. It's been there since the schoolboy that was me, with my treasured French beech-handled penknife, carved it that summer, sitting astride a lower limb. I could see those beeches on the hill-top from my bedroom back in the town. They formed an avenue at a place called the White Gates, although the gates themselves were long gone. A walled garden survived, the ground within now re-seeded with rye grass like most of the surrounding landscape. It sometimes contained a bull, and the ruin of a small outhouse attached to the wall at one end, where we could attempt Butch Cassidy heroics, albeit minus the bicycle. Sometimes we might even have a Katharine Ross figure or two to show off to, if we were lucky.

One of the most dramatic bird spectacles I witnessed around this time was a September gathering of Swallows in and around the reedbed that fringed the loch. The sward was thick with Daddy-long-legs that evening, and the Swallows were filling up on the blundering beasties in the dairy fields around the loch basin. The reeds seethed and swayed with perching Swallows, while other birds zipped and dipped around them before settling: a carnival of wings, for *Hirundo rustica*, a gathering of the clans to banquet, ready for the long march south.

It was the era of food mountains linked to excess production in the European Community. The Treasury had paid out £90 million in 1978 on buying and storing surplus food. It might have been expected that governments would seek more imaginative ways to deploy subsidies than with policies that continued to sponsor the dismantling of habitats. Battle had begun with the Ministry of Agriculture over how it should be using its funds. The ministry seemed determined to insist that it could not use these funds for any purpose other than intensifying agriculture. It also appeared to think that it was above regulations requiring government departments to conserve the natural beauty and amenity of the countryside. The President of the EU had to be called in to disabuse them of this view. As government at last began to show signs that it understood public concern at the loss of the best sites for wildlife, it proposed to properly protect only a few. It was still resisting the idea that landowners should be incentivised to manage estates containing important wildlife sites.

The Wildlife and Countryside Bill had its second reading, and a debate that evoked much of the loss that had been felt in the landscape since the war. It had become clear that the proposed law was not going to be fit for purpose. It was plain to most that the NCC needed more power and funding to set up management agreements with landowners that would prevent special sites being damaged. As it stood, only one in every 40 of these places was safe.

Three years after the publication of the list of the 735 best sites for wildlife – the ones of national and international importance, and the minimum the country should be expected to conserve – four had been completely destroyed and 53 seriously damaged. Unsympathetic farming and forestry operations were the usual causes.

'The Forestry Commission's remit is too narrow,' the RSPB told the Lords, which was also looking into forestry issues. 'The practice of maximising timber production in monocultures is too limited to be considered as a proper national forestry policy.' Experience was showing that the commission needed obligations, not just encouragement.

On its wetland protection duties, government seemed to be shirking. Five years after signing up to the Ramsar Convention on protecting wetlands, it finally got around to adding some more sites to the UK list (of 13) for protection. Six were added, which sounded like progress, until the RSPB pointed out that five of these were sites owned by nature conservation organisations. They were *already* protected. The sixth was a reservoir, effectively also *already protected*. The real net increase in sites being given protection was therefore nil, although it did no harm to have these further six confirmed, and on the list. 'The Government contrives to look well in the eyes of the international conservation community,' wrote Ian Prestt, 'while in fact making no additional commitment whatsoever.'

Marion Shoard's hard-hitting book *The Theft of the Countryside* raised the temperature of the debate. It conveyed the author's anger at the lack of restraint on those who were removing the best bits of the countryside, and what she called the 'toothless watchdogs' standing by as this despoliation was going on. The foreword was contributed by Henry Moore, better known as a sculptor than for his views on the complete destruction of the English countryside that he predicted. 'There is almost universal ignorance of the imminence of this catastrophe,' he warned.

Shoard made plain her fears. 'The English landscape,' she said, 'is under sentence of death … Already, much of the east of the country looks disappointingly familiar to tourists from the American Mid-West.' She called it a 'so far undiscussed onslaught', and 'a major national scandal'. It was now calculated that 140,000 miles of hedgerow had been removed since the war. The advent of guaranteed prices through subsidies had made the drive to convert more woods and hedgerows and wetlands to agriculture difficult for many to resist.

Shoard drew attention to many startling stats underlining the loss of life in all its forms from the farmed landscape. In 1950 there were 300,000 working horses on our farms, and now almost none. In their place were half a million tractors. There were 430,000 fewer farm workers than in 1948. This meant that just one in four still had rural jobs. Of course all of this can be seen as the inevitable march of progress, of technological advance, world markets, greater efficiency. But the point was that the market hadn't necessarily created this situation. Public subsidy had. And if the population was paying to make farm businesses viable, was the public not entitled to a greater stake in it?

In 1980, each farm was receiving on average £8,500 in subsidy from taxpayers and consumers, five times what the average British Steel employee was receiving in subsidy, for example. The figures for grants being given out to make roads, uproot bushes and trees, install fences, kill ancient meadows and pull the plug on wetlands were eye-watering; with little apparent government concern for the wider interest the public might have in the purpose of the rural landscape around them. Nor were grants ever means-tested. It didn't matter how wealthy recipients might already be, in the money-go-round of agriculture. Grants of more than £100 million were being contributed by the taxpayer – up to three-quarters of the cost of improvements to farm businesses. These didn't have to pay rates, and were unconstrained by the planning system. Any conservation system in these circumstances would clearly depend on the goodwill and sympathy of those who owned the land.

Like many families we used to watch a sitcom called *Butterflies*. At face value it was light and safe BBC pre-watershed entertainment for a prime-time audience, but even to my young mind it was heavy with pathos and symbolism, portraying the underlying pain and frustration of the suburban English middle classes. Mum was always a devotee of butterflies – real ones. We had posters in the bathroom and even some pinned-and-mounted Ugandan specimens on the stairwell wall. Huge beasts. She drew our attention to the extinction of a species called the Large Blue in Britain that year. It's a butterfly with a bizarre and complex life cycle, inextricably linked with ants, which tend and raise its caterpillars underground. This improbable life story was no longer being lived out in Britain. The Large Blue had gone. Not because someone pinned and mounted it in a glass case – although by the end of course that wouldn't have done the butterfly any favours – but because its habitat, its food plants and its ants had been destroyed. No Large Blues left to collect.

As the seventies drew to a close, I would have been gratified to learn that the 1980 River Quality Survey and Outlook by the National Water Council showed that 'gross pollution' had declined, although the rate of improvement of water quality had slowed. Meanwhile, something that went largely unreported and unnoticed, but may have been a taste of things to come: across the piece, 1980 was the warmest year ever recorded. The eruption of Mount St Helens in North America would have something to say about the weather to come. In western Scotland at least, things would only get wetter.

The Eighties

1981

The new decade began with a seamless transition into more of the same as the polluted seventies. January would go down in history as one of the worst months ever recorded for oil pollution incidents. More than 42,000 dead and dying birds were counted. Had gale-force winds not brought the corpses ashore, this death toll, like so many others caused by oil slicks out at sea, would have passed unnoticed.

I recently unearthed an old photograph: a particularly arresting image of an oiled Guillemot in the middle distance, surrounded by a vast expanse of sandy shoreline. The bird is facing seaward, towards a line of grey breakers and a low brooding sky. Its wings are held open but drooping, wingtips trailing on the wet sand, maybe for balance. The bird looks slightly crumpled, its bill raised as though in final defiance. It could equally be read as pleading, surrendering. It is a visual statement of farewell, to a beautiful world with a badly tarnished heart. There were half a dozen oil spill incidents this year, and double that the next. The problem wasn't going away.

A lively Lords debate in mid-December had created widespread interest in the progress of the embryonic wildlife law. Amendments had flooded in. Several hundred were tabled in advance of the committee stage in late January. The RSPB's efforts to moderate some of the excesses it saw in the activities of wildfowlers were rebuffed. But the extra protection it sought for the Curlew, Redshank and Bar-tailed Godwit received lots of votes, against government advice.

The House was packed out for the debate on protecting habitats.

This centred on the limits that could be imposed on landowners doing as they pleased with the special places for nature under their ownership. It was a debate about responsibility for land, and nature. The voluntary approach favoured by the Conservative government had sounded laudable in theory, and had been the *de facto* situation until now. It had been hoped that owners would be caring, trustworthy and willing to do the right thing in looking after special places. But fresh reports were being fed into the debate that showed this trust had been breached too many times. Many special places had already been damaged.

The day before the critical vote in the House, government produced a new clause which would offer further encouragement to owners to cooperate in looking after these places. It wasn't ever going to stop a given owner from damaging a SSSI, but it was something, and probably as much as could be expected in the circumstances. And the vote went government's way – although it was surprisingly close at 109 to 100.

The bill went back into the Commons. Some of the concessions won in the Lords were lost again. The Curlew and Redshank lost their protection from hunting, now back on the list of species that could be shot. The government's majority was carrying the vote on these and other issues. Opposition MPs began to question some of the fundamental issues and whether government's determination that the approach should be 'voluntary' would result in legislation with any real authority. More survey results came in from the NCC showing that up to 15% of SSSIs had been damaged or lost last year, especially in lowland farmed areas.

The concept of 'reciprocal notification' was introduced. Landowners would have to let the NCC know if they had any plans to damage a site. The NCC had in turn a duty to let the owner know what sort of things might damage it. There were further deliberations over money. Would the NCC have the cash it needed to make the new approach work, where compensation for income foregone by an owner might be needed? In a final twist, the Lords voted once again that Redshanks and Curlews should not be shot any more, and the government's MPs reluctantly backed down on this point.

For the time being at least, conservation-minded people would have to trust the goodwill of those who owned the land, and their tenants or contractors. The profile of these special places had at least been raised. Perhaps now, with the spotlight on them, landowners would feel more inclined to be seen to be doing the right thing and managing these places for their wider nature and public benefit, rather than for short-term economic gain. Ignorance would no longer seem like a valid excuse for mismanagement either. Conservationists could but hope.

There were some other small wins in the long list of matters covered by the bill. Subsidies for agriculture could now be offered for conservation outcomes, for example. Drainage boards and water authorities would also now be expected to take a 'positive attitude' towards conservation. They would have to consult with the NCC before doing anything to a special wildlife site.

The environmental impact of open-cast mining became an issue. My pals and I had been only vaguely aware there might be risks associated with swimming in a disused quarry 'up the country'. 'The Blue Lagoon' we called it, with more than a hint of satire. In fact it was sage green, in certain lights, and its surroundings fawny-brown, with the hardier wildflowers just gaining a toehold. The Lapwings liked its spoil for the clear views and sense of abandonment, and nested there in good numbers, while we used its steep muddy banks to practice our Tarzan high-dives. I shudder sometimes to think back to the madcap world of adolescence, pre health and safety neuroses. The grass-covered slurry pits we used as bouncy castles, the scrapyards and the builder's yard obstacle courses, the rope-swings high over rocky stream-beds, the willowherb spear fights, the high-wire tree climbing, the stampeding bullocks.

Day of the Triffids was serialised on prime-time television. It may have influenced the scare stories circulating about a plant called Giant Hogweed which loomed out of damp ditches and looked a bit scary. One letter writer called it an 'exceedingly dangerous plant to some people'. Its sap can cause blistering. Some of us discovered this when utilising the thick, hollow stems as blowpipes. But we lived and learned. Post-industrial Britain could be fun for the young, if you happened to lead a charmed life.

Not many people noticed that 1981 was the new warmest year ever recorded, warmer even than 1980. We certainly didn't, as our training shoes disintegrated in the wet and our jeans got soaked to the thigh. And it was little remarked that the Wryneck had gone. There were no longer any records of this strange little woodpecker breeding successfully in England. It had been common in the south-east at one time. A tiny number clung on in Scotland, though not in our neck of the woods. We had the place pretty well covered, even for cryptic little birds like this one.

1982

'Autobiography can be a laying to rest of ghosts as well as an ordering of the mind. But for me it is also a celebration of living and an attempt to hoard its sensations.' The words are those of Laurie Lee. I think it was Mrs Lockley our English teacher who encouraged us to read this, although it may have been Mum, who was always a fan. The essay left a lasting impression on me, and articulated and nurtured an instinct I felt; especially this bit: 'The spur for me is the fear of evaporation – erosion, amnesia if you like – the fear that a whole decade may drift gently away and leave nothing but a salt-caked mudflat.'

That was it. I became a dedicated diarist. Or at least I tried to. The will was there, but there wasn't always the time. Often, the diary would be full and daily until springtime came and life became an outdoor occupation once again. If I wasn't recording the events of this short life, it nagged at me in a way I could probably describe as existential now, if not back then. 'What indeed was that summer if it is not recalled?' Laurie Lee chided, many times over. 'To whom did it happen if it has left you with nothing? Certainly not to you ...' OK, Laurie. Give us a break.

The gaps in diaries I can partially fill because I can plot later life around football matches and popular songs, which of course have fixed dates that can usually be recalled, and checked if necessary, and notes I made about birds heard or seen, wildlife encountered. I know that in the summer of 1982 we camped in Cambridge. To my young eye here was a balmy, flat, dry place, a pleasant if slightly featureless field with a dusty hedgerow along which to fossick. We were on the long road south to a Channel port, stopping off to visit a family my parents had been close friends with since Ugandan days in the sixties. I know because in the background – as the grown-ups chatted, about Uganda now post-Idi Amin and picking up the pieces – Kevin Keegan's England were trying in vain to win a match in the World Cup in Spain. I always rooted for England too, although the pundits didn't always make it easy.

Two decades had passed since the publication of *Silent Spring*, and it seems a fitting marker that the much mulled over and hotly debated Wildlife and Countryside Act 1981 finally became law. It would provide the context for nature conservation in the UK for the next 20 years. But how much would it really help the cause of birds? A test case of its effectiveness arose soon after the act was passed.

One of the last remaining wet meadows on an important Essex marsh was set to be drained. The NCC didn't object, believing that it had to save its limited funds for bigger battles to come. The RSPB was dismayed. The NCC had about one-fifth of the budget the RSPB believed it should have, if it was to work out management agreements and compensation payments for landowners blocked from carrying out operations that would damage a SSSI. 'Resources are massively stacked against conservation,' pleaded the NCC.

There would be no shortage of other examples of system failure. In 1976 the RSPB had surveyed 40 important upland sites in Wales. Only nine were intact. The NCC agreed that these should be notified as SSSIs. Five years on it had yet to even begin to notify any of them. One had been let go to development ruin. For two others, they intended to notify only parts; the parts that were unsuitable for agricultural improvement in any case. The system was failing first of all to identify complete SSSIs, and second by delaying their creation. Sites were not being notified for their scientific worth. The RSPB took legal advice to seek to oblige the NCC to fulfil its statutory duty.

There would be no obligation on farmers and landowners to protect SSSIs. They and government had resisted laws to make that happen. Instead there was to be a voluntary code. When this was drawn up, owners of SSSIs would receive a copy. They would be asked to cooperate with the NCC, but there would be no penalties if they chose not to. It was, as the RSPB noted at the time, 'an enormous act of faith'. The RSPB was consulted on the code. There were several concerns. There was, for one thing, still no commitment to conservation from the agriculture departments of government, or the Forestry Commission.

'The document is rather bland and cynical,' concluded the RSPB. 'Instead of explaining that an SSSI ought to be a source of pride for a landowner, it concentrates on the administrative procedures for objecting to the creation of SSSIs and for claiming compensation.' There were already signs that some landowners were opting against cooperation. Two proposed SSSIs had been wilfully damaged by farming operations while all the consulting and producing of codes was going on.

The voluntary approach appeared not to be working for hedgerow protection either. A Labour member attempted to introduce a bill to protect the bare minimum, most important hedgerows: those along parish boundaries, footpaths, bridleways and roads. These are often the oldest and most valuable in terms of public amenity, as well as species interest. An objection by a government spokesman prevented the bill from becoming law.

A campaign for woodlands began. The House of Lords committee had recorded that since 1950 somewhere between a third and a half of the ancient semi-natural woodlands in Britain had gone. It had taken four centuries for as much as that to have been lost beforehand. They recommended that broadleaf woodlands should not be allowed to decline any more, which hardly sounds like a radical campaign goal but perhaps reflects the modest ambitions of the age. 'In the past, relations between forestry interests and countryside organisations have varied from a state of suspicious truce in some cases, to open hostility and conflict in others,' the RSPB acknowledged.

In the USA, there were fears that any environmental gains made in the seventies were going to be undone with a new administration in place. President Reagan appointed a new Secretary of the Interior so unpopular that within months a petition had been launched by conservationists to have him removed. It amassed over a million signatures, one of the largest petitions ever presented to Congress.

'The anti-environmental policies of the Reagan administration have acted like a shot of adrenalin,' said the head of the Sierra Club, whose membership soared this year. The National Audubon Society made clear that 'the American people will simply not permit a return to the environmental dark ages, when our air and water were fouled at will by those who profited from using our life-support systems as their sewer'.

The ICBP – with six staff operating out of a Cambridge Portakabin – published *Endangered Birds of the World*. Migratory birds had become of particular concern. Michael Heseltine opened the world conference, and underlined growing public interest in the environment by pointing out that more people were now watching the BBC's *Wildlife on One* than *Match of the Day*, which may also have said something about the state of English football. The conference discussed ways to use scientific knowledge to convince other governments of the value of conservation. It also looked at how we might channel funds to poorer countries, which were now repeating familiar mistakes with persistent pesticides.

Conference turned to a subject that not many people had yet encountered, but that would become one of the major issues of the coming decade. 'It started in the 1960s as a fairly local problem in Scandinavia. Fish and other aquatic organisms vanished because of the increasingly acid water in lakes and streams.' Acid rain had arrived. Delegates heard about the damage this was doing to forests in Bavaria and to lake systems in Scandinavia.

In August, the latest International Ornithological Congress brought nearly a thousand people together in Moscow. The RSPB screened its Osprey film twice, by popular demand. Peregrine Falcons were at this time declining all over Europe, but not, any longer, in the UK, where they were by now recovering, despite an astonishing 276 nests known to have been robbed since 1976; thieves getting in quick before the new law came in.

Two pairs of Golden Eagles reared a youngster in the Lake District, the first time that both pairs had succeeded. It had been hoped that Rum's White-tailed Eagles would by now have raised young in western Scotland, where they had been reintroduced in 1977, but no luck so far.

1983

Aldous Huxley's *Brave New World* was a set text for our English O-Grade exams, and made a deep impression on me. John the Noble Savage provided a new kind of anti-hero to adopt. I loved this future-gazing stuff. *The Time Machine* caught my imagination too, shown as part of a science fiction movie season on BBC2. It is based on the short story by H. G. Wells, written a century ago and describing a time that we have not yet reached. That time in the future described is already starting to sound familiar, not least on the subject of plants and animals, and how we use them.

I borrowed the book. Of his own Victorian period, Wells's time traveller said: 'We improve our favourite plants and animals – and how few they are – gradually and by selective breeding, now a new and better peach, now a seedless grape, now a sweeter and larger flower, now a more convenient breed of cattle. We improve them gradually, because our ideals are vague and tentative, and our knowledge is very limited; because Nature, too, is shy and slow in our clumsy hands. Some day all this will be better organised, and still better ... Things will move faster and faster towards the subjugation of Nature.'

Wells was a visionary. If anything he underestimated how quickly this vision of the future would become the present. In a speech at the Royal Institution in 1902, he said: 'It is possible to believe that all the human mind has ever accomplished is but the dream before the awakening.' I also got hold of his *Short History of the World*, which he wrote 'to meet the needs of the busy general reader ... who wishes to refresh or repair his faded or fragmentary perceptions of the great adventure of mankind'. I'm trying something similar now.

Early spring was exceptionally cold and wet. The YOC's migration phone-in recorded Sand Martins returning in dribs and drabs over a seven-week period. Then a wave of migrant birds flooded in towards the end of April. A major wetland in Somerset was confirmed as a SSSI, an isolated piece of good news for the new law. There had been several years of deliberation, during which time important parts of the site had been leaking away through drainage. Even then the main farming union accused the NCC of being hasty and continued to argue for a much smaller area to be protected. Farming had begun to intensify in the Somerset Levels from the early seventies. They were drained so that herbicides could be added, then ploughed and re-seeded with grass seed that would be more productive. This increased hay and milk production but removed most of the wildlife interest of the meadows. Aquatic plants died under herbicides and oxidisation of the drying peat. Farmers demonstrated in February against it being designated, backed up by a Sherman tank from the war. They burned an effigy of the NCC Chairman and his staff. One of the effigies was aimed at the RSPB. They even burned the papers notifying them that this was now a nature reserve.

The new Environment Secretary let the Chairman of the NCC know that his contract would not be renewed in April. 'It has been widely reported that [he] was dismissed because he was unwilling to bow to pressure from local landholders to exclude their land from the SSSI. If true, this provides an open invitation to others who wish to resist the notification of their land, and NCC's task will become well-nigh impossible. Is this what the Government wants?' asked Ian Prestt.

The Code of Guidance was approved by the Lords and Commons. In Parliament, it was noted that the NCC was under-resourced to do its job, and that the spirit of the code and principle of voluntary agreement had already been widely broken. Owners would now have to notify the authorities if they wished to start doing anything different, such as drain a piece of the land. If the authorities thought this would be bad for the wildlife interest of the site, they would say so. If the owner then agreed not to go ahead with the plan anyway, they would receive compensation.

Back in 1972, the Swedes hosted the UN conference on the environment because they wanted to draw early attention to what acid rain was doing to their forests and lakes. Acid rain was now thought to be affecting Pied Flycatchers breeding near lakes in the north of Sweden. There was increasing acidity in the water table, and heavy metal content harmful to human health. Symptoms of acid rain were also being reported in North America.

A peculiar consequence of acidification had been noted in Sweden: how 'eerily beautiful' an acidified lake could appear: clear, sparkling, undisturbed by movement, free from any of the disturbance caused by organic life; serenely silent, as lifeless as a treated swimming pool. Frogs, Otters, fish and other aquatic wildlife were said to have disappeared from pristine, remote areas of Norway. Effects on birds were suspected but not proved. Birds like Ospreys, Bluethroats, Reed Buntings and Willow Warblers had all been looked at. It was thought that they might be having trouble breeding. Some thought heavy metals were likely to be implicated.

Publicity about the effects of this pollution brought home how little the acidity of water needs to be altered before the life it supports begins to die. It also has the side effect of releasing often harmful metals in soil. Acid rain is caused by sulphur dioxide emissions from industry, coal and oil burning. A solution proposed was to remove sulphur by half, at source. The UK signed an international convention promising to do its bit. It was thought that if £500 million were spent on the problem by the end of the century, toxic emissions could be reduced by half, although this would require electricity price rises of 15%. These measures could also provide employment for a lot of people.

The Black Forest was feared to be dying from acid poisoning. Germany duly brought in laws controlling sulphur emissions. It wasn't the birds that told us about acid rain. It was the dying trees, the lifeless rivers, the dissolving buildings. But like *Silent Spring*, the concept of acid rain resonated in the public mind, in a way that the term or even the concept of 'atmospheric pollution' wouldn't have done. Maybe it was the sense of our emissions mounting a physical fightback, a by-product of our activity that came back to bite us, rather than just being something we passively breathed. And it didn't have to rain for the acid to get to work on our environment. It could be likened to passive smoking in a prevailing breeze, nowadays, knowing that your smoke was wafting all around a neighbour's house, staining their walls and their clothes, poisoning their pets and their children. The USA was as guilty as Britain. Both countries were passing much of the consequence on to near neighbours – Canada and Scandinavia.

The Geneva Convention on Transboundary Air Pollution came into being in March. Nine European countries had promised to cut sulphur emissions by about a third. It was hoped that the USA would also do so soon. The UK had still not signed up, despite being the major exporter, as well as now feeling the impacts itself. Effects of acid rain were now being recognised in south-west Scotland, the Lake District and Wales.

In September, the Central Electricity Generating Board announced a five-year programme of research into what was beginning to feel like an emergency. It could only be hoped this would add significantly to the research already done by the countries which had already been living with our emissions for ten years or more.

The three men who created the bird book our family grew up with, that helped us to identify the birds of continental campsites and their surroundings, *A Field Guide to the Birds of Britain and Europe*, were special guests at the RSPB members' conference.

'You cannot watch birds without becoming an environmentalist,' American artist Roger Tory Peterson told a packed audience. The authors bemoaned the lack of biological knowledge in government. Guy Mountfort predicted that 'with the increasing hardships of the environment, people will need the spiritual uplift that birds can give'.

Of the uplands, the RSPB said, 'It may be that its best prospects for a secure future are to serve wider and more imaginative ends than the production of sheepmeat alone.' A number of fires had raged apparently out of control as moors were burned in late summer. New guidelines were being produced, such as to avoid burning in the spring and summer months, except under special licence. The RSPB sought a total ban, apart from anything so that it would be clear when a fire was an illegal one. Ministers would not accept this but at least the NCC would have a chance to comment on any applications for licences.

There was another interesting test case of the law where forestry was concerned. A SSSI had been identified back in 1974, on a mountainside in the Highlands of Scotland. It extended from the shore of a loch up the glen to the summit of the mountain, with patches of native Birch woodland. A forestry company purchased part of this site then applied to the Forestry Commission for state grant aid to plant the lower part of it with conifers. The NCC opposed the idea. If ministers supported the NCC, it would be expected to compensate the applicant; a tidy piece of business for the company, whatever the outcome. The RSPB asked the Forestry Commission for details of the planting proposals, but the commission refused to share them. The outcome of this test case was eagerly awaited.

In March, two years on from the passing of the Wildlife and Countryside Act, the NCC's deadline had been reached for getting round all owners and occupiers of SSSIs. Even with a five-month extension on this deadline, the NCC had managed to re-notify just 11% of several thousand sites. Until a site was re-notified, an owner or occupier could claim ignorance of it, their role and its needs. Whether by accident or design, they might have damaged it.

There was always a risk of a stampede to 'improve' special places before they were turned into SSSIs. At one proposed SSSI, the owners drained it while discussions were taking place between the authorities and local people. The RSPB alerted the NCC to what was going on. Some weeks later the NCC asked the Environment Secretary to apply a stop order on the drainage of the land, to buy time for further discussion, to save some of the remaining wildflower and winter flood meadows.

Despite all this, government was behind schedule on meeting its obligations under EU law. Measures should have been in place by the end of March to meet the requirements of the Birds Directive. The EU should by now have been told the sites that government intended to protect. Some wetlands had been identified, under Ramsar; but apart from those, nothing.

We lived with the ever-present idea that nuclear weapons were pointed right at us from the east. In west-central Scotland we thought we might be first in line if it all went off, with our nuclear power station, US submarine base and airport. The general threat certainly gave the pop industry plenty of material to sing about. Another general election came and went. CND-supporting Michael Foot's Labour Party imploded, the Social Democrats capitalised but not much, and the Conservatives increased their majority, despite spiralling unemployment. The Falklands War appeared to have turned the government's flagging popularity around, diverting attention from the kind of domestic gloom that made TV series like *Boys from the Blackstuff* possible. It was grim up north, and scant consolation that this was now the warmest year ever recorded. Way down south, the mighty river Niger would dry up completely over the coming winter.

1984

Geography lessons at school led us to believe that the planting of state forests incorporated features to make the plantations more 'natural', benefiting wildlife and people. Planters would mix up the types of trees, edge plantations with broadleaves, provide recreational areas, follow contours, leave space for wildlife to get in and out. These were lessons not borne out by my experience of plantations. Dad was always very scathing about these places. Mum was more philosophical – the country needs the toilet paper, she once remarked. 'Sure, why do you think God gave you a left hand?' I remember him replying. He was rarely this vulgar.

I dreamed of doing a study on Ailsa Craig, also known as Paddy's Milestone, the gigantic lump of rock that guards the mouth of the Firth of Clyde, the way the Statue of Liberty announces New York and the USA to those arriving by boat. But I had no idea how to go about getting there. The word was that no one was allowed. It was privately owned and out of bounds, too dangerous, or something.

So instead, in spring I surveyed the loch basin that I'd grown to know so well – 'the only mineral-enriched, mesotrophic loch in north Ayrshire', apparently. They'd found ancient crannogs in there, including one made mostly of stone. I was doing a bio-geographical study, as part of the Higher Geography course. I think it counted for about a third of the overall mark. There were various types of project you could choose, and I recall the teacher telling me that I was the only pupil in the school to have chosen to take up the bio-geography option – making the link between the physical terrain, the geology, weather, soil and water, the historic human use of the site, such as farming and recreation, and the plants, invertebrates, birds and mammals that lived there. As I was also taking Biology, it seemed like a natural fit. Why no one else would have chosen this option seemed peculiar. To my classmates on field trips I was 'nature-boy', after the song in the charts of that name. 'Dezo' was catchier, but not everyone got it.

My mates outside of school were growing out of the old trips 'up the country' so I was on my own with this research now. I remember my first tentative steps with the project. I harboured faint aspirations to be an artist then, inspired by a careers visit to Glasgow School of Art, and a teacher who thought he'd spotted some talent and did his best to 'broaden my horizons'. I was probably drawing too many birds, and football scenes. I designed an album cover for Gerry Rafferty's

Night Owl in the exam, although the first owls I got properly acquainted with were the day-flying Short-eared Owls that hunted over that loch basin in winter.

I lovingly sketched some of the birds that I'd got to know in and around this loch: Heron, Reed Bunting, Water Rail, something else. I remember Mum showing these, I thought quite proudly, to Dad. He was the geography teacher, after all, when he wasn't running a secondary school, she the naturalist – a French and English teacher, but with a better grounding in natural history than the biology teachers I knew. He agreed these were decent illustrations, in their own way. But how they would add much to a geographical study, even a bio-geographical one, he couldn't quite see.

Of course, he was right. I was disappointed at the time, but six months later I had wised up enough to know what he had been getting at. By then my illustrations were linked with neatly ruled lines and annotations on the physical features of the site. By then I had learned about soil pH, and that tiny adjustments in acidity meant huge differences in what could and couldn't grow. I had familiarised myself with soil types, about nutrient enrichment of the water due to run-off of fertilisers and manure from the shallow basin of pasture land surrounding the loch and its floating marsh. I had learned that the grazing by cattle which, when I first discovered it, I thought was a disaster for the bog's flora, was not necessarily a bad thing, if permitted at the right level. And about how the water collected here and how it escaped. And what the plants were. Mum could name the plant samples I brought home, and if there were any she struggled with, she had the books to consult. There was a species called Cowbane – nationally rare. From the books I could add the scientific names to my report, for that finishing, academic touch.

Parliament debated the shortcomings of the Wildlife and Countryside Act that summer. Not surprisingly, 'the good faith … has not proved quite enough'. New RSPB Chairman Lord Blakenham helped by pointing out the four ways that the act was falling short:

- Lack of resource to re-notify sites, too many delays, allowing sites to be damaged meantime.
- The three-month consultation period was giving an unsympathetic owner time to 'so damage a site that its scientific interest is no longer special'. There were a dozen examples.

- The law required owners to consult the NCC before carrying out any damaging operations. There were numerous examples where they had failed to do so, but the fines were so low that they were not a deterrent.
- The compensation that could be paid to owners for any income foregone could instead be given to voluntary bodies to purchase sites. The example was given of the £1 million the RSPB had raised to buy a wet meadow, with less than 7% of this sum donated by the NCC. Meanwhile, the other two-thirds of the site in private ownership would cost the taxpayer up to £200,000 every year in payments to the owners not to damage it.

The RSPB also called for an end to taxpayer funding for private farmland drainage operations. Too many schemes were wrecking wildlife sites with no obvious economic or other benefits to the nation. Public enquiries were never held.

There was a change of tack by the RSPB on farming and conservation. Until now, the Society 'took the view that losses of farmland habitat and consequent reductions in bird numbers should be accepted because of the benefits which agricultural efficiency brought to the nation. Rather than seeking to change farming policies and practice, we chose to become a prime mover of the Farming and Wildlife Advisory Group. Indeed for a decade we were FWAG's financial mainstay ... Latterly, however, it has become clear that collaboration is not enough.'

The emphasis would have to shift now to influencing policies. Evidence was presented and a case made to the House of Lords committee looking at this. Agriculture departments claimed in their own submissions that the problems had been grossly exaggerated, and that in any case, under the Treaty of Rome, there was no way they would be permitted to use subsidies to protect the environment. Subsidies were for increasing production. The RSPB called on the Department of Environment to fight harder to challenge Agriculture's domination of all things rural, and to take a broader view of the scope of its own role.

European elections were due and the RSPB weighed up what the Birds Directive had achieved so far across the ten member countries signed up. Not one of them was complying fully. UK government, for example, was allowing the shooting of Barnacle Geese and fish-eating birds. It was the kind of non-compliance that might make it awkward for this country to complain about the French shooting migrant Turtle Doves for three weeks in May.

Europe had given conservation clout, as demonstrated by the inclusion of habitat protection in the Wildlife and Countryside Act. There were other encouraging examples from the Netherlands, where the RSPB's partner used Europe's leverage to stop government wrecking wetlands. Europe also understood that conservation costs real money, and had politicians with greater knowledge and concern than was evident at national level. It had been a promising start.

I landed a rare job as an auxiliary nurse in a Kilmarnock hospital that summer, which meant weeks of bleary, dawn-chorus starts to put on a white coat, and no more biting my nails. I was placed in the geriatric ward, the occupants of which were almost all here to stay. As my early shift replaced the night shift we would hear in hushed tones the roll call of incontinence, illness and, on several mornings, death. As tastes of the real world go, it was life-affirming, in a harsh kind of way. And I never really got used to the hospital smell of disinfectant and boiled food. I looked at the clock a lot, but I felt privileged to have had this job with the angels, if a little unsure as to why I had been given it. I longed to be outdoors through those long mornings, 'til liberated at lunchtime, to seize each summer day.

The exam results came through. The loch-basin study seemed to have hit the mark. In fact I had all the grades needed to do university sooner rather than later, so come the autumn I left behind the soggy pastures, onshore winds and hard nuclear targets of Ayrshire for the forested hills and distant peaks of the north. 'Careless Whisper' was number one in the pop charts. The miners were on strike, the Brighton bombing imminent. Small-town boy arrived at Stirling on the pretext of studying Ecology, to develop his love of nature and equip himself the better to save some of it. I was so young I hadn't stopped growing. I had barely started shaving.

The Scottish Wildlife Trust hosted a major conference on acid rain in nearby Edinburgh that autumn. Acid rain, and calls for it to be stopped, had come to represent and to give a focal point to centuries of environmental degradation, reported journalist Tony Samstag. This was an ambient, environmental enemy we could see and name, as well as have gut feelings about.

I now had hills on my doorstep, and what remained of their wildlife still to discover. The fate of uplands like these was coming under closer scrutiny. The RSPB issued a report called *Hill Farming and Birds – A Survival Plan*. Damage to moorland had reached levels that shocked many. Ten bird species were named as being at risk, all of which I now had a chance of getting to know, although my chances of finding them appeared to be diminishing: Golden Eagle, Hen Harrier, Merlin, Red Grouse, Black Grouse, Golden Plover, Greenshank, Dunlin, Ring Ouzel and Twite.

Farming in the uplands was described by the RSPB as 'patently uneconomic', and particularly dependent on public money. It was time that these subsidies provided for the needs of wildlife and recreation. 'Lively discussions' had taken place, with 'harsh comments initially from some farmers' representatives'. There were 'encouraging signs that conservation arguments are now gaining acceptance in an agricultural economy increasingly under siege at home and from Brussels'.

I found Dippers on the nearby Allanwater and the faster stretches of its tributaries. The dapper, rotund little Dipper, bobbing in its tux, has long been a visible sign of a river's health. I hadn't thought of it as a singer. Their world is noisy with rushing water. I was with Mum when one day we found one, singing cheerfully across the water of a calm stretch, as though casting sound onto the surface, to be carried downstream, a message for its kind. It looked a lot like an avian preacher. My mum liked this idea. Maybe it put her in mind of her dad, who had been a man of the cloth. I thought of soul man the Right Reverend Al Green and the song 'Take Me to the River'.

Dippers didn't do well around the plunge pools of my youth, I would have occasion now to reflect. The NCC then found Dippers to be declining more generally in Scotland. A study in Wales by the RSPB and Welsh Water found the same. The water in our rivers was becoming more acidic. The invertebrate life that Dippers are specially adapted to feed on in these rivers, by rummaging around under water, was dwindling as a result. We now had a bird species appearing to confirm what had been long suspected: acid rain was a problem here too; not just an invisible by-product exported on the wind, but a visible threat to our own heritage, along with the dissolving visages of gargoyles and other historic relics on sandstone buildings.

At first industry had been in denial that the problem existed. The Confederation of British Industry had claimed it was a media issue fuelled by pressure groups. A spokesman for the Central Electricity Generating Board claimed that our sulphur emissions came down in places where they could do no harm. 'How,' enquired an RSPB supporter in a published letter, 'does he know?' Industry also pleaded that doing anything about it would be cripplingly expensive. By that autumn, government acknowledged public concern in its published report on the issue. Backed up by independent scientific opinion, it rejected the CBI's stonewalling.

Acid rain effects were also starting to be felt in the southern hemisphere, from Brazilian soil to South African air. But why only now, some people asked, when polluting industry was hardly a new thing? Analysis of tree rings and pollen then showed that the acidification process had started with the Industrial Revolution.

There was some evidence that the environment was being taken more seriously by politicians as an electoral issue, and one to which a substantial number of voters were paying close attention. The concept of 'greening' was gaining ground. In November, opposition Environment Spokesman Jack Cunningham called a debate on environmental issues, especially significant considering how little parliamentary time they were allowed for such calls. Cunningham's motion calling for new laws and bigger budgets for the environment was ultimately defeated.

Surveys were beginning to show numbers of wading birds in freefall, except on nature reserves. Snipe, Redshank, Curlew, Lapwing and Oystercatcher were studied, and more than a thousand sites were checked. The years of subsidised flood meadow drainage were beginning to exact a heavy toll. Most of these species were by now confined to five places, as yet undrained.

Another common bird was vanishing: the Sand Martin. This appealing little brown-and-white, rural version of the more familiar House Martin isn't famed for its contribution to the dawn chorus, or its ability as a singer, but it was starting to be missed over rivers and lakes, and the quarries and embankments where it tunnels its nesting colonies. It had declined by a sobering 70% in just one year, and by more than 90% since *Silent Spring*. It was a visible sign of the drought in Africa that had led to the formation of Band Aid, the coalition of pop stars calling on the public to help feed the world at Christmas.

Of course it didn't take a crash in Sand Martin numbers to reveal drought problems in north-east Africa, when the horrifying images from Ethiopia's famine were beamed into our living rooms. But it was about more than drought. Ethiopia had lost 90% of its forests, and even in a wet year the land was struggling to cope with demands being made upon it. The population of Ethiopia had doubled since the fifties, to around 50 million. The UN predicted a further trebling by 2030. There was a growing recognition that environmental degradation and resource depletion lead inexorably to social strife and suffering.

1985

I didn't care much for the latest lab coat, or the smell of ammonia in the morning. It's a good thing that others did. Towards the end of that first semester of malodorous, four-hour science labs – a blur of white coats, goggles, test tubes and dead tissue – I had a chat with the Film and Media Department about a switch. You could do that in those days – if you were lucky. This was the most over-subscribed university course in Scotland, and the most coveted of its kind in Britain at that time. A Mickey Mouse subject? They set this as an exam question. Cheeky. I would take what I already knew about wild nature – and my semester's-worth of cell biology, organic chemistry and environmental physics – and train instead in the art of communicating, about these subjects.

It was pointless to deny it: I was by instinct more interested in the movement of neo-realists than in that of water across semi-permeable membranes. I had nothing new to tell the world about mitosis. My memory for facts is patchy. Film, media, English lit, the arts and education were more suited to a conceptual mind. I would study things that could be debated into the small hours, till the sun – or the Sub-Warden – came up, till the warblers rang in the craggy woods hanging over the hall of residence.

I was drawn to the journalism, and worked on the student newspaper *Brig* for a few years, including a spell as Editor. 'Surely this boy is too young to be at university?' someone scrawled next to my name on the ballot paper. I can see now that they had a point. Youth – and formal education – were in some ways wasted on this youth.

I recall perhaps most vividly that spring semester – the first in my new course – studying the work of the auteur director Nic Roeg, including environment-themed movies like *The Man Who Fell to Earth*, and *Walkabout*, which featured in the end-of-term exam. This 1971 film, and its John Barry score, became anthemic. It captured for me what our own lives were: the beauty of our setting, the thrill of discovery, the kind of movie we'd all have liked to be able to make, to change the world (the point, after all, of human activity, as Marx maintained). It also said a lot about what we were doing to the environment, that film, and to ourselves in the process.

If I think back to that time, in my mind's eye there is a crane shot – not the bird ... actually yes, the bird – that pulls back from the lecture theatre. There's a stuffy exam, Starlings squalling in the roof, me chewing on a pen, daydreaming like Jenny Agutter, trapped once again in her Sydney apartment. The retreating camera reveals the rooftops of campus, the canopy of the woods and crowns of the crags, the sweep of the valley floodplain, the snaking Forth within, Flanders Moss to the west, the mountains beyond, and the Ochils and Edinburgh way to the east. The John Barry score strikes up, the Housman poem ...

That is the land of lost content, I see it shining, plain.
The happy highways where I went, and cannot come again

In the contemporary world beyond the campus, the media was a fast-evolving organism. The print unions were resisting new technology that would soon enough make typesetters of us all. *Brookside* was setting new standards in soap opera. In cinema, the British were said to be coming. Irishman Neil Jordan had just made *The Company of Wolves*. I devoured this visual feast at the campus arts centre, which made the night walk home afterwards through the wintry woods a vivid – if nerve-tingling – experience.

And what of the environmental movement? A lot was happening in Scotland. Licences were being issued for the killing of fish-eating birds like cormorants, goosanders and mergansers. The RSPB reminded government that such licences should only be granted after serious damage to fisheries had been proved. It would have 'no option but to take the matter to the European Court,' said Richard Porter, now Head of Species Protection.

There was jubilation when, ten years after the project began to bring them back to Rum, the first young White-tailed Eagle flew from a Scottish nest. The eagles had first started trying to breed two years earlier, without success. The birds were inexperienced, still. This year there were four nests. Three failed early, and the last one was closely supervised until the young eagle finally took wing. The 'sea' eagle was properly back.

A bill was introduced to amend defects in the Wildlife and Countryside Act, such as the three-month consultation period, which had had the unfortunate consequence of allowing some owners of a site about to be designated as an SSSI to carry on with damaging operations. Since the act had been passed, no fewer than 14 SSSIs had been damaged or destroyed in this way. The bill was brought forward by the opposition, with all-party support. It wasn't expected to encounter any obstacles, but this turned out to be wishful thinking.

In the end, the three-month-loophole clause amendment got through. Two of five clauses were blocked and the others substantially diluted by government. Among these were efforts to strengthen protection for badger setts, which was unpopular with fox-hunting interests, who claimed it would interfere with their need to dig foxes out of the ground for the chase. Another was a move towards creating inshore marine nature reserves, which the ministry and inshore fishing interests opposed. An attempt to require the Ministry and the Forestry Commission to have a duty to further conservation was also beaten back.

The insult added to this list of injuries was described by Ian Prestt: 'Our final disappointment ... is the way in which some members of Parliament have seen it as an opportunity to increase the number of species that may be shot. Redshank, Curlew, Brent Goose, Barnacle Goose and Stock Dove will, if some MPs and Lords have their way, be added to the list.'

He went on, through gritted teeth: 'It is hard not to conclude that the Government has made a serious tactical blunder. Following recent signs that it had begun to see the importance of nature conservation, it has succeeded in amazing the entire conservation movement ... The Government has shot itself in the foot ... completely failed to gauge the mood of the nation ... Disappointing is not the word.'

Local authorities were at it too. One county council bulldozed a reedbed shortly after the NCC announced its intention to add it to a neighbouring SSSI. In Northern Ireland, where SSSIs were called ASSIs, RSPB staff noticed diggers moving in to start work on a wet meadow. When they contacted the authorities, it became clear that the owner was oblivious of its status. The government hadn't told him.

Essex police were called in to a rare meadow full of Green-winged Orchids that was in the process of being notified as a SSSI. The owner was in the throes of spraying the site, with a view to adding houses. Protestors had to be kept at bay. The Department of Environment issued a 'stop order', which may have saved some of the rare plants.

There were by this time fewer than 200 Cirl Buntings left in Britain. News came in that a Devon hedgerow, where some of these surviving birds nested, had been torn out. In its place now stood a wire fence – something for the now homeless birds to perch on, at least. This is just one among countless examples that could be cited. And the cost of this act of vandalism, intentional or not, was borne by the taxpayer.

Across the Channel, there was a confrontation and even a defused bomb incident in south-west France. Six hundred protestors had gathered to protest against illegal shooting of Turtle Doves. It was a decent turnout for a demo of this kind, but four times as many hunters confronted them, beyond a thin line of gendarmes. The protest was the culmination of a campaign by the RSPB's French partner, which took its government to court and won. France would have to honour the EU's Birds Directive, like all other member states. So too would Greece, which had been trying to use the French example as a precedent, to dodge its own obligations. There, spring migrants of all kinds were still being shot, under cover of a permission to hunt Turtle Doves.

The nation had mourned when Eric Morecambe passed away in 1984. He had continued to develop his love of birds in later life. Birds had been 'a joy for him,' his son Gary recalled. 'He was often distant and distracted while out ... He loved the exotic colours of European birds. And when he matched one to a bird in his spotters' book he was in a state of great excitement for hours.'

There was considerable showbiz involvement in conservation at this time. The RSPB's Eric Morecambe Appeal was launched in May at Fortnum and Mason, with guests-of-honour his widow Joan, and Joanna Lumley. A concert by the Royal Philharmonic Orchestra was held at the Barbican, attended by royalty. A nature reserve and visitor centre was opened in Birmingham by *Blue Peter* presenter Simon Groom and Goldie the dog, joining Max Nicholson, current but soon-to-retire President of the RSPB.

I recall warm summer days on the hills, but overall it was a year of very poor weather. The hide used by staff and volunteers to keep tabs on the Golden Eagle nest high in a Lakeland fell blew away in a gale. Luckily there was no one in it at the time. The RSPB reintroduced Otters to Minsmere. The Otter Trust provided three captive-bred adults – a male and two females. They were seen again occasionally, along with tracks and other signs, but there was no sign yet that they had bred.

Before 1985 not many people had heard of the Flow Country, even in Scotland, but it was about to become one of the biggest conservation causes célèbres of all. 'In recent months we have witnessed massive commercial afforestation programmes on these blanket peats ... long considered virtually unplantable,' reported the RSPB. Tens of thousands of acres of this tundra-like wilderness landscape of north Scotland had been ploughed and planted, and over £10 million of public money poured in. It had never been designated a SSSI and this, coupled with its remoteness, may explain how it stayed outside the radar – until now. Senior RSPB staff visited in the spring, and soon after called on government to halt drainage and planting until a proper evaluation had been carried out, and a strategy drawn up that considered wider interests. The Secretary of State for Scotland refused.

Term ends at Stirling with the end of May, as spring becomes summer. I woke up on 1 June in a quiet room in a Victorian villa, on a leafy residential road on the edge of the woods. The contrast with the tumult of campus and the scramble of thousands of students to pack and leave could not have been more stark; traumatic, even. But it quickly dawned on me that the summer stretching ahead was alive with possibilities. In between visits to the Job Centre I would have time to get to know these sylvan surroundings better, on bike or desert boot.

As luck would have it, a student who shared my love of football, music and – uniquely – birds had moved into the study bedroom next door to mine the previous term. We shared DJ-ing duties at the union and clubs locally. Through Nick I got to know some post-graduate biologists writing PhDs on Dippers and Sand Martins. This broadened my horizons greatly. These guys knew loads, and had the use of a car. They were looking at things like the role of commercial conifer plantations in making upland rivers more acidic. So there was legwork, usually on very wet evenings, but there were magical insights too. Between checking nests of their study species, and taking weights and measures, we found some of the hidden treasures of the Trossachs: birds like Black Grouse, Long-eared Owls and Peregrines. And on one unforgettable midsummer evening, I found the Osprey.

I had borrowed a rowing boat and was ferrying some friends to an islet in a loch, for the solstice. I didn't know there were Ospreys here, and so the large bird in the distance was probably anything but. No doubt a Heron. It was flapping languidly closer, and I began to wonder … I pointed it out to my passengers, who weren't too interested in birds. Still closer it came, until I was in no doubt it was an Osprey. Its unhurried wing-beats high against the evening sky brought it circling overhead. I wondered if it might be homing in on a fish. Surely not? It had a whole lot of loch here to choose from, and the chances of it fishing so close to the only boat for square miles around seemed fanciful. But to my (and the crew's) astonishment, it folded and plunged, talons extended, exploding through the placid surface a short distance from us. Our boat rocked as we struggled to contain our whoops, and laughter. Funny how you laugh in response to such moments. And it got its fish.

I found out from those in the know that this was a secret Osprey nesting location, so of course I too was sworn to secrecy. The Ospreys were spreading slowly, reclaiming the land from which they'd been shot to extinction by the Victorians. This was as far south as they had yet reached. I wasn't able to tell anyone that story. At least not until quite a few years later.

At dawn on another midsummer's day, after spending the shortest night on the hill, we stumbled across a roost of Black Grouse in a block of spruce on the edge of the moor. The birds retreated to cover, making peculiar noises. I noted the spot and backed away respectfully, not wishing to disturb them unduly. I knew of the growing concern for the prospects of this remarkable and improbable species. Across Wales, all the male birds had recently been counted at the dawn display sites they use in early spring, known as leks. 'A modest number but more than expected,' Roger Lovegrove called it.

A Black Grouse lek site can lay claim to hosting the most surreal performance put on by any birds in these islands. It functions like one of those dances in a costume drama. The males arrive in all their finery, a bright navy-blue uniform with neatly curled coat tails, flouncy white petticoats and shirt frills, and scarlet eyebrows, like epaulettes stuck in the wrong place. Heads tilted back, wings out, they strut and scuttle around each other, making a bizarre bubbling sound, bumping into rivals, occasionally coming to blows. All the while, the modestly attired females look on demurely. You can almost imagine them fanning themselves, nudging each other and nodding in the direction of the combatants, part in admiration but mostly in amusement. I can't help wondering how much our own rituals might have been influenced by their example.

Instinct tells me that Black Grouse society doesn't function very well in a fragmented landscape. This is a bird that needs space and critical mass of population to work. They need a combination of open ground, and cover, the sort of upland landscapes that are most pleasing to look at, by and large. It seems tragic to report that almost half the Welsh leks found in 1986 had just a single male bird turn up, displaying alone, uncontested.

The best remaining Black Grouse lek site in the Peak District was also under pressure. Large piles of slurry had been dropped on it, a sign of further 'improvements' to follow. The RSPB contacted the Environment Minister. He issued a conservation order blocking any further development. The NCC had asked for the same thing earlier, while discussions were taking place over the future of the site. Their request had not been actioned.

A number of Herons had been found dead, and of the five examined by the ITE, four had high levels of pesticide in their livers. Organochlorine pesticides remained in circulation, despite the voluntary ban introduced two years earlier. Incredibly, after all this time, dieldrin was still killing birds. The RSPB again asked the public to report any large numbers of sick or dead birds. The struggle continued to have DDT and dieldrin completely banned. Their use was still possible under the voluntary regulations on use, sale, storage and import.

It was the summer of Live Aid. I rented a corner of a temporary flat in Stirling, with the ornithologists, while my room in the woods was rented to Edinburgh festival-goers. I'd seen enough from Wembley, and cycled out to the Gargunnock hills, to a favourite spot on the river there, a plunge pool in a glade, for a swim, and to look for Dippers.

Autumn brought storms, and another house move, to a flat close to the campsite my returning family had used nearly 20 years before, on the plains of the River Forth. Mercifully, news came through that the rains had also returned to East Africa, bringing some respite.

1986

Stirling's US-style semester system means January off. New year dawned over another house in the woods, further up in the foothills, with an outlook across the Forth valley to Ben Lomond in the west, the Campsie Hills shielding Glasgow to the south, and with the Ochils on its doorstep, a short stroll through the woods. From the Witches' Craig the widening river fades to the horizon, the distant hill at Edinburgh known as Arthur's Seat sometimes there, sometimes not. And the petrochemical works of Grangemouth sometimes loomed, middle-distant, from whence a fabled band called the Cocteau Twins had come, making the musical backdrop to this and many years to come. Elizabeth Fraser vocalises like the most animated songbird, Robin Guthrie's guitars and keyboards shimmer around her. The listener must add their own interpretation of the 'spoken in tongues' lyrics, as you might for a bird.

Our house was idyllically placed. The catch was we had to sleep three to a room. Luckily I got a top bunk. There were Merlins on the moors above, a bird that 'symbolises the Society's alarm at the pace and scale of land use change in many parts of the uplands,' as

Ian Prestt put it at the time. It also told a familiar tale of pesticides. One population of Merlins had dropped from 25 pairs in the sixties to just six. There were symptoms consistent with the effects of DDT poisoning. Other bird species, bats and Otters had also been reported dead – poisoned. New regulations were debated in Parliament. The RSPB helped to point out a major flaw in the proposals, which would have allowed virtually any of the UK's (by now 5,000) SSSIs to be threatened by aerial spraying of neighbouring land.

The Peregrine has long been the headline-grabber of the falcon family, but the Merlin was twice as scarce. The RSPB was concerned that the odd upland nature reserve and SSSI wouldn't be enough to sustain Merlins at the rate the hills were being shorn of their heather and other habitats. A new concept emerged from Europe to try to meet this need: the Environmentally Sensitive Area (ESA) was born. It remained to be seen if government would identify enough of these, and in the right places. So far six had been named, although mainly for landscape reasons rather than for the sake of threatened birds.

The Forestry Commission had at long last begun to talk about broadleaves and was able to give grants for schemes that weren't all about timber production, but had wildlife aims. Government was looking into timber as a farm crop. The trouble is that trees tend not to provide an income for at least 30 years. Could government make it worth a farmer's while by providing an annual income, as it did for often surplus cereals? A few ideas were circulating, to find ways to increase native broadleaf woodland planting on farms.

Max Nicholson retired as RSPB President and called for his successor to be female. He saw the organisation as a national asset, in inauspicious times: 'We offer a shining example to a nation which is torn by divisive squabbles, whose manufacturers are in steep competitive decline, whose unemployment levels touch new records, and in which no crime or violence is too sordid or nasty.' On birds, he was of the view that 'they have certainly never been better recorded, understood, appreciated or cared for'. Nicholson was replaced as President by Magnus Magnusson, best known as presenter of *Mastermind*. TV's Bernard Cribbins was elected to RSPB Council.

Springtime can sometimes be cruel. With the resurgence of life comes nature at its most raw and unforgiving. The weather can be capricious, bringing snow and even gales to strip the blossom like confetti. A shadow was cast over the European spring in late April when we woke to news that the Chernobyl nuclear plant in Ukraine had exploded. Over the course of the following days, its fallout drifted on the prevailing wind across a huge area and deposited its invisible threat on the hills. Some people think that nuclear power stations are our only hope for a low-carbon future. But the lesson of Chernobyl confirmed others in the belief that its risks are too great.

Mechanical cutters had changed the ways of management of the hedgerows that remained, with more and more being cut back from late summer. In the past, this had been a winter task, which gave wildlife a chance to reach fruits and berries late in the year. The era of the giant peat-harvesting machine had arrived. Commercial operations were now busily stripping peatlands and bagging up the material for sale, piled high in garden centres. Only in Ireland did substantial peatland areas remain, but they were living on borrowed time.

Government had failed in its obligations under the Birds Directive to protect a peatland on Islay, on which geese depended in winter, when visiting from Greenland. They hadn't even carried out an assessment before giving the go-ahead to a very large pharmaceutical and drinks manufacturing company to drain and cut the peat. There were other places that could be used, argued those concerned to protect this internationally important site. A public meeting attended by TV botanist Dr David Bellamy and several hundred islanders ended in chaos. Some kind of compromise was eventually reached, but only time would tell what the geese would make of it.

'Some conservationists attempted to further the case by holding a public meeting on the island and attracting publicity,' said Ian Prestt. 'We took the case to the European Commission as we believe the site is protected under an EC Directive. Officials of the Commission have now taken up the issue with the British Government and we are optimistic that this will help to save the site.'

Road developments were becoming an increasing pressure on special sites. The RSPB objected to a proposal for road development that would threaten a Stone-curlew site on chalk downland. Fewer than 200 pairs were left, mostly in southern England. Around half of these nested on farmland. Meetings were taking place with farmers to discuss how the species could be kept going.

In June the NCC published a detailed account of commercial forestry's impact on the wildlife of the uplands. Forestry interests also now acknowledged that there was a case to answer. The claims of the RSPB and others could no longer be ignored. All the while, the draining, ploughing and planting of our last wilderness places like the Flow Country of north Scotland proceeded. Since the turn of the decade, government had encouraged the private sector to lead the way in funding commercial forest. There were attractive tax breaks for private investors. High-rate taxpayers would receive £280 of support for each £400 per acre bought. It was possible to buy more land, more cheaply in remote places with poor quality soil. Places like the Flows. Even forestry interests admitted it was unlikely to produce worthwhile timber.

'We don't advise our land owners to plant trees on a commercial basis in the far north of Scotland,' one company representative revealed, 'because we don't believe the financial yield or the investment will compare adequately with those yields from commercial tree planting further south. A combination of climatic conditions together with the extra cost of harvesting and marketing the timber would largely liquidate the profit to the woodland owner.' The profit incentives were the same, irrespective of land quality. Ten years or so later the investor could sell on at profit to a pension fund, almost tax-free.

No special designation had been given to the Flow Country that might have helped the struggle to protect it. There were no controls to represent the interests of wildlife – the NCC would usually be consulted only if it were a SSSI. The National Parks system in England and Wales had helped to stem the spread of forestry plantations. Scotland didn't have these. The RSPB continued to encourage government to incentivise forestry in the farmed lowlands instead.

Six ESAs had been named, in England and Wales. Agriculture departments now had a direct responsibility for conservation of wildlife in some of the most important parts of these countries. But there was a mounting problem of pollution from farm silage and slurry, which had reached record levels in 1985.

The law was starting to show its teeth. At a Welsh site, an owner was shaping up to clear-felling woodland that supported Pied Flycatchers, Wood Warblers and Redstarts. It was a SSSI. An order was made to halt the work while the NCC tried to negotiate an agreement with the owner. An injunction was then needed to ensure the order not to proceed with the felling was observed.

Estuaries faced a 'vigorous new phase of destruction'. Thirty coastal sites faced development threats, with half a million waders and 300,000 wildfowl at risk. Five were threatened by the possibility of tidal barrages. All five were supposed to be listed as Special Protection

Areas and Ramsar sites. Government plans to privatise the water industry in England and Wales had become a source of some anxiety. Would these environmental safeguards be sufficient in this new era of profit-driven management?

1987

The 25th anniversary of *Silent Spring* arrived, with the RSPB still pressing for a complete ban on the use of organochlorine pesticides. Government researchers at the ITE were still appealing for corpses of birds of prey and fish-eating birds. 'Organochlorines are still disturbingly widespread in the environment. They find their way into all food chains – every single sparrowhawk body or egg analysed since 1963 has been found to be contaminated.'

Europe's food surpluses remained a source of public scorn and political embarrassment. In the spring, government revealed plans to do something about it. It had come up with a scheme to encourage the planting of woodlands on lowland farmland. While this was something that conservationists had been suggesting, as ever there was little to be gained from planting the wrong type of trees in the wrong places. The details needed attention. Meanwhile, government's proposal to increase the blankets of conifer on upland moors and peatlands was inexplicable.

There would be more investment in ESAs, to encourage more sensitive, traditional farming, but overall the package of reforms was disappointing. Where was the detail, and specific advice to local authorities on how to ensure protection for the best bits of the countryside for wildlife? On offer instead was some vague encouragement to preserve 'good' bits. 'Taken together, these measures portend a weakening of the protection afforded to wildlife habitats,' the RSPB concluded.

People had begun to comment on the disappearance of the Lapwing. Mapping showed them retreating to the north and west. Two-thirds had disappeared from south-east England since *Silent Spring*. It was already uncommon as a breeding bird in East Anglia, reduced to small pockets elsewhere, reflecting the loss of damp pastures as autumn cereals advanced. Lapwings can't nest in autumn crops, which are too high when spring comes. In dairying areas cattle were trampling as many as three out of five Lapwing nests. 'Perhaps farmers could be persuaded to leave some marshy or rough patches unreclaimed, or at least to increase their vigilance when using machinery during the breeding season,' suggested the RSPB. The Stone-curlew population, meanwhile, had reached an all-time low.

It was European Year of the Environment. I signed up for volunteer conservation work, doing things like dry-stone walling in the foothills of the Highlands of a Sunday morning. I picked up a Greenpeace leaflet with a bold statement on its cover that made a big impression.

Planet Earth is 4.6 billion years old. If we condense this into a conceivable time-span we can liken the Earth to a person of 46 years old. Nothing is known about the first seven years of this person's life, and whilst only scattered information exists about the middle 35 years, we know that only at the age of 42 did the earth begin to flower. Dinosaurs and the great reptiles did not appear until one year ago, when the planet was 45. Mammals arrived eight months ago; in the middle of last week, human-like apes evolved into ape-like humans, and at the weekend the last ice age enveloped the Earth.

Modern humans have been around for four hours. During the last hour we discovered agriculture. The industrial revolution began one minute ago. During those sixty seconds of biological time, humans have made a rubbish tip of paradise. We have caused the extinction of many hundreds of animal species, ransacked the planet for fuel and now stand gloating over this meteoric rise, on the brink of the final mass extinction. We have almost destroyed this oasis of life in the solar system.

These are the kind of terms pressure groups used to have to use to make an impact. It certainly made an impact on me. I had it on my wall as a student, at a time when like many people I was increasingly pessimistic about the likely fate of the world, and the general apparent lack of concern at large, and politically. Things have changed and Greenpeace has toned down the guilt trip a bit, which is a tribute to their and others' success in making more people sit up and take notice.

A general election loomed. There were some encouraging signs of increased interest in green issues from the political parties. Voters were encouraged to quiz candidates on habitat protection. The UK was five years behind schedule on notifying Special Protection Areas (SPAs), as the spirit of the EU's Birds Directive required it to do. Almost 200 potential SPAs were identified, and just 20 had been notified.

There was some encouragement for the Flow Country. The Forestry Commission agreed to consult with its environmental advisers on any future grant applications for afforestation. This was an important first step, after two years of campaigning. An application to cover 15 square kilometres was currently on the table. The RSPB called for this to be refused pending proper discussions about the future of the Flow Country as a whole. The National Audit Office had carried out a study that concluded that, let alone the damage to wildlife, it might for economic reasons be better to plant no trees at all. It raised doubts about the claimed benefits for the environment and for jobs. 'It would be absurd to allow uneconomic forestry to continue to destroy one of Britain's most valuable areas for wildlife,' said Ian Prestt.

The RSPB continued to object to the moves to put forestry plantations in the uplands, while government ignored the apparently obvious opportunity to 'bring forestry down the hill' and take lowland farmland out of crop production to cut grain surpluses and grow broadleaf or mixed woodlands there instead.

An NCC report in 1986 had asked government to review forestry policies, produce a Green Paper on rural issues, and generally take a more rounded view of how and where to plant trees; a bit of vision, really, to enhance the beauty of places, adding more life to them, enhancing rather than blighting landscapes and burying diverse nature under darkening, acidic needles. The response came in late 1987. Industry had appeared to close ranks, much like a swelling grid of Sitka Spruce. After an 18-month delay, the Scottish Secretary issued a response, more or less rejecting all of these entirely reasonable ideas. The Treasury and Forestry Commission also paid scant regard to the points raised, leaving onlookers to wonder why government had commissioned the study in the first place, at more public expense. There were continued calls for forestry to come under planning controls. There were also concerns from local authorities at the lack of local input and say in forestry.

Meanwhile, the Department of Environment reported that the overall improvement in water quality up to 1980 had gone into reverse. The RSPB gave evidence to a government enquiry, with suggestions on how things could be improved. No fewer than 30 estuaries were threatened by development. Two in particular looked disastrous for the environment, and the RSPB did what it could against the might and wealth of the developers, and private members' bills that could bypass the planning system and proper public scrutiny. A bill like this approved 45 acres of mudflats being turned into a boating lake. An extension to this aimed to spend £55 million to create a water park, in the process destroying an outstanding area for nature. The RSPB suggested an alternative plan – an urban nature park that would also provide clear value for the visiting public.

A few more Ramsar sites were added to the list of wetlands to be protected under the European Birds Directive. There were now 35, and 26 SPAs. All governments were expected to report every three years on how they had applied (or adapted) the directive. Only Britain had done so, and only Denmark had listed what could be considered a reasonable number of SPAs. Belgium and Italy became the first countries to be taken to the European Court for failing in their legal duties under the Birds Directive. The RSPB called it: 'Pitiful. If they needed a court case to force them to pass bird protection laws, how can we hope that they will ever enforce those laws once made?'

A survey of the Somerset Levels showed that in the decade since 1977 Snipe, Redshank, Lapwing and Curlew populations had gone into varying degrees of collapse, because of drainage followed by increased numbers of grazing animals and earlier cutting of hay and silage, which destroys eggs and young. The lack of birds being found in Northern Ireland was giving cause for alarm. So many wetlands had been drained it was now critical that what remained be protected if Lapwing, Curlew, Redshank, Golden Plover, Dunlin and Snipe were to survive.

There was further good news in Scotland when the peatland on Islay was saved. The brewery that had been shaping up to strip it of its peat to make whisky were told they could use the other source of peat that the RSPB had identified as being much less damaging to the rare geese that depended on the island. It was a victory for common sense over confrontation.

The reputation of weather forecasters and ignorers of available evidence everywhere suffered a famous setback in October when the BBC man told the viewing nation that they'd received a call earlier in the day from a viewer in the Scilly Isles warning that we were about to be hit by a hurricane. 'Don't worry,' he assured us, 'we're not.' The following morning, those (and it seems to have been a surprising number of people) who'd slept through the 100mph winds woke to find much of southern Britain flattened, and treeless. The RSPB set up an emergency appeal to help pay for the damage to nature reserves. A thousand trees had been knocked over at Minsmere alone.

The Otters had produced young at Minsmere early in the year. Tragically, the male and one of two cubs seen crossing the entrance road with the female Otter were killed by cars. The Otter Trust rode to the rescue when it provided a replacement male. Not far away, Britain's last remaining pair of Red-backed Shrikes bred.

It was time for an Avocet makeover. The RSPB revamped its logo, zooming in on the Avocet's head, and going with the acronym rather than the name in full; aiming for a bolder, snappier, more contemporary feel. A converted double-decker Bird Bus arrived, now a mobile information and exhibition centre. It was billed as an 'Aladdin's cave of displays and videos' as it hit the road. The YOC's membership now topped 100,000, after a slight slump reflecting the lower birth rate of the early seventies. The combined membership of the RSPB and YOC exceeded half a million. Thanks in part to evidence gathered by young people, most types of lead weight were to be banned from use in angling, to protect swans.

The Brundtland Commission produced a landmark report, *Our Common Future*, in response to mounting UN concern about accelerating deterioration of the global environment, the ozone layer, climate and 'compromising the needs of future generations'. The goal was 'long-term environmental strategies for achieving sustainable development to the year 2000 and beyond'.

It was the centenary of the death of English nature writer and essayist Richard Jefferies, whose writings had inspired Rachel Carson. 'The hours when the mind is absorbed by beauty are the only hours when we really live,' he once wrote. 'These few lines,' Carson said, 'so impressed themselves on my mind that I have never forgotten them.'

It was pretty 'Baltic' in my winter cottage again come new year in Stirlingshire, but the bigger-picture calculations showed we had a new warmest year on record. Last year had been only the fourth warmest – a blip.

1988

Work began to gather data for the *New Atlas of Breeding Birds in Britain and Ireland: 1988–1991*. This would provide for the first time an accurate view of how the distribution of bird species had changed, although some scientists thought it too soon after the first atlas for these patterns to have yet emerged. As the project developed, it became clear that there were indeed some clear-cut changes emerging.

Readers would have to wait until 1994 for the completed atlas to be published. When it came, it would help create a clearer system for setting conservation priorities.

The Flow Country was attracting attention and support from experts overseas. International authorities now recognised the global importance of this place, as near to wilderness as anywhere in the UK could seriously claim to be. They called on government to protect the most important wet bits as Ramsar sites. There were even calls to make it a World Heritage Site, such was its natural value.

At the start of the year, Secretary of State Malcolm Rifkind made a long-awaited statement acknowledging the international importance of the Flows. It was agreed that more SSSIs should be established there, to protect around half of the area. But it wasn't clear whether this would be binding, or protect these areas from drainage and afforestation, or whether in effect this might be read as an open invitation to drain and plant the other half.

In the March Budget, Chancellor Nigel Lawson bowed to pressure and announced the ending of tax concessions for forestry investment of the kind that had wrecked large areas of the Flows in the first place. The Environment Secretary then announced that permission for large-scale commercial forest planting in the hills of England 'should not normally be given'. As hoped, there would be new incentives to plant broadleaf native woodlands on lower ground no longer needed for other crops or livestock. There would still be over 80,000 acres of new forestry per year, so it seemed likely that this would be carried out in Scotland's wide open, thinly inhabited spaces; out of sight, out of mind. But the grant aid available for more exotic conifers was hiked up again, significantly higher than for the much-needed broadleaved woodlands, and the details remained sketchy (if they remained at all) on how exactly the promise to make this planting 'more sensitive to the environment' was going to be achieved.

Conservation was steadily mobilising its armoury. Europe had recently brought in a directive requiring an environmental assessment of any project – including commercial forestry – likely to damage an important site. Perhaps it would work as a deterrent. 'It will be a sorry state of affairs if the EC and others have to force our Government and its grudging Forestry Commission to fulfil their responsibilities towards Britain's wildlife,' Ian Prestt warned.

At the final count an estimated 15 million trees had been blown down in last autumn's storm, with the south and east of England worst hit. A scheme was announced that might result in 30 million new trees, it was said. The value of trees in a global context was better recognised, with 27 million acres of rainforest now being reported lost to logging each year.

Scotland escaped the worst of the hurricane, which was just as well. In the Highlands only 1% of the Forest of Caledon survived from 500 years earlier. A quarter of what was left had been lost since *Silent Spring*, much of this because of a recent process called 'under planting' for commercial reasons – or out of ignorance of the damage being done – of Scots Pine with non-native, fast-growing species like Sitka Spruce and Lodgepole Pine. Grants were available for planting native pines, but very few people were taking them up. The RSPB wanted the Scots Pine to qualify for the same level of support as native broadleaf trees like Oak, Ash and Elm. Apart from anything, Scots Pine is fine timber for furniture making. The RSPB was already selling a surplus tree or two to the Post Office for telegraph poles.

Unusually, a relic part of this near-extinct habitat came onto the market, at Abernethy. A marker was put down when the RSPB raised the funds needed to buy the arguably priceless tract. It cost £1.8 million. Nature reserves are normally measured in acres, or the later hectares, so Abernethy's 30 square miles was easily the biggest single land purchase ever by a European wildlife charity. As well as forest, the area included heather moorland and mountain-top and was home to Golden Eagles, the high-altitude grouse we call the Ptarmigan, and that beautiful migratory wading bird the Dotterel.

Local authorities were issued with new guidelines on how to play their part in protecting the best places for surviving nature. This included being equipped to reject proposals to develop areas earmarked as SPAs. In a landmark court case, a Sussex landowner was successfully prosecuted for hedgerow destruction: not because it was a valuable hedge, per se, but because it had nesting birds in it. The defendant pleaded that this was incidental to what he was doing, a defence permitted under the law – a bit like saying I didn't really mean it, the nest was just sort of in the hedge I was demolishing. Crucially, the fact that neighbours had pointed out to him that there were Blackbirds and Song Thrushes nesting in the hedge meant that he had knowingly destroyed the nests of protected species. This was of little consolation to the nesting birds, or his now hedge-less neighbours, but on top of his fine he agreed to donate £50 to the RSPB.

Many new species were given protection under the law following its five-year review: Wild Cat, Dormouse, Pine Marten, all whales, dolphins and porpoises, sea turtles and 31 species of flowering plants were added. American scientists mounted the biggest search yet for the Loch Ness Monster, and although they drew a blank, the Plesiosaur was never, to my knowledge, finally declared extinct.

In the summer, having graduated, and encouraged to fly by my *alma mater*, I found myself adrift in the largely job-free wider world of eighties Scotland. It had been bleak enough before the autumn's Black Monday crash. Back then, a government scheme enabled a young graduate to eke an existence in the local foothills, and continue to indulge his love of his surroundings – an inexpensive hobby, in the end. It also got him off the unemployment register.

My allowance gave me time to become completely immersed in the history and natural history of my local patch, 'interestingness beating upon me from all sides', as historian John J. McKay had put it. I loved the teasing clues about the goings-on in history, from Logie's old kirkyard – 'in truth there is a witchery about the spot, even in more prosaic days', as Katherine Steuart said of it in the 19th century – to the Allanwater playgrounds of Robert Louis Stevenson's youth, including a cave at the river's edge. I developed a particular interest in folklore, and the communication of history and myth in pre mass-media days. 'History records not so much what happened, as how people reacted to and thought about it.' Discuss? I wrote a short book and published a few copies for friends and family.

The Common Agricultural Policy (CAP) had its 25th birthday. It seems that throughout its existence it has been subject to reform, as a succession of critics has lined up to point out its faults. Its underlying mission to guarantee prices for farm outputs had fuelled the headlong rush to increase production at the expense of the life within the landscape.

Eighty per cent of the landscape was now said to be farmed. Much of the unfarmed remainder was urban. A new idea was introduced – 'set-aside' – the latest measure aimed at addressing the surpluses being produced. Participating arable farmers would be compensated for taking 20% out of production for five years. It sounded like a huge opportunity to restore the wildlife interest of the arable landscape. The scheme had an option of converting the set-aside back to grassland, with grazing animals. It could have been a chance to restore damp meadows in lowland river valleys, which in recent years, with their dropping water levels, had haemorrhaged wading birds. Regrettably government, under pressure from other farming interests, blocked this. It was also possible that the non set-aside land would be farmed even more intensively, so the RSPB proposed that the 20% reduction in output should apply across the farm, to add value to the measure.

Late in the year the Agriculture Minister issued details of a new farm grant scheme aimed at combating pollution, restoring wildlife habitats and protecting traditional buildings, replacing grant aid for drainage, roads and new buildings. Some optimists believed that the drive to drain and plough up the best of the countryside was now at an end. Thirty-five wetlands in the UK had now been listed and given protection as Ramsar sites.

To mark the coming centenary the RSPB hired a biographer, and *For The Love of Birds*, by Tony Samstag, was published in September. The author was briefed to do a 'warts and all' job, and he didn't disappoint. Refreshingly frank in some ways, mischievous in others, Samstag brought an American's outsider eye to proceedings, and a Fleet Street journalist's nose for a yarn. The resulting book is, if nothing else, a decent read. It was reviewed by Max Nicholson, who was faint in his praise, concluding: 'Many discriminating critics, as well as supporters of the Society, will regret that it could not have made a more profound and constructive contribution, without being any the less candid.'

A milestone in environmentalism was reached when Margaret Thatcher gave a speech to the Royal Society. She majored on three themes – greenhouse warming, the ozone hole and acid deposition. The five warmest years in the last century had all been in the eighties. 'Stable prosperity can be achieved throughout the world provided the environment is nurtured and safeguarded,' she told the assembled science community. Protecting the balance of nature would be, she concluded, 'one of the great challenges of the late 20th century'. It was an intervention that, in the words of Robin Gove-White, 'gave unprecedented prime ministerial legitimacy to the idea that environmental concerns ... now required new forms of coordinated political action'.

I was backstage at the local arts theatre on a bitter December night when word began to filter through that a jumbo jet had been blown out of the sky less than a hundred miles away, over the tiny village of Lockerbie to the south-west; chilling news to round off what was now, to those in the know, the new warmest year on record.

1989

The old year ended and the new one began with me in panto. I'd taken a job as a stage technician at the arts centre, no white coat required, thankfully. It meant rubbing shoulders with Snow White, seven dwarves, and some well-kent faces from the cast of *Gregory's Girl*, *Rab C Nesbitt*, *Take the High Road* and *Grange Hill*. Two months of panto double bills was in places an unusual, *Groundhog Day*-style torture, but left me with memories I still savour, as well as free movie tickets. I still snigger guiltily to recall how the dwarves would try to trip each other as they 'hi-ho-ed' in file onto the stage. And how, to help keep things fresh, I made unofficial interventions on the script, furnishing the handsome prince with a range of 'ugly' animal names with which to mock the wicked queen. 'Trout' went down particularly well, I seem to remember. Political correctness had yet to mature as a movement, but in any case I'm confident Ben Elton and co would have approved.

In my spare hours I continued to write a book about the history and natural history of the local area, covering the estate in which the university stands, and the former spa town of Bridge of Allan. I had a room in one of the old hotels there, where Robert Louis Stevenson had stayed, brought here as a sickly child to take the waters and escape the smog and stress of Victorian Edinburgh. He had scratched his initials on one of the windows, an act of vandalism soon forgiven by history.

Stevenson was brought here regularly, and grew to love the setting, especially the riverbank and its paths. 'All the way along I was thanking God that he had made me and the birds and everything just as they are and not otherwise,' he wrote in a letter, 'for although there was no sun, the air was so thrilled with robins and blackbirds that it made the heart tremble with joy.'

A report in January seemed to encourage the acceleration of forest plantation in the Flows. Aerial photographs showed the vast peatland landscape by now scored with row upon row of furrows, ploughed into the centuries-old peat. It could almost be another planet, pockmarked with black-hole pools of clear water and larger lochs like craters. Huge proportions of many rare birds depend on this place: Greenshank, Dunlin, Golden Plover, Scoters, divers and birds of prey.

'No land use is quite as catastrophic for moorland birds as planting conifers,' as Derek Ratcliffe, Chief Scientist of the NCC, put it. A would-be forester could propose to plant up a known special place for wildlife, in the knowledge that when this permission was refused, they could be compensated for loss of income from sales of timber, and also of the public grant they would have received to do the planting. Government finally took steps to remove the foregone grant element of this compensation.

Another attempt was made in January to bring in protection for at least some of the best and most important surviving hedgerows. This had support from politicians of all parties, and sought to make it an offence to destroy hedgerows forming parish boundaries or bordering public roads and bridleways. A government MP again blocked the bill.

The RSPB's centenary brought notes of congratulation from the main political party leaders, Margaret Thatcher, Neil Kinnock and Paddy Ashdown, among many other politicians and notables. The Green Party announced its arrival as a significant player on the political stage when it cornered an impressive 15% of the vote in the European elections. A Green Party representative highlighted a rising issue of the day when he asked the RSPB: 'How many members have changed to unleaded petrol?' The number of vehicles in use was unlikely to diminish, as the government published a White Paper called *Roads for Prosperity*, 500 development schemes billed as 'the biggest road-building programme since the Romans'.

'We insensitive overgrown mammals are at last awakening to our huge and perilous deficiencies,' wrote Max Nicholson in his tribute. 'We dimly see some of the ways in which birds can show us how to achieve fulfilment through the harmony with nature which they so happily and successfully demonstrate to us. May not this be the guideline to inspire the Society's second century?'

And there was this touching dedication from Francesco Mezzatesta, head of the RSPB's Italian partner LIPU, among the many that the Society had mentored. 'All at once I saw that LIPU's future could be just the same: protecting birds and nature by setting up a scientific background, professional promotional techniques, and an extraordinary structure ... history runs its course and in Italy the time is coming when people will watch joyfully our winged friends ...'

Margaret Thatcher joined in with the celebrations, taking time out to launch the Action for Birds campaign at Kings Cross station, where a locomotive called the Avocet was unveiled. As a special centenary concession, the Bird Bus was allowed to park near Westminster where it was visited by MPs, lords and ladies. The Bolshoi Ballet toured in the summer, with a new production of *Swan Lake*, granting the RSPB the honour of a gala centenary reception at the premiere.

But perhaps the greatest birthday present of all came when government announced that all remaining approvals for the sale, supply, storage, use or advertisement of products containing dieldrin would be revoked from the end of March, and aldrin and chlordane from the end of 1992.

Two decades after the *Torrey Canyon* disaster, the start of spring was blighted by images of oil apocalypse when the *Exxon Valdez* ran aground off Alaska in late March; the worst oil spill in US history. An extraordinary 1,300 miles of coastline were coated, and 11,000 square miles of ocean.

In April I travelled north with a group of friends to a rented cottage in Gruinard Bay, in Wester Ross – a stunning and secluded corner of the coastline, with a tarnished past. The island in the bay was the setting for an anthrax biological warfare experiment by military scientists in 1942. In 1986, an attempt had begun to decontaminate the island, and its entire area was sprayed with formaldehyde in seawater. At the time of our visit, the island remained out of bounds, and it wasn't known whether it would ever again be safe to visit, although its sheep flock seemed to be grazing quite normally. We kept our sea kayaks at a sensible distance.

The EU's Habitats Directive was now on the horizon. The RSPB wondered if government was intent on trying to block it, after representatives made scathing remarks about the plan. 'If Britain's record is so good,' asked Ian Prestt, 'what is there to fear?'

A shadow of uncertainty was cast over National Nature Reserves when government asked the NCC to look into whether it was necessary for the state to own them all. It then announced plans to break up the NCC, which set alarm bells ringing, not least because the move was made without consulting the NCC itself. The fear was that the function could only be weakened by this fragmentation. 'We see no benefit to conservation in this strange proposal and the Government has been unable to offer any,' said Ian Prestt. Chris Patten was asked to think again, and examine where the real problems lay. The NCC seemed to be paying the price for criticising government, which it was entitled to do – that, in the end, was an aspect of its role. 'The break-up is a political move designed to remove this independence of thought and action,' said the RSPB.

It was a warm summer, this so-called second summer of love, the more so for me as I spent part of it in the balmy south, in Bristol, where my girlfriend had a summer job. The male Red-backed Shrike returned alone (and would again next year) to the place a pair last bred. Extinction now looked certain. An ambitious scheme was launched to bring the Red Kite back to southern England, and the first young kites were flown in from Sweden to a secret location. Two were found poisoned soon afterwards, indicating that success was far from assured. The state of fisheries and the marine environment gave cause for alarm, as Arctic Terns failed spectacularly to raise young in Shetland for the sixth year running. Kittiwakes, Puffins and skuas were also toiling.

A bill to privatise the water industry in England and Wales was published in the autumn. It had improved since its first draft two years earlier, at which time it proposed to allow water companies to be in charge of water pollution control – when they themselves were often major polluters through failures in sewage treatment. River pollution had worsened through the eighties. Farm slurry and silage waste had become even more of a problem than untreated human sewage. Much of the wildlife value had been lost to the reshaping of rivers to stop them spreading over their natural floodplains, and the removal of bank-side trees and shrubs.

Responsibility for pollution, flood defence, fisheries, recreation and navigation would rest with a new body, the National Rivers Authority. What would happen to the land currently in the hands of the state-owned water authorities? Would its conservation value be maintained? The new policies and awareness among river engineers offered hope that the era of destruction had ended. There was some good news on aquatic wildlife. The number of swans poisoned by lead had halved in two years since tighter controls on lead weights in angling were brought in.

Scientists had begun to talk publicly about a new phenomenon they were calling the greenhouse effect. I could claim to have been unaware of the problem and the contribution I might be making to it when I boarded a jumbo jet at Heathrow in December, to fly to California and visit friends studying there on exchange. The flight alone was one of the most exhilarating experiences of my young life, as we flew into almost perpetual sunset, and I had grandstand views of Iceland, Greenland, the eastern seaboard, the Great Lakes, the Rockies and the vast, unpopulated plains of the Midwest. I couldn't understand why most of my fellow passengers were watching James Bond.

I was tipped out of the sprinter bus from the airport in south-central district's Greyhound bus depot, very late on a Friday night, by a driver who looked genuinely fearful for my prospects of survival. I didn't rate them much higher. The next morning I woke in San Diego, to watch a spectacular Christmas parade downtown in blazing sunshine. Welcome to the land of contrasts, of vast empty wilderness and teeming, scary cities, eerie downtown ghettoes and conspicuous, uptown wealth.

I visited the zoo, where the world's few surviving California Condors had been taken into care for captive breeding. Some would be released the following year, as the effort began to save the wild population from extinction. We did the beatnik, first summer of love thing and went on the road in a beat-up van over Christmas and new year, to Mexico, then Arizona, and San Francisco. I came so close to a Golden Eagle dining on carrion in the desert I could see its blonde mane. We even found a black panther, called a Jaguarundi. America was as you'd expect: bigger, closer, more colourful, bursting with variety and possibility. The nineties era of Reaganism was just ending. It hadn't been environmentalism's finest hour. George Bush Snr had replaced Reagan as President. Gazing down into the vastness and silence of the Grand Canyon, I wondered if the Witches' Craig would ever look quite the same again.

1990

As the new year began, we crossed the Golden Gate Bridge on a pilgrimage to Muir Woods, 'the best tree-lovers' monument that could possibly be found in all the forests of the world', as the man after whom it is named, Scots-born godfather of US national parks John Muir, had himself described it. America blew me away, but the main culture shock was returning to midwinter Stirling, and realising that I lived somewhere closer to Warsaw than to California: home seemed suddenly so old, grey, cold and defeated. But it was January, to be fair, and the Berlin Wall had just come down. Perhaps things were about to pick up.

Robert Louis Stevenson wrote, on his deathbed in Samoa in 1892, of 'lying back and seeing the child, that once was me, wading knee-deep in butterburs' by the Allanwater. I share his lingering fondness for the place. I can still see that former me-child, knee-deep in revellers at the Grange student club where I DJ-ed occasionally, perhaps not fully grown even when graduating at 21, fledging uncertainly, and making those first tentative wing-stretches in the world. I still hanker sometimes for those 'blue-remembered hills' of the north though: the

Ravens over the Ochil hills, the Bluebell woods in May, the creative buzz of the campus editorial office and recording studio.

I bought a second-hand Amstrad word processor and taught myself to touch-type, started work as a trainee with the Scottish Wildlife Trust, and with more than a tinge of regret left behind the playgrounds of Stirlingshire to move 'through' to Edinburgh, taking everything I owned on the train, over the course of several journeys. The Trust's offices were at that time in Leith and in the shadow of the 'Castle in The Air'.

Stevenson was no great fan of the capital. He described it as having 'one of the vilest climates under heaven', but then he was consumptive – a very sickly child. 'For some constitutions,' he wrote, probably meaning his own, 'there is something almost physically disgusting in its bleak ugliness.'

Nelson Mandela was released in February, bringing a mood of optimism, that things could change after all. At any opportunity I escaped 'Auld Reekie' for the Highlands and Islands, booking cottages and mobilising friends, all the while trying gently to kindle their interest in nature. From a base in Achiltibuie I organised the group for a visit to Handa Island, which lies just off the north-western extremity of Scotland. A fisherman ran us across in his fishing boat and we clambered out onto the beach. We had the afternoon to walk across the gently rising island, as the famously hostile Bonxies, aka Great Skuas, cruised overhead, until we reached the cliff-top at the western end. Here, the world falls away from in front of you, in the most spectacular amphitheatre of sea cliffs and seabirds, their squawks and their smells wafting upwards on the sea's spray. It was 18 years since I'd been here and the snapshot image of the place taken by my five-year-old mind's eye remained intact. Happily, it survives comparison with the Grand Canyon, by now a distant dream.

My achievements in converting chums to the cause of nature have been mixed. To foster his interest I made a gift of a cassette called *The Soothing Sounds of Nature* to my friend Maceo. This had come free with *BBC Wildlife* magazine, but of course it's the thought. It featured real-life, orchestral-in-scale dawn choruses from around the world, from English oakwood to East African acacia forest. These multi-participant natural orchestras featured much more than birds, with gibbons, frogs, Hippos and insects adding to the vernacular cacophonies.

Maceo reported that he'd really enjoyed the cassette. He had thought it might be cool to listen to in bed; a relaxation thing before nodding off. So he stuck it on one sultry summer evening, when he got in from the pub, and lay down in a darkened bedroom to be suitably soothed. He was just drifting off, he said, when a huge bumblebee came in through the open window. Lucky Frank, as he is also known (he's accident-prone, is Maceo) is allergic to bee and wasp stings, so understandably he panicked a little, scrambled out of bed to fumble for the light switch, sent a pint glass of water spinning off the bedside table and, dazzled by the light, searched frantically for the offending bee, only to discover that it was ... on the cassette. Just one more of the soothing sounds ...

Parliament debated the Green Bill, a piece of legislation mainly concerned with tackling pollution. But it also contained moves to replace the NCC, and nothing about the shortcomings of the laws in place to protect SSSIs, which continued to suffer from neglect and mismanagement. Conservationists went on questioning why the NCC didn't have the same powers over special places for nature as existed to protect listed buildings.

Industrial-scale stripping of peatlands had by now become frightening in scale. The Prime Minister was said to have been encouraging consumers to buy and use this peat. Prince Charles was being more helpful in the campaign against peat use. Only 4% of raised peat bogs survived, and the NCC predicted that these would disappear by 2010. Planning permissions given in the past for peat extraction pre-dated the SSSI process. Even newly protected sites were still being dug up, quite legally. The need to find alternatives to peat for gardeners was now clear and pressing.

The fight for special places raged on. The RSPB took a local council to court over a planning decision. The case concerned an estuary that was due to become an SPA because of its international importance as a feeding and resting place for migrating and other birds. A proposal for port development had been approved, without the RSPB being consulted, even though promises had been made that consultation would take place. If it had, the RSPB would have asked for an environmental assessment, and a public enquiry.

The case reached the High Court, which found in the RSPB's favour, agreeing that the case was in the public interest and that the council should have consulted. Hitherto unclear areas of the planning process could now be addressed. Unfortunately, the court didn't reverse the planning permission because the judge deemed it would cost the port authority too much and because, he said, the case had not come to court quickly enough. So, conservation case vindicated, site lost. But the fight had been worthwhile. What had been learned could be taken up with the UK and European parliaments. Local authorities would do well to take heed.

At this point in history, 10% of the UK's Corncrakes survived in County Fermanagh. Researchers started work with farmers to find ways of trying to keep the birds going. The species had declined by 60% across Northern Ireland in just ten years. Government needed to designate more protected areas. There were currently seven, and only one was a wetland.

Surveyors heard just 17 Corncrakes, compared to the 70 recorded two years earlier. The rest of the province produced just ten, down from 60. They were known to be declining, but these latest figures still came as a shock. It was felt that the creation of an ESA was the only hope for the birds, and perhaps for small-scale farming as well. The RSPB was encouraging farmers to cut later, and to cut from the middle of fields, so that the birds and their chicks could escape from the blades. The scheme was to be tried in Scotland and the Republic of Ireland next year.

Sand Martins had now declined by an astonishing 92% since *Silent Spring*. A bulldozer driver was persuaded to postpone an operation at a sand quarry, where 80 pairs of Sand Martins were nesting in holes in the banks. His manager saw things differently, however, and ordered him to get on with the job. They were both charged and duly convicted. The charge against their company was dismissed, which meant that they had taken individual responsibility.

There was much talk back then of 'thinking global, acting local', and 'taking only photographs, leaving only footprints'. We talked a lot about the Cairngorms in the offices of the Scottish Wildlife Trust. A long-running battle for these mountains reached a satisfactory conclusion when the Secretary of State for Scotland rejected proposals for ski development in Lurcher's Gully in the Cairngorms. More than 7,000 letters of objection had landed on his desk, dwarfing the 135 letters in favour. The Save the Cairngorms campaign appeared to have worked.

We fought hard as a movement, with RSPB alongside, to stop a special place called Glen Dye being damaged by commercial forestry planting, and to stop a housing development on green belt land along the Allanwater towards Dunblane. I became immersed in both cases through researching and writing campaign features.

A league table of Europe's offenders saw Spain come top when it came to protecting special places. It had been issued with 57 threats of legal action for violation of directives since 1986, ignoring legislation and putting roads across its best wetlands. A fifth of the funding for these developments came from another part of the EU, paid for by Europe's taxpayers. Twelve of the most important wildlife sites in the Mediterranean region were under threat. There were comparable cases happening here, and across Europe. Belgium had received 46 warnings, the UK 31.

We lost a bird. The Red-backed Shrike became extinct as a breeding species in Britain. The male returned alone for the second year running to the place the pair last bred. But again no female bird joined him. The impact of this loss was felt by those who had known the bird, such as Hazel Hunt of Avon, who wrote:

> The phrase 'for the first time no shrikes nested in England' left me desolate. Instantly I was a seven-year-old again, in Somerset, called by my grandfather to see the strange bird perched in the garden. He was like no other bird I have seen, flamboyant and arrogant, scolding us with his harsh 'chack-chack'. From that moment began a love-affair with wild birds that has lasted all my life. I soon learned where he nested, deep in a railway cutting in forbidden territory to me.
>
> Every summer he proudly brought his young brood, usually five but once seven, to show off. His mate had none of his flamboyance although neither she nor the fledglings had much fear of the small child curled up on the seat ... How can such a brave and beautiful bird be lost to us? I can lie awake at night and listen to the waves on the shore, the calls of the waders, the haunting cry of the curlew – but I would exchange all of them to hear again the familiar 'chack-chack' of the bird that touched my childhood with magic.

The White Paper on the Environment, the first major government statement on the subject for two decades, was greeted with disappointment and described as 'lightweight'. It was failing to meet head-on most of the tough political challenges and what would actually be done around coasts, renewable energy scheme impacts, wildlife crime, ESAs and the best sites. Environment Minister Chris Patten was recognised as a man with ideas and commitment to the environment, but there was much left unsaid and little that was novel in the proposals. There was little to improve protection of SSSIs, nothing on estuaries and coasts, nothing to reduce afforestation of the uplands. Opposition spokesman Bryan Gould committed his party to SSSI and coastline action. Agriculture Minister John Gummer was pressed to help reform the CAP and link environmental protection to the issue of over-production.

Through the summer months, it emerged that developers in America had been weighing up the possibility of building Eurodisney on Rainham Marshes in east London, rather than a site near Paris. There was a snag with Rainham – it was by this time a SSSI. It also had no major road through it, although there was also a plan to build a six-lane motorway across the site. Conservationists had a different vision for Rainham, which was to turn it into a proper nature reserve with visitor access and facilities, within easy reach of the major population centres of London and the south-east. There would be a public inquiry over the road plan. Disney would no doubt be awaiting the outcome with interest.

'The whole area is bleak marsh land, littered with tired factory buildings and hundreds of containers ...' as one letter-writer described it. 'To talk of a major wildlife reserve and visitor centre is rather grand, but far too late in the day.'

The RSPB tried 'to persuade MCA that the destruction of this site is not in their best interests', and encourage them to think about a less sensitive site to the east. Chris Patten declined to call a public inquiry. The Thames Estuary as a whole was under pressure. 'Will the "protected" areas remain undamaged? Or will they disappear under concrete and spoil?' the RSPB wondered. A national estuaries campaign was launched.

The BTO's Common Bird Census showed that seven bird species had now reached their lowest levels since the survey began in *Silent Spring* year, 1962: Turtle Dove, Little Owl, Tree Pipit, Spotted Flycatcher, Starling, Bullfinch and Yellowhammer.

The RSPB published an environmental manifesto for the nineties, introducing terms like sustainable development, true costs to society, precautionary principle – when risks are not clearly known, but possible – and environmental education. There was much talk in the press about organic farming, lead-free petrol, catalytic converters and a new term coined in the USA – 'greenwash'.

An era and a decade with a particular political flavour ended when Margaret Thatcher's 11-year reign as Prime Minister drew to a close late in the year. She had clashed with former Environment

Secretary Michael Heseltine over Europe, and when it became clear she didn't have the necessary backing from her cabinet to continue, she had no option but to step down. Chancellor John Major emerged from the shadows to win the power struggle to succeed the 'iron lady'. Thatcherism had spanned the eighties here. Politics, and the environment cause, were about to enter a new phase, albeit one that would be a good deal harder to define. The biodiversity years might be one way of describing it. The struggle to save nature was about to go global.

The Nineties

1991

In January *The Times* ran a news story under the headline: 'How Thatcher's dream park vanished in the marsh'. The saga of Disney for Rainham was over. Conservation had won this battle, but the takeover of MCA by another company was probably key.

I became reacquainted on a regular basis with the dawn and the headlines when I started work in a media monitoring company. In fact I was up before all but the street light Robins, and it meant 3am alarm calls, and cycling over the cobbles of Edinburgh's deserted new town to get the scalpel out and unbundle the day's papers. Our clients were mainly banks, oil companies and nuclear interests. It was all useful research for me, combining my interests in environment and media.

There was never any shortage of oil coverage, but the scope was set to widen. The early part of the year was dominated by hellish images of conflict in the Gulf. Oil fields burned and spewed, bombs and bullets flew. While first and foremost a human tragedy, the environmental impacts were also stark. *Private Eye* ran a cover photo of a Cormorant coated in oil, in a lake of the stuff. It looked like a figurine drowning in chocolate. The speech bubble coming from the bird's beak said simply: 'It's not about oil.'

What is it about birds and oil? You'd think the average *Eye* reader would be able to cope, but I recall vehement letters of complaint in the magazine, and resignations by subscribers who felt this was a satire too far.

The Socotra Cormorant was the species of most conservation concern among the 50,000 birds snagged by the oil from the sabotaged Kuwaiti oilfields. Two million birds of 40 species were known to move through the region in spring. Tired and hungry migrant birds mistook the spilled oil for freshwater lakes. RSPB expertise was called upon. David Sexton visited, and reported seeing migrant Swallows swooping to dip their beaks in these black lakes of oil, one of them being dragged under, the others flying on, stained, presumably choking, to die soon after. The extent of the losses of birds could only be guessed at, until and unless full survey work could be done, which would of course be logistically very difficult. Saddam Hussein's troops had destroyed vast areas of the Mesopotamian marshes in south-east Iraq, by diverting rivers, to displace half a million Marsh Arabs. It was one of the most extreme acts of ecological sabotage ever inflicted on the planet and its people.

Back home, the February cold snap took its toll on birds. It took its toll on me when a rare city centre white-out wiped out my driving test. Another crown jewel of the Scottish landscape was up for sale. The Mar Lodge Estate covers 120 square miles of the Cairngorms, and was on the open market. Conservationists urged government to buy it for the nation, but government declined. The RSPB then joined forces with the World Wide Fund for Nature and the John Muir Trust to boldly pledge half the buying price, to encourage others to come forward to fund the shortfall. There were substantial management costs to factor in as well.

I visited Mar Lodge that spring. I had been able to spend more time in the Highlands, not far from the estate. A friend of mine had the use of a wonderfully basic and splendidly isolated old keeper's cottage, and a few of us would escape to it at weekends – longer when we could. It was here that I got to know a Stoat or two, which provided the inspiration for an essay I called *Celebrities*. The Stoats had been using the cottage, and I'd had close encounters the previous autumn. In spring, I found them again. 'As I sat outside, I recognised the sense of frenetic activity that heralds the entrance of celebrities. They came into view, ducking and weaving among the boulders and roots, jinking this way and that, manic as ever; more so, if anything. I could see my own feelings of elation on that fresh, windy afternoon reflected in their mannerisms: that urge to run, leap and breathe fresh air, all the things that winter and city life seem to preclude.'

It proved an unexpected turning point for me as the piece was published in *BBC Wildlife* magazine, and led to commissions from the Natural History Unit in Bristol where I worked on television documentary scripts with actor/narrators like Andrew Sachs and Bill Paterson, and later on natural history books. Ties in Scotland prevented me from trying to make the move south a permanent one.

I visited Devon, where it was now all-systems-go to save the Cirl Bunting. Just a hundred pairs survived in the south of the county, with a few more hanging on in the Channel Islands. Before the Second World War the Cirl Bunting could be found all across southern England and parts of Wales. There were still around 300 pairs in 1970. By 1982 this number had halved. Research had given a strong clue that stubble fields in winter are essential for Cirl Bunting survival. Not only had these stubbles dwindled in the farmed landscape, but any left have much less spilt grain and few wildflower seeds within them, due to modern efficiencies and herbicides. The increase in field sizes has also been a problem, as foraging birds don't like to be too exposed. They prefer the sanctuary of a hedgerow close to hand. Nationally, another fifth of what was left of our hedges was removed from the landscape between 1984 and 1991. Grants for hedge removal, having been routinely issued until the eighties, were now being provided to put the hedges back.

The NCC came to an end and was replaced in April by separate bodies for England, Wales and Scotland. In May, a renewed campaign was launched against the import of wild birds into Europe. Tragically, three-quarters of wild-caught birds were dying before they even reached pet shops. Legal trade was being used to mask countless illegal transactions. The regulations were so complex and so varyingly applied in different countries that they could be widely flouted. The taking of European wild birds had already been banned, so it seemed reasonable that the same should apply to birds taken from elsewhere.

A general election was due within a year, and an environmental manifesto was sent to all candidates. The 10-point plan called for greening all aspects of policy-making, and included SSSIs, farm subsidies linked to environment protection, creating marine nature reserves, stopping bird of prey persecution, mandatory environmental education in all schools, ending the wild bird trade and illegal killing in the Mediterranean, and addressing greenhouse gas emissions.

The summer would be remembered as another dreary one. I left press cuttings and broadcast transcriptions and took another, slightly better paid and more sociable job in promotions with the Edinburgh

Festival. Most of my friends were by now in paid jobs, so in the face of the drizzle ten of us decided we could afford to bail, and rent a holiday *gite* in southern France. It was a far cry from an Edinburgh tenement, or even Stoat Cottage in the Highlands. Here was a picturesque limestone plateau, traced with dusty white tracks and heat haze. Poppies decorated the field edges with stabs of crimson, the warm summer air rang with the sound of Orioles, frogs and Nightingales.

I recall a magical afternoon stalking with a camera a calling Golden Oriole in an Oak and Poplar grove. The whole place shimmered like ticker tape from the heavens, while the bird and its mate haunted me with their occasionally repeated, liquid, fluty calls, teasing me with glimpses in the flickering, kaleidoscopic leaves of the trees. The sylvan sirens evaded me, but I was consoled by a Red Squirrel foraging nearby, and a Hoopoe that flashed in to strut among the fallen twigs on a cloak of black-and-white moth-wings, probing the leafy earth with its sickle bill, crest bristling and slumping alternately. They nested in an old woodpecker hole in the Walnut tree next to our *gite*, and hoo-hoo-hooed most mornings.

Two weeks of communing with the birds, relaxing by the pool and exploring the Cevennes, had been, you might say, *très, très jolie*. By the end of the sojourn we were very relaxed, as we headed to Toulouse for the flight home. An escapade ensued. All my chums managed to board the correct flight. How I managed not to remains a little sketchy.

The last thing I recall is fishing in my pocket for the boarding card, momentarily taking my eye off Trish, the chum ahead. I presented my card, which was checked, then put through a scanner. I took my bit of it back, and tramped down the gangway to the plane. Or perhaps I should say *a* plane.

I figured it was sit anywhere, as there was a large French gentleman in what my boarding card suggested was my seat. I got buckled in nearby. We took off. There was no sign of any pals, though I craned forward and back. I took it they must all be beyond the partition. I buried my face in a magazine. I was vaguely aware of announcements in French – and French only. I didn't think this unduly odd. I wasn't a very experienced flier, and, well, the French are like that, aren't they? Speaking French a lot. I noted the in-flight magazine was only in French too.

I craned harder, and again in vain, for a familiar face. I began to think that maybe I was on the wrong plane. But then I stopped myself – don't be daft, no one gets … etc. *No one.* Imagine. I wanted then to find my friends just to tell them 'Hey, you know what ... ho-ho!' How we would laugh.

The lights came on giving the go-ahead to unbuckle. I hurriedly wriggled free to go and have this amusing conversation. Wrong plane, indeed! I looked in vain. I had a moment of painful realisation that something had gone badly awry.

'Excuse me,' I ventured to a steward in the aisle. 'But where is this plane going?'

'*Comment, monsieur?*'

'*Ou va cette avion?*' I mumbled.

She looked a little alarmed. Plainly this was beyond her experience or training. Some nearby passengers were also looking twice.

'*Un moment,*' she muttered, hastening in the direction of the cabin. I followed, feeling gormless. The head steward appeared. My main concerns at this point were: where were we going, and would they make me pay to get home?

'I think I'm on the wrong plane,' I told him.

'You don't worry about anything,' he answered immediately. It was, of course, mostly his and their problem. He rushed off, I guessed to make some calls. I established that we were en route to Paris. At least it wasn't Quebec.

Meanwhile, the other plane, the one I was supposed to be on, had taken off without me. My pals had had their suspicions that I was missing confirmed by the apparent anxiety of their cabin crew. They of course were one head count short of the number of bags in the hold. A major security alert was imminent, complete with immediate landing. There was relief all round when my friends proposed to them the 'Passenger Jameson is missing' scenario. Contact between the two planes and air traffic control confirmed *le coq* up. Hilarity ensued, at least on their plane.

My foster airline looked after me. They gave me a meal and bussed me from Charles de Gaulle to Orly for the flight to London. And no, I didn't have to pay. The adventure ended some hours later, after my bus round *le périphérique* of Paris, and I was greeted by the smiling faces of my group as I exited Heathrow. Our bus to Edinburgh wasn't due for another couple of hours anyway.

I've dined out on this story many times. I never made anything publicly of it at the time, although back then we lived in times of supposedly heightened security, with the first Gulf War of George Bush Snr. His New World Order ('to shape the future of the world for the next hundred years') was in its infancy. I won't embarrass the airlines concerned by naming them – it could, in the end, happen to any airline. Or airlines. I'm not sure how often people get on the wrong plane. Straw polls of people I have known employed by airlines suggest, well, never. Not that airlines would exactly publicise such incidents. So I am the friend, or the friend of a friend, who got on the wrong plane. It may have reinforced an image of me that is scatty, mishap-prone, or just unlucky. For a long time I think it certainly did this even with those who know me well.

Barbara Young succeeded Ian Prestt as RSPB Chief Executive, bringing a fresh brand of leadership from her background in the health service, as the growing organisation shaped up to the new and varied challenges of the nineties. There were, for example, new fears that the system of protection for SSSIs in Scotland was being undermined by moves to review it. 'Ministers have abandoned all their pledges, broken the trust established with the RSPB and weakly capitulated to one interest group,' she wrote.

The Habitats Directive was close to being agreed in Europe, after three years of negotiation. To begin with, the UK and Spain had stalled its progress. Spain feared that it would get in the way of development. Powerful hunting interests and some MEPs delayed a report for a year, and European President Jacques Delors held it up further. Spain continued to object, for wider political reasons. The directive had become 'a piece in a much bigger game', according to the RSPB, but there was optimism that the Dutch Presidency could resolve the problems and the directive could be adopted by Christmas.

The Shetland sand-eel fishery had been closed to allow fish stocks to recover. A dramatic improvement in breeding success by seabirds ensued. Thousands of young Arctic Terns fledged for the first time in eight years, while Puffins and Kittiwakes did better than for several years. It was too soon to say whether the closure of the sand-eel fishery had done the trick so soon, but time would tell. Shetland still had its Corncrakes, but the sad news coming to light was that this formerly widespread species was now effectively extinct as a breeding bird in mainland Britain, surviving only in County Fermanagh, the Hebrides, Orkney and Shetland.

It was now hoped that one of the Corncrake's final refuges, the Hebridean island of Coll, would be able to hold on to the remaining birds that still returned there each spring. The RSPB had bought four square miles of land there that could be managed in a way that supported the birds rather than killed them, as seemed to have happened almost everywhere else. At the time of purchase it was thought that the reserve had around five calling male birds.

There was another unfortunate twist in the pesticide saga: even more products were now being misused deliberately to kill birds and other wildlife – targeted at them in lethal concentrations on baits left out illegally.

1992

I got a break when I was offered the job of editing John Lewis's staff magazine. So, at the turn of the year, I traded the Oxfam-bought Hardy Amies classic suit that had somehow got me through the interview, purchased something double-breasted and 'much more Partnership' from the shop floor, and took up position at the Editor's desk. The spirit of its founder, John Spedan Lewis, lived on in this idiosyncratic, philanthropic business, which knew how to look after people: staff (I should say Partners) and customers alike. It had a profit-share scheme, a democratic infrastructure, never advertised or opened on Sundays or Mondays, and still used arcane slogans like 'never knowingly undersold'. Lewis had been a naturalist too, and a charitable trust in his name still provides grants to encourage young naturalists.

From the New Town, Edinburgh's profile is dominated by the bulbous outline of the John Lewis building, where the jagged row of spires, flagpoles and chimney stacks falls away to the lowland east end. We had a roof terrace, and sometimes the Edinburgh climate even allowed it to be used. It afforded glorious views east over the vast, unplanned urban sprawl of tenements and warehouses, and landmarks including Meadowbank, Easter Road stadium, Leith docks and the Botanic Gardens, with the mouth of the Forth and its islets, and Fife sometimes visible on the northern horizon. Calton Hill stands shoulder-to-shoulder with the shop, crowned with the classical pillars that call to mind Auld Reekie's other nickname – 'the Athens of the North'. Comedian Jeremy Hardy suggested that the name derives from the number of English people being sick here in the summer, during the Festival.

At last in April the Habitats Directive was adopted. Like the Birds Directive before it, its success would depend on member states taking the action it required of them. It was therefore timely to reflect on how well the obligations of the Birds Directive had been honoured. For some, the UK's record might have been cause for embarrassment. Of the 240 sites of international importance that had been identified under the terms of the directive, only 41 had been designated as SPAs. This amounted to a lower percentage of the landscape than most neighbouring countries. Britain was ninth in the league table. Three more SPAs were designated but all were RSPB nature reserves, probably less in need of confirmed protection than any of the other sites as yet undesignated. Only 21% had been confirmed by this stage.

Native woodland is not without its management conundrums. Capercaillies and Black Grouse were being killed by flying into fences designed to protect woodland from deer. It was just one cause of the steady decline of the Capercaillie. The RSPB was removing internal fences from the Abernethy reserve to alleviate the problem. Deer numbers in Scotland had doubled to 300,000 since 1959. Along with sheep, they can be a serious impediment to woodland regeneration in unchecked numbers.

Mar Lodge would not be added to the list of challenges, as the consortium set up to try to raise the money to buy and manage the estate was forced to withdraw as it had been unable to raise the shortfall in funds. The estate remained on the open market.

The Forestry Commission at last recognised the value of native woods, including Birch and Oak, and damp woods dominated by Willow and Alder. Grants and advice were made available from the spring. Safeguards for SSSIs were being improved too. Scores of them were still being damaged each year. More ESAs were to be designated in England too, adding 12 more to the existing 10. It was hoped that this model could be used in other European countries, to improve the farmed environment for wildlife. The RSPB was increasing its support for European and other partner organisations, in Poland, Spain, Romania and Sierra Leone.

Commercial foresters had made another application to drain, plough and plant 900 hectares of SSSI within the Flow Country. There were huge areas that had been identified as acceptable for planting, away from the most important parts. But in the end, if you really want to protect a special place for nature, you can do a lot worse than purchase it. So the RSPB showed it meant business and bought its first piece of the Flow Country jigsaw. It wouldn't be the last.

* * *

There was considerable optimism around the Earth Summit in Rio de Janeiro, Brazil. 'Never before has there been so much concern among politicians and the general public alike about the state of the world's environment,' said the RSPB. It spawned the word 'biodiversity'. Global agreements were duly signed on this, and climate change. The latter had many loopholes, and the USA in fact refused to sign it, but it did give new legal impetus to conservation worldwide. The countries that did sign were now expected to exercise their 'best endeavours' to make sure emissions of greenhouse gases were maintained at 1990 levels come the year 2000. The 800-page Agenda 21 (as in 21st century) document also resulted. Countries had now to produce sustainability plans.

In spite of this global backdrop, environmental issues were far from prominent in the general election campaign, which was won by the incumbent Conservatives under John Major. It was 'the Sun wot won it' this time, apparently, and few would argue.

Government published a report called *Britain's Environment Strategy*. Despite this, too many government policies, development proposals and actions continued to threaten the environment and special places for wildlife. There was a sense of 'here we go again' when Rainham was threatened by proposals for a Channel tunnel rail link, but it had been a record year for the designation of SPAs, with 72 now on the list; 65 Ramsar sites had been designated too. But when Environment Secretary Michael Howard removed an area of mudflats called Lappel Bank from the proposed SPA on the Medway Estuary in Kent, to keep it free for development, the seeds were sown of one of the biggest test-case battles of all.

The six-month UK Presidency of the EU ended in December. It culminated in a summit meeting of political leaders in Edinburgh. From my editor's desk on the top floor of the John Lewis building on Leith Walk, I had a grandstand view of a huge neon sculpture by the artist Ian Hamilton Finlay on the roof of the government buildings next door. It said 'European Heads', although the word heads was upside down, which could be read as subversive.

The main issue on the table was the question of which responsibilities should be Europe-wide, and which ones should lie with an individual country: the so-called 'subsidiarity' question that emerged from the Belgian city of Maastricht and the treaty signed there. UK government, perhaps smarting a bit from its own poor track record in honouring its obligations, put forward the view that European environmental legislation was intruding on national affairs and should be weakened, or even withdrawn. But environment was probably the last area that should be devolved, as it cut across all areas of policy and land use and had to be evenly applied across all countries and borders, to ensure a level playing field. If any given country was permitted to relax its standards or protection laws, then others would soon cry foul, and follow suit.

Democrat candidate Bill Clinton was elected US President, but it had been a year to forget for the royal family, the Queen famously calling it an '*annus horribilis*' in a speech late in the year.

1993

January witnessed the dreaded return of the tanker disaster to UK shores when the *M V Braer* hit the rocks off Shetland and discharged 84,000 tonnes of oil. In the wake of this, conservationists and others called for controls on the routes that oil tankers could take, and the areas they must avoid. It also called for tighter control of old and substandard ships.

Later in the month RSPB investigators travelled to Amsterdam to inspect around 300 crates of wild birds just arrived from South America, in a batch worth nearly £1 million. They found crates packed with macaws, parrots and toucans. Very little was known about the conservation status of these species in the wild. About a quarter of them were destined for the UK. A year had passed since the launch of the campaign against the wild bird trade, but government's position was unchanged: 'Our general policy is to endorse the sustainable use of the world's resources and reviews by our scientific advisers last year confirmed the potential benefit for wildlife of such an approach.'

The idea here is that if a market exists for wild-trapped birds, then the places where these birds come from will be preserved. For some people this is a persuasive ideal: that a tropical forest, for example, can provide a renewable harvest of birds and therefore be preserved intact as a resource for local people. But it overlooks the fact that the harvesting is impossible to regulate, cannot be guaranteed to preserve all species, and there is no evidence that the trade is actually benefiting any birds or habitats.

Beyond the conservation arguments, and the hair-splitting over exactly how many of these wild birds were dying before, during and after export, was the basic question of decency. And to anyone who had witnessed the condition in which birds were being caught, caged, boxed and exported, the offensiveness of this business was stark and beyond dispute. Apart from anything, most of the species suited for captivity and worth keeping as pets can, by definition, be captive-bred. US government, meanwhile, had already introduced new laws that would effectively ban the trade. Michael Howard's department offered the following in defence of the suffering and mortality rate of trapped birds: 'Overall, birds are likely to live longer in captivity than in the wild.'

The 20th anniversary of CITES was celebrated in March, with 118 countries now participating. Trade in 156 species of bird was now banned, and 1,209 other species could be traded only if scientists in the exporting countries advised that it wasn't harmful to the species. In spite of these controls, the legal trade continued to mask illegal activity, and made enforcement nigh impossible. The RSPB was prepared to accept a shortlist of species where it could be shown, using reliable scientific evidence, that trade did not jeopardise these birds.

In early March the RSPB took on its role as the UK partner of the newly formed BirdLife International, based in Cambridge. It called the moment 'a major turning point in the fortunes of bird conservation'. BirdLife would have global reach, with partners in 100 countries, and growing. Of the thousand seriously threatened bird species in the world, 29 were in Europe, three of them found in the UK: the Red Kite, Corncrake and White-tailed Eagle. The most threatened birds tend to be in countries with little money or wherewithal for conservation. It was hoped that this imbalance could be overcome, through the partnership. Habitat loss was identified as the most serious problem. 'Hotspots' were mapped, to show where the threatened birds with the smallest ranges were found. Most were in the tropics. Indonesia topped the league table for threatened species, followed by Brazil, China and Peru.

The partnership identified five main areas of work:

- To get the facts.
- To make plans based on the facts.
- To change government policies.
- To work in the field.
- To build the strength of partner organisations.

I migrated south in spring, to live and work in Cambridge in search of a different life, a fresh perspective and, if nothing else, better weather. I had friends there, who helped me to find the kind of place

I'd daydreamed of – a draughty, 16th-century, timber-framed, brick-floored cottage with a walk-in fireplace. It was just south of the city. There wasn't a straight line in the place. It was beautiful. Its oak beams were warped as liquorice sticks. 'If a house has been standing that long, it's not going to fall down now,' went the thinking. Where I'd come from you can stand by and watch while exposed timbers rot. The orchard out the back had an old church pew for a bench below a fossil of an apple tree. Beyond was a tangle of bramble, which I wasted little time in partially clearing for a pond and wildflower meadow. As I wrote at the time, I prepared the tilth, planted wild meadow grasses and settled down for the summer to watch them grow.

My old mate from Stirling University, Dan, who'd found the place, liked it so much he decided to live here too. He was a postdoc by now, nurturing a dream of his own around this big idea they were calling the 'world wide web', and setting up a cafe, like they had in a few places in the States, that would provide public internet access. We debated endlessly the possibilities presented by this new internet thing that summer, on long evenings in this strangely balmy, al fresco country, as the Swifts screamed around the barbecues, and the church bells clanged. Sure enough, Dan lived the dream and soon afterwards opened CB1, one of Britain's first internet cafes.

I felt at home here, though I missed the hills, my people in Scotland. But this was my chance to live the Gilbert White dream. It was 200 years since the death of the parson-naturalist. I noted this from one of his letters: 'Frequent returns of deafness incommode me sadly, and half disqualify me for a naturalist, for, when these fits are upon me, I lose all the pleasing notices and little intimations arising from rural sounds: and May is to me as silent and mute with respect to the notes of birds ... as August.'

I discovered that I'd been here before. Spookily, my parents' best friends from Uganda lived round the corner. Dr Church was sewing my head up one day (another mishap) in the local surgery. 'The last time I attended to your family was when I delivered your sister,' he told me, all matter of fact, as I tried to avoid catching sight of the needle and thread.

I revisited the campsite we'd used back in the late seventies. I suddenly recognised this not-so-foreign land, saw the young teenage me firtling in the hedgerow. I remembered the rope swing at the end of the Churches' garden, over the river now at the end of mine. It was a life-affirming if unsettling feeling, to suddenly apprehend the gap between child perception and young adult. The world never felt so small, nor time so shrunk. I had to resist feelings of pre-destiny, of homecoming, but it definitely helped with the sense of belonging in this now not-so-foreign field.

The weather also helped, and the outdoor space. It was like being abroad, on holiday, even; if only my Scotland could have been so blessed. News came through that a pair of White-tailed Eagles had seen their nest tree uprooted in an Atlantic gale. The young eaglet had fallen 80 feet, but somehow survived, unscathed. Birds are quite good at falling, as a rule. It was rescued and placed in a hastily constructed nest platform, installed in a neighbouring tree. Happily, the adults resumed parental duties and this chick became one of the five produced that season in Scotland, in what was described as an 'atrocious' summer, bringing the total to 34 since the scheme began. Ten more Norwegian birds were released to give the population a further boost.

Meanwhile, back in the English lowlands, I found myself back in chemistry, a creative copywriter with the Royal Society of Chemistry, which had its base at Burlington House in Piccadilly, and state-of-the-art premises in Cambridge's high-tech Science Park. To keep my hand in with conservation I signed up as a volunteer at BirdLife's Secretariat. Spotting my journalistic background they set me to work launching *Africa Newsletter*, with a French version we called *Bulletin Afrique*. I also joined a group of local conservation volunteers, to get my hands dirty managing what was left of ancient woodland in this mostly arable county. It's not much, I have to report.

Conservationists awaited action from governments on producing the action plans to which the 1992 Rio Earth Summit had committed them. 'Information about our flora and fauna is patchy,' the RSPB acknowledged. 'But this is no excuse for inaction. The Convention itself says that lack of precise information must not stall progress.'

There was some cause for optimism. UK ministers had achieved some decent results, leading Europe's other farm ministers in introducing the ESA scheme, and later measures to limit farming's environmental damage. The role of other government departments in environmental protection became more critical than ever. A plan was expected by the end of the year. Success in this would be, in the RSPB's words, 'a prize that has eluded conservation for 50 years'.

A review of the ownership and management of state forests had been called, in keeping with the ongoing privatisation agenda of the

Conservatives. It might lead to the break-up and sell-off of parts or all of the national forest estate. The environmental track record of the Forestry Commission may have been poor, but there had been signs of improvement, and slow but steady progress in recent years. The possibility of a fragmented and privately owned forest estate being any better for wildlife seemed remote. 'Is the Government intent on fixing a "problem" that does not exist and in the process littering its path with yet more avoidable banana skins?' the RSPB wondered.

Land taken out of farm production seemed to offer an obvious means of providing for the needs of declining birds and other wildlife in the farmed landscape. These so-called set-aside fields now came under closer scrutiny, as fields left fallow in the short term were not realising their potential to provide food and nesting sites for birds. UK government proposed to European partners a scheme whereby fields could be set aside for a number of years, to provide habitat like restored grasslands in the longer term.

October brought government's long-awaited paper setting out how it intended to make the Habitats Directive work. The Department of Environment had been trying to manage expectations in the lead-up to the publication of this paper. And well it might. It bore the usual hallmarks of pressure from other departments not to impose any taxing demands or constraints on their activity. There was little on special site or marine protection.

Meanwhile, a number of government decisions and actions had undermined confidence in their willingness to really grasp the need to protect the best places. They had now allowed the damming and flooding of another internationally important part of Cardiff Bay, despite alternatives being proposed during five years of wrangling. A debacle and ecological disaster, conservationists called it. Formal complaints were taken to Europe.

A conference was held in London in November, called Sustainable Development: the Key to Maintaining Biodiversity. Addressing it, Environment Secretary John Gummer indicated that government had got the message. He warned delegates that the world faced 'devastating danger … We need to create an entirely different way of looking at the world … it is a battle for people's minds, to change people's attitudes. … Government,' he accepted, 'has got to set an example, and cannot back out of its responsibilities.'

His colleague at Agriculture announced that his department was spending £70 million on environmental schemes. Ten years earlier this figure had been zero, so it represented progress, while the figure was still a drop in the ocean of subsidies for arcane, damaging practices. English Nature was set up as government's new-look official wildlife advisory body.

Not far from my cottage, an attempt was being made to save a little-known amphibian called the Pool Frog. It used to thrive hereabouts, but disappeared in 1847, after widespread drainage of its fens. There was a surviving population in Norfolk, but this rapidly declined until there was just one frog left this year. It had been hoped it could be paired with frogs of its kind from Sweden, but it died in captivity.

Peter Conder died in the autumn, in Cambridge. 'He was highly inspirational,' wrote Richard Porter in an obituary in *The Independent*. 'It was, I feel sure, this inspiration, his deep love of birds and a basic nous and intuition that were the catalysts for the meteoric rise of the RSPB from 1962 to 1975.' He 'hated modern conservation jargon … if the term biodiversity had been suggested to him, he would have said "Go away, chum, and think up something the public will understand".'

When winter came I was to learn that they also have sub-zero conditions here in the eastern prairies, and that the cottage was irretrievably draughty. Jays and Nuthatches came for the acorns I put out by the back door. Emblematic of the bone-deep chill of midwinter was the eerie Black-headed Gull frozen solid into the River Cam where it swam, in now suspended animation, below the bridge at Kings College, where my girlfriend was completing her PhD. Last-minute shopping on that icy Christmas Eve I quite by chance bumped into David Payne, an old friend from Stirling. He'd studied bird behaviour there, and was now working for the RSPB, along with his partner Ali. The Lodge wasn't far away. I'd already been casting covetous eyes in that direction, and explored the reserve there, admiring the setting. I'd taken my folks and the Churches there for a day trip, when they visited for a reunion. Dave and Ali promised to tip me off if any vacancies arose in the comms line.

1994

Civil servant jargon or not, biodiversity was fast becoming the environmental catchword of the nineties. The UK's Biodiversity Action Plan was published in January, as the Department of Environment showed its hand on Rio, and government set out how it intended to honour promises made at the Earth Summit. There remained a lack of commitment across all parts of government to achieving sustainable development. Perhaps it was dawning on them what this actually meant: that development could not carry on as before; untrammelled, unconcerned about anything but itself and short-term profitability. The RSPB carried out a survey of local authority strategies across the UK, to show how government's plans could work at local level.

A bewildering 75,000 dead seabirds were washed ashore in February, the length of Britain's eastern coast; two-thirds of them in Shetland alone. Tests indicated that the birds had simply starved due to lack of fish. Ominously, June marked the 150th anniversary of the extinction of the Great Auk, once of our north Atlantic islands, now lost to the world.

The *New Atlas of Breeding Birds* was published. I bought my copy in Cambridge, flinching a little at the price, but considering it well worth the pain to own my own copy of this milestone work. It was the most comprehensive attempt yet made to show how our birds were faring. It presented maps not only of distribution and for the first time density, but also maps of change for each species since the early seventies and the previous, less comprehensive and detailed atlas. It would become the foundation stone of much conservation decision-making, a definitive source of information on where birds are, what they need, and where they are struggling. It was produced by the British Trust for Ornithology, the Irish Wildbird Conservancy and the Scottish Ornithologists' Club.

It inspired me to attempt the Breeding Birds Survey, just launched. I'd be part of the small army of volunteers providing the intelligence that, added together, makes up these maps. I was assigned a survey square in the arable prairie of south Cambridgeshire, and I set off one Sunday afternoon to visit the man I was told owned the land in question, for permission to carry out the site visits through spring. I was to visit three times, if possible, as early in the day as I could make it, to catch the birds when they are most active, most likely to be making their presence known through song, calls, movement ...

There is a pain barrier to be broken through at 4am on a Sunday morning, when it's not quite light, far from warm, and just way too early to be dragging yourself out of bed on a weekend. But it is ultimately rewarding, to catch the spring sunrise, and to be in at the launch of the dawn chorus. I had to leave behind the swelling birdsong of the gardens and trees of the village, and venture out into the plains beyond.

Here, things became very much quieter. My survey square, one of those selected at random across the land to cover a representative spread of types of habitat, was too far from home to reach by bike. I parked in a lay-by, on a road not yet busy with traffic but that would be by mid-morning, and walked the tracks I'd agreed with the farmland owner. He was interested to know what I found. I walked my two transects, which is two straight lines, parallel to each other, across the land, as consistent as I could make them. I didn't count much. There wasn't much to count. The highlight was a large covey of Grey Partridges (aka English Partridges), adults and chicks, that I photographed as they dithered on the track ahead of me. I found the exercise in general dispiriting. This was heightened by the lack of entries I could make on the recording sheets.

A local farmer with 2,000 acres of neighbouring arable land was profiled in *The Sunday Times*. He posed for a photograph standing in one of these enormous wheat fields, looking pleased. 'I am a happy man,' he told the world. 'Not just because the harvest has been easy this year, but because by Christmas I will receive a little brown envelope. The postmark will be Guildford but the cheque inside, for almost £200,000, will come from Brussels. It is my share of the CAP.' He may have been cashing in, but he was also publicising the iniquities of the system, and made a televised documentary on the issue soon after.

The scale of the payments was becoming more transparent. The Minister for Agriculture answered a question in Parliament, showing how many farm and landowners had received huge cheques of this kind. Five thousand, for example, received 'more than £50,000' in 1994. Part of this was payments of £138 per acre for land set-aside, taken out of production. Even this land was failing to provide the environmental benefits that conservationists were seeking as a basic requirement of public subsidy.

I gave up on walking these fields; I found them so lifeless and soul-destroying. Even a sunny morning couldn't redeem them. I signed up as a volunteer with the local Wildlife Trust, and joined a work party to carry out management of a rare scrap of not very ancient woodland. I volunteered at the RSPB's Fowlmere reserve, which had become my local sanctuary, clear bubbling springs and watercress beds feeding an oasis of life amid the sterility of the arable plain around it. Here were orchids, dragonflies, Pike in the ditches, Water Rails grunting and squealing. Like the loch of my childhood, only warmer, much less muddy. I helped local kids' groups with pond-dipping, the highlight when we landed a Great Diving Beetle after what felt like a titanic struggle; a beast of an insect by normal UK standards. But not as monstrous as the Great Silver Beetle I fished out of the maturing pond at home – a terrifying creature, but strictly vegetarian, I discovered in the book. Fowlmere was my Sunday evening bolt-hole; for quiet contemplation and a fix on nature before the working week ahead.

I loved exploring this new world, with its quaint villages and thatched barns, sagging churchyards and medieval ruins. I also took to the River Rhee, tributary of the Cam, in a kayak I picked up from a local jumble sale for about £10, after I'd persuaded the grown-up selling it that I was also a grown-up. In fact I was old enough by about 10 years, by this time. I suppose I should have been flattered instead of irked. In any case I now had a means to explore hidden Cambridgeshire, even though in places the river was so low I'd be grounded on gritty sand-spits, and risk regular capsize leaning away from the clumps of nettles clamouring on the undercut banks. Most of all the memory is of glittering pink-and-white kaleidoscopes of a tall flowering plant that swarmed at midsummer on both banks of the narrow channel. Pretty, like an impressionist painting, and thick with Banded Demoiselle damselflies. Himalayan Balsam, I discovered it is called – an introduced plant in the early stages of taking over the nation's waterways. I was down with the Kingfishers now, and the secret hideouts of Mandarin Ducks. These were long hot summers, in mid-nineties Cambs, of pubs with gardens, a strange local gentlemen's custom called cricket, and after-work, jumpers-for-goalposts kick-abouts on Parker's Piece with participants from every part of the world.

I sometimes had to remind myself this was a country in recession, even though I was surrounded for three years by people talking a lot about something called 'negative equity'. Anyone who bought a house in the late eighties or early nineties had probably watched its value plummet by about a third, even in Cambridge. It wasn't so in the agricultural landscape, mind you. Just outside of town, land prices were rocketing. The price of the best arable land – and we had quite a bit of that near here – almost doubled in three years to 1995. The income from it was more or less guaranteed, after all.

Concern was mounting about the decline of common species like the House Sparrow, Starling and Song Thrush. Ann S. Pope of Surrey wrote to the RSPB of her concern for the demise of the latter. She proposed the theory that slug pellets might be to blame. 'What beauty is there in a garden in which songbirds have been silenced, in pursuit of perfection?' Song Thrushes had declined by half since Atlas One.

Debate raged in the newspaper letters pages about the reasons for the decline of these birds. Not everyone had noticed, or could remember, the massive changes the landscape had undergone in the last few decades. What they had noticed was the return of Sparrowhawks and Magpies, and had seen for themselves the death of some smaller birds in the clutches of these newly returned and conspicuous larger birds.

'Some songbirds have declined in the countryside and these changes may be reflected in gardens. But the reasons are far from clear,' the RSPB responded. 'Many point to increased numbers of magpies and sparrowhawks as the reason for a decline in garden birds. These form the current burning issue: but it's not that simple.'

The virtually complete absence of the Sparrowhawks from southern England in the sixties had provided an opportunity to study whether their absence had resulted in lots more small birds. But had anyone been keeping records before, during, and after this period of absence? Luckily they had. There were two study areas for which comprehensive records had been kept. One was in Surrey, between 1949 and 1979, in an oak wood. It showed that the presence or absence of Sparrowhawks was immaterial. What mattered were changes in the structure of the wood over time. Hard weather also had a short-term impact on small birds like the Wren. None of the 13 species in the wood, all of which would feature in the diet of the Sparrowhawk, were significantly more numerous when Sparrowhawks weren't there.

The records of Blue and Great Tit numbers in woodland near Oxford showed the same thing. While Sparrowhawks eat a lot of these smaller birds – it is, in the end, what they eat – the smaller birds produce a lot of offspring, year after year, to replace birds lost to predation, and were it not predation it would be cold, hunger and disease.

Skylarks were also being lost at a frightening rate, with more than half gone in 20 years, but there were signs of change. Set-aside fields with a mix of wildflowers in them supported four times as many Skylarks. Only around a quarter of our Tree Sparrows, Corn Buntings, Grey Partridges and Turtle Doves were left. The BTO began to research Song Thrush populations in different sorts of habitats.

Meanwhile, the one calling Corncrake left in Northern Ireland fell silent around this time, and no one was suggesting Sparrowhawks had anything to do with it. There was encouraging news from the island of Coll in the Hebrides, where the number of calling males had trebled since 1991. They were also increasing on Islay and Tiree, where the RSPB was making things right for them. But it was clear that the Corncrake was going to test the resolve of government to save a species. A fifth of all those clinging on in the UK had disappeared in just five years. Calling places ESAs might not in itself be enough, if farmers and crofters could not be persuaded to do the basic things necessary to keep the birds going.

It is probably one of the lasting regrets of conservation that the best places for wildlife had to be blighted by the name SSSI. RSPB Chairman Professor John Lawton now came up with an alternative: 'cathedrals of natural history'. A proposal emerged for a stretch of new road in Wales that would damage no fewer than six of these areas. European intervention was needed to stop even more being trashed by road developments. The Twyford Down motorway was opened, after years of bitter controversy, protest camps and civil disorder. A new grassland was created on part of the old road, to compensate for the SSSI that had been destroyed. A government committee now concluded that building more roads only encouraged more traffic, and that the best way to limit pollution and congestion was to manage demand, not accommodate more vehicles.

Government finally published its plan to protect sites and species under the Habitats Directive. The best marine sites remained at the mercy of a system of protection that was optional, and there was little new thinking in the plans for land. The Land Drainage Act 1994 might at least now allow ministers to intervene to save wetlands, if they wanted to.

The RSPB asked the courts to decide whether government was entitled to cite economic grounds when leaving the mudflats of Lappel Bank outside the boundary of the part declared an SPA. Whether development was later permitted was a separate matter. But it seemed fundamentally dishonest and against the spirit of the endeavour of designating the most important protected areas to ignore the evidence of what was there, and to simply plot a distorted line around a different or smaller area. It was, in the RSPB's view, unlawful. The Lord Justice in the Court of Appeal agreed, but was outvoted in a split decision. This was now being appealed against too. There was also the question of government providing compensatory habitat for displaced migratory birds, for example if an SPA that the birds depended on must – in the state's view – be destroyed.

There was much at stake for conservation, and financially, as pursuing cases such as this is not inexpensive. But it was vital to test what Europe intended with its environmental protection laws, and to make them work. All of Europe – if not the world – was watching, in this new global game of saving biodiversity.

Winter brought the first reunion of the states that signed the Convention on Biological Diversity in 1992. 'The UK must lead by example,' the RSPB exhorted. A year had passed since the UK produced its Biodiversity Action Plan, and since then some work had been done on a 'modest suite' of targets and actions.

'Do we have any biodiversity in Britain?' Professor Lawton was asked by a Member of Parliament. 'I think,' he reported, 'but I am not convinced, that I managed to persuade him that we do.'

1995

It was European Nature Conservation Year. Greenpeace was campaigning to prevent Shell dumping the Brent Spar oil platform in the North Atlantic. Far from nurturing its internationally important marine environment, or its image as a nature-loving nation, Britain had been dubbed 'the dirty man of Europe', because of the amount of sewage it continued to spew into coastal waters.

Government published its White Paper on Rural England, and a separate process began for Scotland's rural landscape. It was the first time that such an endeavour had been attempted: viewing the countryside in terms broader than solely farming.

Local Agenda 21 was one of the drier-sounding outputs of Rio. It required local councils and others at local level to plan for sustainable development in communities. The RSPB issued an *Environmental Challenge* document for local authorities, a manifesto they could adopt, to manage and conserve their environment. More advice was being issued to citizens and business on how to reduce their 'footprints'.

At the same time, government was cutting budgets to its nature conservation agencies in each of the four countries, despite the increased responsibilities that came with European law and Rio. More special conservation areas were being designated, including 36 in Wales, but there was concern that there would be a lack of resource to look after them properly. Government was also making noises about unloading state nature reserves onto others less well resourced or qualified to manage them effectively.

Europe's environment ministers agreed to begin action to protect the marine environment outside territorial waters, although they didn't commit themselves to a deadline. Talks about tackling over-fishing didn't get so far, but further talks were promised. Canada's Cod stocks collapsed, which ought to have helped to focus minds.

The RSPB's Charter was updated and reworded, to set out more clearly the organisation's core purpose of conserving wild birds and the places they depend on, to recreate such places, encourage others to conserve, and to promote education and research. It also made clear the role of supporting people and organisations at home and abroad, and now to acquire land, if necessary, overseas.

I was reacquainted with that Sparrowhawk painting from the cover of spring 1972 *Birds* magazine on the sunny October morning when I was interviewed for an editorial job at The Lodge. There it was, the ravenous raptor, by artist Ken Wood, along with a number of other paintings that had fronted *Birds* magazine in the period, framed on the wall of the interview room in the main house here. I took it as an omen. I also couldn't help myself blurting out to my startled interviewers the significance of the picture, at least for me. I got the job, despite – or perhaps partly because – of this interruption.

December saw the launch of the Biodiversity Steering Group's report. Here now were rescue plans for 116 of the most threatened species and 14 types of habitat. This had been the focus of joint effort for the past year, and stemmed from Rio '92. The plans were detailed and the costs were set out too. More would follow. It wasn't perfect, as it didn't adequately cover marine issues and species of the wider farmed environment, but it did a fair job on species that could benefit from targeted action. Government's response was eagerly awaited.

The RSPB raised the profile of peatlands with a peat-free garden at the Chelsea Flower Show. Four hundred miles north, my beloved Flanders Moss was saved from commercial peat-milling when Scottish Natural Heritage intervened and bought for the nation the rights to do this, which of course it would leave in a filing cabinet, while the Moss went on being a peatland, supporting a unique ecosystem, and holding on to its carbon.

1996

It was beginning to feel like an annual tradition. In February the *Sea Empress* ran aground off the coast of Wales. There was hope to begin with that the ship would hold on to its cargo of oil. But in the following days, repeated attempts to dislodge the ship resulted in more and more oil spewing into the sea. At the final count, 70,000 tons of crude had bled out.

After years of headlines and bitter argument about the pros and cons, the bulldozers moved in to start work on the Newbury bypass, one of the most high-profile road development controversies yet known. It threatened damage to three SSSIs. Government made its biggest moves on transport for nearly 20 years. It was up front about the problems that our reliance on the motor car was causing, but the Transport Green Paper said nothing about protecting wildlife sites.

The Advocate General of the European Court agreed with the RSPB that government had acted illegally when it omitted Lappel Bank from the SPA for economic reasons. The European Court as a whole would now have to agree, but this appeared a formality. Later in the year it finally announced its decision on Lappel Bank, which by now had been converted – from a vital feeding ground of international importance for many thousands of migratory birds – into a car park. It agreed with the RSPB. It was hoped that this would now mean government couldn't pull such a stunt in future, and that it would make compensatory habitat available somewhere else.

The RSPB was bidding to become champion for the Skylark, one of the 116 species listed in the Biodiversity Action Plan. Latest figures now showed three in five Skylarks gone since the early seventies. The set-aside scheme offered the chance to put back two features that had been lost from modern agriculture – fallow field and winter stubble. As food mountains shrank, the case for set-aside became less clear. It had been reduced to just 5% of cropped land, and now it might be phased out altogether. The RSPB and others came up with a solution – another kind of scheme that would provide these benefits for wildlife. The Ministry of Agriculture decided not to take up the suggestion, even though it would have cost about £1 million; not so much, in the context of the £1 billion being paid to arable farmers and agribusiness in public subsidies for which there were no environmental conditions.

A Department of Environment survey found that almost a third of people in England and Wales were by now 'very concerned' about the environment. A little more than half were 'quite concerned'. It was clearly a matter for politicians to take seriously. Prime Minister John Major pledged encouragement for the Biodiversity Action Plan, calling it 'a challenge I wholeheartedly welcome, and it has the Government's full support. Many of our species are in decline, and there is no room for complacency'. It was considered a world-leading biodiversity plan: the millions needed to do the job had been set out, but instead there were rumours of further cuts to the very agencies that would be needed to carry out the work.

In the five years to 1996, one in five SSSIs had been damaged in England and Wales; half were now in 'unfavourable condition'. One chalk grassland SSSI was ploughed up and the owner ordered to repair it, after the intervention of the Secretary of State. The ploughed earth had to be righted and pressed back into place, but a lot of SSSI damage was much less conspicuous, and owed more to long-term neglect or misuse.

There had been heated debate around a proposal to build a funicular railway to the top of the Cairngorms. Conservationists were concerned that it would damage the fragile wilderness it was supposedly bringing people to see. They proposed consideration of something more sensible, even if its name didn't sound particularly so – the Glenmore Gondola. Scottish Natural Heritage withdrew its objection to the funicular, even though one of its own senior staff had pointed out that 'a thoroughly unsatisfactory proposal of this sort, rushed through in an atmosphere of controversy, is the last thing that should be foisted on one of the most important mountain areas in northern Europe'.

When summer ended I moved into an unfurnished shell of a farm cottage, with very little to indicate which room was the kitchen. It was within cycling distance of The Lodge, in a rural community with its roots still very much in the landscape around it. It had a strong sense of its own internal life, a vibrant local pub and a family greengrocer.

The RSPB established the nature reserve of Glenborrodale, on the Ardnamurchan Peninsula of Western Scotland, the closest part of mainland Britain to North America. For a much-needed fix on wilderness I rented a cottage there at new year and dragged some friends along. I brought along a book about the history of this remote place – *Night Falls on Ardnamurchan*. Author Alasdair Maclean tells of the losses he had witnessed: 'In the last ten years I saw my last molehill and my last roe deer, I heard my last corncrake. I bade farewell to woodcock, partridge, pheasant and sand martin. There were eagles as close as Plocaig once; not any more ... Sanna is a bare place now, stripped of much of its cover and many of its inhabitants and deprived of many delightful creatures.' He was writing about the year 1970.

1997

My latest old cottage had a long back garden that sloped gently down to a brook, and gave on to an open field beyond, from which it was separated only by a public footpath, much used by dog walkers. In that first winter, it all seemed a bit bleak and exposed, as much of our arable landscape can at this time of year. It was crying out for a hedgerow. So, over the course of several murky weekends, I cleared the rank grass, built a fence out of reclaimed timber, then sourced and bought the plants – 150 of them, mixed native species. The hedge would follow the boundary of the garden, and define both it and the footpath beyond. I dug and heeled-in each plant, in two rows, from outhouse to brook. I laid a plastic sheet along its length to prevent the worst of the weed growth that can outcompete a hedge in its early years, and I left the plants – in most cases just thin, bare stems – to grow.

It wasn't much to look at in the early days. As the weeks passed to spring I carefully nipped out the weeds that strained for daylight through the sheet, added water during dry spells and, one by one, the stems sprouted buds and then leaves. The long, steady journey to hedge had begun.

My next-door neighbour was Old Frank: a countryman, by anyone's definition. He'd lived for most of his life in this row of cottages of which Johnny-come-lately – me – was now sharing a part. He was nearing retirement age, although it was unlikely that he would in any conventional sense ever actually retire. He would just carry on being the odd-job man for the estate, smoking his pipe and vaulting the gate of a morning, until it was time for him to leave.

He stopped me one morning. 'Cat brought a big rat in, last night,' he announced, with a hint of pride, through what was left of his teeth, confident I'd be interested in such a development. I followed him to his back door, a matter of yards from my own. The 'rat' was laid out in a dish. It was quite large, right enough, but not unduly so, for a rat. It was a little ruffled, but with no obvious injuries. There were features of it that did not say 'rat' to me. The tail, for instance, was much too short. It was furred, not bristly. The nose was blunt, not pointy. This wasn't a rat, as such, although in fairness to Frank he may well have meant Water Rat – which is the old countryman's name for the Water Vole that we were looking at. Kenneth Grahame's *Wind in the Willows* vole was called Ratty, after all, to add to the confusion.

'It's a Water Vole,' I offered, adding, 'Brilliant!' Not brilliant that it was dead, of course, but I knew what I meant. In any case Old Frank didn't seem too troubled by the distinction. Mere semantics, he might have been thinking, if not in so many words.

There was a brook at the bottom of the garden. I like to think that I would have discovered the Water Voles here soon enough, but it took the dead one to alert me to the possibility of them. I paid an evening visit to set up a vole vigil. What surprised me was just how easy it was to watch them here, on the banks, as they scurried along their well-worn paths, by their burrows, and even in the water itself, as they torpedoed along, stirring the mud.

Unlike with real rats, it's not hard to sympathise with Water Voles. Plump, short-sighted, set in their ways, easy to find, active in broad daylight, cute, harmless, disease-free (probably), not in the attic, vegetarian (mostly – I was interested to read that they do eat fish, from time to time). What is also less well known about Water Voles is that they are not confined to aquatic places, and can thrive equally well on dry land.

Their decline is well recorded, thought to be as much as 90% in just two decades. The main cause will be loss of habitat, but they are also persecuted, I am sure in many cases in the mistaken belief that they are *rat* rats.

My local colony seemed pretty secure, but shortly before I moved on, disaster struck, in another guise. The drainage authorities dredged the brook – as dredge they must – and transformed this 100-metre stretch of waterway into a denuded trench. I discovered the desolation on my return from work. I was shocked to see forlorn and visibly traumatised voles clinging to the near-vertical sides of the newly scooped ditch. They really did look like a bomb had hit them. The following spring, it became an offence to damage Water Vole habitat under the Wildlife and Countryside Act – too late for my voles, but likely to help them in future if they could recover.

It was another general election year, and conservationists were working harder than ever to convince the parties that the environment was a consideration for all areas of government. The economics of conservation grew in prominence within the debate. There was louder talk of future generation needs and a mounting sense that the environment might be unravelling for people too.

Deep down we knew we had a beleaguered government riddled with allegations of sleaze that had become largely unsupportable, and that after 18 years the nation was ready for a change. But no one was quite prepared for the extent of the election rout. With the ascendancy of Tony Blair's Labour government, we entered what became known as the age of spin, as though this was the first government to employ news management techniques or weasel words. These were also the honeymoon years of Britpop, and 'cool Britannia'. Bands like Oasis, Pulp and Blur would all write songs inspired by birdsong. It boded well. Things, we were promised, could only get better.

Amid the hype, it was quietly hoped that the new government would find the funds needed to turn the biodiversity aspirations into results. Labour had promised to 'improve the protection of wildlife' in its election manifesto. It was a major task. The UK's 6,400 SSSIs had many thousands of owners, with an average of more than 200 cases of damage each year. Most of the previous government's major road-building schemes were suspended.

Another of our birds and its distinctive springtime sound seemed to be on the way out: the reedbed-dwelling Bittern, once so widespread in the fens they piled them high at medieval banquets. A count of male birds 'booming' like distant foghorns barely reached double figures, an all-time low. Money came from Europe to help keep it here, primarily through the restoration and recreation of its fenland habitats.

A survey of the wild plants of more than a hundred arable fields was carried out, to repeat a survey done in the year of *Silent Spring*. Besides the predictable decline of a number of arable plants, one of the most dramatic changes was the ascent of a grass called Barren Brome, so-called because even livestock is reluctant to eat it. It was found in more than three-quarters of the fields, having been entirely absent in 1962. A new scheme to put some of the plant and other missing life back into arable farmland was to be trialled by government.

News of the car crash involving Princess Diana and Dodi Fayed came through on that sombre Sunday morning as August ended, a resolutely drizzly day with the tragic reports unfolding on television. The public outpourings of grief and shock reflected how well the public felt they knew her, how familiar she had become in our everyday lives. We had family tragedy too, that summer. Life's fragility and uncertainties were suddenly laid bare. I knew before then I had to move again, to bid farewell to this rural cottage and foundling hedgerow. But I would be back one day to check on the old place, on the planting.

When I arrived at my new (and current) home in the early autumn, the front garden was just one of many restoration challenges to be met. The estate agent spoke of this lifeless, gravel-covered carport as a virtue, and I'm sure it added to the price, but I knew that as soon as I was freed from DIY duties indoors I would convert it all back to the leafy green elegance retained by one or two of my neighbours' gardens. The car could sit on the roadside beyond. This was, after all, *supposed* to be a garden. By early spring I was busy bagging up gravel and prising two-by-two paving slabs from the cold, damp plastic sheeting beneath. There was hardcore and brick rubble to fork out, like some kind of fossilised root crop – and a bumper one at that.

My neighbour was now Old Fred Bettles, as he introduced himself to me. He'd lived all his 80 years in this village, once on the farm and now in this row of houses, since they were built after the war. Fred was an endless source of local knowledge and useful pointers. His cousin, Old Mont, still lived on the farm up the road. He helped me heave the masonry aside and bag up the spoil and hardcore which he would use on his farm track. He was in good shape, for a man in his seventies. 'I've got to keep going,' he puffed, lifting a sack of rocks onto his ancient tractor. 'If I don't, I shall die,' he added, laughing. I told him about my wildlife garden plan. 'Each to their own,' he wheezed, in his deep whispering voice, with his Norman Wisdom grin, and it was my turn to laugh.

I donated the gravel to colleagues, and set about preparing the soil, compacted under years of vehicular activity. Hours of treading and crumbling followed – a uniquely meditative pastime – as I massaged air and life back into the consolidated earth, and raked off blackened lumps that turned out to be stray chunks of breeze block. The lingering cement – muck, the local brickies call it – crumbled beautifully to stir like cake mix into a free-draining, friable soil on this finger of alluvium soil, pointing east from the river Great Ouse.

Eschewing the vogue for expensive Ikea, ground-level futons, I found a cast iron, framed and sprung bed among the clutter of Mr Boglin's Treasure Trove, the local junk emporium. The bed is high enough to allow a grandstand view from the bedroom over the front garden, passing birds overhead and the fields to the south. There is a play area opposite the house that serves as a tiny football pitch for the kids in the road, boys and girls alike, of all ages. Old Fred told me the play area is on the site of the old village pond – Frog Hall, they called it. The carts used to stand in it overnight, to swell the wood wheels tight to their iron rims. To the right is an unsurfaced area, where the Martins and Swallows gather mud from the puddles in spring after rain, the thrushes bathe and the doves eat grit. When it is dry the sparrows gather to dust bathe, and to fight.

'You don't 'alf make work for yourself, boy,' Fred would say to me, puffing on his pipe, watching with kindly amusement my sweaty toils to fix the place up. He told me I shouldn't be putting Field Maple in the hedgerow I was planting. And he was right.

There is a barn close to the play area, one of those open-sided affairs with eight iron legs and a corrugated asbestos roof, keeping rain off the bales. Collared Doves and Pied Wagtails inhabit the rafters, and Kestrels sometimes arrive in the evening to roost. Beyond it is the rest of the farm, with its sagging tiled roofs, where Swallows nest. One summer night I was woken by the screams of Little Owls issuing from it, screams so persistent and anguished I got up and stumbled over to investigate. I assume a fox, or possibly a cat, was the cause of the disquiet, but until that dark moment I had had no idea the Little Owls I occasionally see in the splintered willow up the road, and hear at dusk, would be nesting so close to me.

Another willow hangs over the play area, all tumult in a strong breeze, writhing this way and that, 'as restless as a willow in a windstorm', indeed, as per 'It Might As Well Be Spring', by Rodgers and Hammerstein. Mistle Thrushes sing from the top of it, earning the local name Storm Cocks, because they breed early and often have to sing in rough weather. Their song is like a nervous attempt at the Blackbird's, as though they were too self-conscious – or too *hard* – to see it through, or to attempt the whole verse. Theirs is one of the first murmurs of spring.

I moved into this house because it had House Martins nesting on it. Well, partly. It was a factor. I thought, well, if they like it here, then there's a fair chance I will too. At the time I arrived, this was the only house in the row with Martins. Why this one exactly, I couldn't be sure – particularly given the resident cat. Maybe the birds just liked the flight path, something about the lie of the land. Not long after I arrived the Martins departed for the winter. I hoped to have the front garden sown with grass and framed with hedge plants by the time the Martins came back from Africa. *If* they came back.

* * *

The RSPB attended the Kyoto climate talks in December, along with the Wild Bird Society of Japan, its partner organisation there. It presented a report on the effects wildlife was already experiencing due to a warming world: from Costa Rican cloud forest to the Antarctic, from the Alps to migrant birds in North America. None of these examples proved conclusively that we had caused the changes, but the findings corresponded closely with the expected effects of climate change. There were still vocal opponents of the idea that human activity was changing the climate of the world, but few voices were raised against it in Kyoto.

The UK government took a strongly pro-environment position at Kyoto, which promised much for future action. Many of the things that conservationists were calling for, in the climate change context, were simply sensible things to do anyway – energy efficiency, green technologies and cleaner technology, better transport systems to reduce reliance on cars. These would produce other benefits, in employment, competitiveness, cleaner air.

Climate change was now being described as 'perhaps the biggest challenge that mankind has ever faced'. Despite this, the conference set a target to reduce emissions that was way below the level recommended by scientists in the know. It was also full of loopholes. But it was a start, and a framework, and even the biggest emitters seemed to be taking the problem seriously. Britain had committed to a 20% cut in greenhouse gas emissions by 2010.

1998

'Could pesticides be to blame for farmland bird declines?' ran a national newspaper headline. Latest analysis showed that of the farmland bird species in decline, most had begun a downward trend between 1974 and 1985. Given all that had happened in the 35 years since *Silent Spring*, it might have seemed obvious that pesticides had played a major part. But was there enough actual *proof*?

'Now we see farmland bird declines again,' the RSPB reported. 'But if pesticides are involved in current bird declines, the evidence suggests it is not a *direct* effect – no dead bodies, no thinning eggshells. How about an *indirect* effect?'

'Can you imagine a spring without the first cuckoo?' asked author and journalist Simon Barnes. 'The joke is that not only have we permitted the ruination of our farming countryside, we have paid handsomely for the privilege.' Forty species of birds on lowland farmland were studied: 24 were in decline, 16 stable or even increasing.

For 11 out of 12 declining birds, the major declines could be traced to the time when the use of herbicides, fungicides and insecticides was ramped up. The evidence suggested that the indirect effects of pesticides might be a factor in Skylark, Turtle Dove, Lapwing, Swallow, Blackbird, Song Thrush, Tree Sparrow, Starling, Linnet, Bullfinch and Reed Bunting declines. It wasn't just birds. A survey of Harvest Mice found these at less than a third of the places they'd lived in the seventies. Great Crested Newts had declined by half since *Silent Spring*.

Mistle Thrushes nested at the top of Old Fred's spruce tree, a ghost of Christmas past now 15 feet tall. Fred was a great collector and planter of seeds. He loved Scotland, and the two Scots Pines at the end of my garden are a legacy of his travels in the north. I also owe my nicely maturing orchard trees to him.

Spring 1998 was a wash-out for many things, but for grass growing it was nirvana, and my bents and fescues soon bristled from the seedbed, at first a sheen of lime green, then a coat, and then a mop, ready for its first trim. I went for a seed mix to suit a thinner soil and endure the rainless phases of an eastern summer. I wasn't looking for AstroTurf: I wanted character. The front garden is on the southern side of the house, and I hoped the loose, fine soil would encourage delicate annual wildflowers and inhibit vigorous perennials.

Magically, Creeping Camomile appeared, and to help it establish and spread I carefully mowed around it, and the Bird's-foot Trefoil. Grasshoppers colonised, from who knows where. And the final seal of approval in late summer was a juvenile Yellow Wagtail, accompanied by a more streetwise Pied Wagtail, also adolescent, passing acquaintances blown in on a westerly, looking for insects on the sward.

The car on the roadside was increasingly obscured by the hedgerow plants I installed. I got the hedge 'whips' from a local nursery, a mix of thorns and Beech, with some Hazel, Dogwood, Dog Rose and Wild Privet. I was delighted to find an old Hawthorn stump refusing to submit and sending up fresh stems, and traces of Blackthorn too, when I removed some stray Cypresses. Fred's immaculately maintained Elm hedge next door sent a sucker under the path that separates our two gardens, to add to the diversity and help make the link between our two hedgerows. Fred and Dorothy would give me their grass cuttings to spread as mulch around the growing plant stems.

I added some Cistus shrubs, for a Mediterranean 'maquis' feel, for scents in the summer sun, and for year-round green and drought tolerance. I also decorated the hedge bottom with Primroses, and slipped a few Snowdrop and Bluebell bulbs between gaps in the plastic, disguised with some leftover gravel. I lined the garden path with Lavenders, Broom and Box. A cutting of Gorse from the greensand ridge heath rooted well, added in the corner, where I could enjoy the spring sunlight radiating from its golden flowers. And nearby I squeezed in a plump Foxglove, fattened and ready to produce a flowering spike the following spring. Foxgloves with Gorse would remind me of Scotland, and Dumyat, the hill that glows as the summer sun sets over Stirling.

The House Martins were delayed. The RSPB launched an emergency survey, in response to widespread reports that the birds were much reduced in number. Volunteers like me delivered simple record cards asking householders to note how many Martins nested this year, and how many last year. Local press also carried the forms. Over 4,000 replies were received, recording almost 15,000 nests. It didn't support the theory that there had been a population crash since the year before, but the birds had returned significantly later.

In due course all three of my Martin nests – a terrace of them – were reoccupied, after the winter-roosting Sparrows had been displaced. In late April, construction of a fourth nest began; only not an end-terrace, but a detached property, about 10 feet away.

I signed up for another one-kilometre Breeding Bird Survey (BBS) square. Luckily my square, randomly selected by the British Trust for Ornithology/Joint Nature Conservation Committee and RSPB, was right on the doorstep. On a May dawn I found my local woodland canopy a free-for-all of warbling as I paused to make notes, to extricate one song from another, Robin from Robin from Blackcap from Blackbird from Dunnock from Wren from Wren. The May visit was the second of three, between April and June. I emerged onto my street, with its teams of House Sparrows, Collared Doves and House Martins. The square straddles a major road, and part of it is on the other side, leading down to the River Ouse. In April I counted up the nests in the rookery – an extra task in the survey. They were easy to count then, but by now they had disappeared behind the unfurling leaves.

The riverine habitat boosted the total with Kingfisher, Common Tern, Grey Wagtail, Cuckoo, Rabbits x10 (mammal info important too). It's tempting to think 'the more the merrier', but square discipline is important. If it's outside the square, it doesn't get in.

Line one complete, I nipped down the edge of the square to the start of line two, which brought me back from the river past the church, under its bulging Chestnut trees. I noted with pleasure that the Spotted Flycatchers had come back, between pasture and graveyard. I crossed the road again to walk between an unmanaged, Sycamore-dominated strip of woodland on one side, and foot-high winter wheat on the other. Not so much to record here. By 9am I was back home, clutching a cup of coffee and feeling connected, if slightly glazed.

The RSPB was calling for a peat tax and tax on pesticides, coal, gas and polluting cars. Charges for water pollution and abstraction were also needed. The Budget produced some new measures on car taxation and public transport funding, but otherwise the Chancellor passed up the opportunity.

With the RSPB now a million members strong, the by-now Baroness Young departed from The Lodge to become Chairman of Natural England, after seven years at the helm. At the time she took over, she had asked if wildlife sites were safe in government's hands. As she left the RSPB the same question was still being asked. Lack of progress had not been for want of good old traditional RSPB 'prodding'. She would now be in charge of government's own advisory body on nature conservation and vowed that it would 'work its socks off' to conserve these places. Graham Wynne was promoted from Director of Conservation to become the new Chief Executive.

More and more people were reporting House Sparrow declines, and a bad year for Swallows and Swifts, as well as Martins. The Black Grouse was now declining faster than any other UK bird species. Half of those surviving were dependent on SSSIs. One of the most prominent, Rainham Marshes, was threatened again, this time by a business park. It might yet become the biggest SSSI so far trashed in England. There were brownfield sites that could be used, gaps in the urban landscape, that wouldn't require millions of pounds of public money.

'The market would do a better job of feeding people and providing a rich and diverse countryside,' argued Graham Harvey in his newly published, hard-hitting critique of the farming system and how it is financed by the public purse, *The Killing of the Countryside*. Harvey raised an intriguing question: what if the fortunes of farming had been left to the marketplace, without the help of subsidies from the state? At the very least it seemed reasonable to ask again why so much collateral damage had been inflicted, with so much public support.

Organic farming was now much in the news. At this time it occupied just 0.3% of the UK's farmed landscape. The RSPB called for this to be increased to 5% by 2002, and even more thereafter. A new scheme called Arable Stewardship was piloted, to help larks, buntings, thrushes, invertebrates and wildflowers in the lowlands.

On the biodiversity action front, the RSPB was given the lead role on saving a number of the priority bird species, but also some less well-known, non-bird and unglamorously named species like the Medicinal Leech, which is found at Dungeness nature reserve, and a plant called the Stinking Hawk's-beard. One by one, the priority species were allocated to lead and joint-lead organisations.

Overall, summer would be remembered as something of a damp squib, yet drought was adding to the problems of our remaining wetlands, with too much water being sucked out of them. Drought didn't help the Song Thrush, but it beat the Blackbird to number one in a vote to find the nation's favourite songbird organised by MORI and the RSPB. It had declined by almost three-quarters in farmland, and by half in the woods.

In October, Europe threatened legal action against ten member states, including the UK, for failing to submit adequate proposals to meet their obligations under the Habitats Directive. They were supposed to have done so three years ago. It was also continuing to fail on the Birds Directive, by not confirming protected area status for the most important sites. Europe was now thinking ahead to enlargement and the likelihood of Eastern European countries repeating the mistakes of the west in industrialising agriculture at the expense of supporting life. Perhaps inspired by the UK government's attempt to pull a fast one in the drawing of convenient boundaries around SPAs, the Greek government tried the same ploy. Also that month, the Scottish Court of Session rejected the legal case brought by the RSPB and WWF Scotland against aspects of the proposed funicular railway in the Cairngorms.

I bought an old moped, thinking that this might be the environmental transport of the future. I just needed to kick-start the trend. The trouble was I could barely kick-start the moped. On a bright but unusually cold Sunday morning in October I was along the road, pedalling like mad to get the neglected machine to ignite, struggling to catch my breath and feeling the cold, petrol-tainted air sharp against my lungs. I met Old Fred's son-in-law looking sombre. He told me Fred had just died.

Later that morning I crouched in the orchard he had planted, in quiet contemplation, wondering where I had been, exactly, at the moment he had fallen, two hours earlier, at his back door. He was well into his eighties, and sharp as a tack to the last. He was edged out of farming by the process that almost all our families have been through, sooner or later. I don't think the modern farming revolution would have suited Fred anyway. He was always lamenting the loss of wildlife from the fields around us, the draining of the 'Mashes', the blocking of the streams, forced into pipes underground, the removal of small paddocks, consolidated into huge cereal fields, places he used to be able to walk, now out of bounds. Compared to some places, I didn't think we were doing too badly. We still had our Corn Buntings, for one thing. But then I'd never known the super-abundance of Goldfinches, and Brown Linnets (as he called them) and Common Frogs, and even Grass Snakes, that he had known. I suppose I, like most of my generation, are used to making do with occasional sightings, aware though, and a little troubled, by the fact there could and should be so much more.

At the end of a momentous year in which much political authority was devolved from Westminster, another major milestone was reached in the struggle to have conservation taken more seriously for its broader benefits to humanity: government announced its indicators of quality of life – the measures of sustainable living. There were 13 of these and among them an indicator of achievement on wildlife conservation: 'numbers of wild birds'. This and the other indices like health, education and emissions would be measured year on year, and published annually, to show whether government was making progress or not in creating a more sustainable world, and a better quality of life. Until now, only economic measures like gross domestic product and employment were taken as meaningful. Here at last was official recognition that life is about more than material and financial advancement. Welcome to the Skylark Index.

1999

Even now, with the benefit of distance, it's tricky to put your finger on anything that could be usefully said to have defined the nineties; or why it lacks the identity of the decades before it. There are almost no books about it, whereas its precursors have had authors queuing up to encapsulate them. As far as contemporary music goes, I had completely lost track by the end. The tale becomes steadily harder to tell as the post-modern world widens and fragments simultaneously. 'You must resist the temptation to say everything,' my one-time guru John Izod once scrawled in the margin of a film essay, and I have always tried to apply that wisdom.

Until it finally came, the year 1999 always had that slightly futuristic, important-date-to-have-reached kind of feel to it. Perhaps because Prince, who by this time was 'the artist formerly known as Prince', had sung as long ago as 1982 about the year 1999, as though somehow, with the turn of this particular new year, partying would take on a whole other dimension and range of possibilities. It might also, of course, be everyone's last *chance* to party. Prince's song articulated the nagging sense that such a futuristic-sounding number as '2000' must bring with it something apocalyptic.

There had been many doomsayer nods to Nostradamus, but happily, we survived. Perhaps the end of the world would take a bit longer, and could be averted if we would all just get a bit better at recognising the warning signs. But conservationists by the end of the millennium were no longer just talking about the loss of what to most people might seem important but obscure, remote and unfamiliar things. It was around this time for example that I, like a lot of people, stopped taking my House Sparrows for granted. A sequence of events headed off any danger of complacency.

For a start there were testimonies like this one, from Norfolk farmer Marie Skinner. 'Just 25 years ago sparrows were considered a pest on our farm. At harvest time, thousands would fly out from Norwich, swelling the numbers of our resident sparrows. Together they would descend upon our fields of uncut wheat. Swarms of house and tree sparrows would eat the nearly ripe grain and, through sheer weight of numbers, flatten the crop, causing considerable damage. Five years ago all that remained on our farm were two or three nesting pairs of house sparrows and no tree sparrows. What had happened? How, in such a short time, had these common birds turned into a potential rarity? If numbers can fall so rapidly, what might happen to other birds we currently take for granted?'

This farm decided to do something about it. They made sure there was a roof the sparrows could access to nest in. They let hedgerows grow thick and tall near where the birds could feed. And they provided enormous feeders, made from drainage pipes. Because of this they got their House Sparrows back – a colony of around a hundred. Some kind of solution, but was it sustainable?

'It sounds like a success story,' said Marie Skinner, 'but it is not. What is needed is for every farm to have specific habitats for wildlife. At present, the subsidy system counts against this happening. If we leave uncropped land around our arable fields, we have money deducted. To receive area payments in full, we must plough up close to roadside, ditch and hedge, whether we want to or not.'

On a bright spring morning I opened the front door to find a small cardboard box on the doorstep. Inside it was a dead House Sparrow. There was no note, which made it all the more disconcerting. If this was an unfriendly neighbourhood, or if I were of a more pessimistic disposition, I might have taken it as some kind of warning. But I assumed it to be from a well-meaning neighbour. Sure enough, a few days later, a local farmer I'd introduced myself to when seeking permission to carry out a winter farmland bird survey stopped on his bike and told me it was from him. He told me that his friend on a farm down the road had been finding Sparrows dead at a roost site in the rafters of his pigsty. He wanted to know if I, as the village RSPB man, could work out the cause of death. 'I'll see what I can do,' I reassured him.

I called the ITE, whom I knew to be still in the market for dead birds of prey, and other species higher up the food chain, for analysis. Perhaps they could squeeze in a Sparrow. A man there said sure, send it in. He told me they could test for certain things, like rat poison, but not for all possible causes of death. Back at home I went to retrieve the Sparrow corpse from the garden, but one of nature's undertakers had already claimed it.

I am lucky enough to have a resident colony of House Sparrows, visiting for dampened crusts. Mostly they are peaceable and sociable, sharing the crumbs and the birdseed in a civilised way. But from time to time there are squabbles, and the settling of disputes can be vicious. Mobs rampage into the hedgerow, and there some kind of conflict resolution takes place, summary justice, amid a frenzy of chirping, hidden from view. Order is restored, with the group hierarchy no doubt reinforced or slightly rearranged each time. House Sparrows can't sing, as such, but their insistent chirping, the one-syllable urgent yelps, are as much a signal of spring as any fancy warbling. *THE – SUN – IS – UP: GET – OUT – OF – BED!* They seem to yell, on or near my windowsill.

My Sparrows nest in holes in the gable end between brick and tile. 'You wanna get those filled, mate,' the cavity wall insulation man had told me. 'You'll get birds in there, and all sorts,' he explained. Blimey, I thought. *And where are me sparras gonna nest then, eh?*

I later wondered if I could provide the sparrows with alternative accommodation – maybe wean them off the gable end. I came across an old box in Treasure Trove, my local junk store – or, as I preferred to think of it, the museum of local erstwhile furniture fashions, like the dusty props from *Abigail's Party*, where you can not only touch but *buy* the exhibits, take them home and give them a new lease of life. With the simple addition of two partition walls and a frontispiece with three holes in it, I made an experimental row of sparrow flats. I hung it on a wall in the back garden, above the sparrow breakfast bar. A Great Tit checked it out a couple of times, but the sparrows would take a bit of time to get used to it, and the idea of nesting this colonially.

Besides my friend the farmer, many people had noted a recent decline in House Sparrow numbers, and others had reported seeing them dying or finding them dead. The newspapers had been full of it. The *Independent* newspaper even offered a £5,000 reward to the scientist who could come up with the best explanation. The RSPB enjoyed the privilege of being both judge and potential entrant. The bookies must have stopped taking bets.

It is quite likely that one of the downsides of being *Passer domesticus*, living where it does and in such a gregarious way, is that this makes it prone to contagious diseases. But it is also at the mercy of farming and its new-found efficiencies. The official decline figure at this stage was 64% since the early seventies.

Just as the House Sparrow marched in step with urbanisation, so the Tree Sparrow was our comrade in the agricultural revolution. *Passer montanus* likes trees, but it likes them well spaced out. The removal of dense forest for farmland suited it just fine – up to a point. In the UK it has become as elusive as the House Sparrow has been familiar. It is by comparison a refined, specialised rural thoroughbred, sophisticated and dapper. It has found the UK countryside of the late 20th century not exactly to its taste.

I grew up with Tree Sparrow blindness. They weren't in my visual vocabulary. It's an easy species to overlook. I see now from the guidebooks that they do (or did) occur in Ayrshire. The 1971 edition of the *Hamlyn Guide* has a fully-shaded distribution map, and describes the Tree Sparrow as common. But before I moved south the maps were being re-shaded.

In fact, I don't think I'd ever actually seen a Tree Sparrow in the UK until the previous March. Not properly, at any rate. Not one I'd found myself. I struck lucky on a walk across the Marlborough Downs in Wiltshire. By the time we were descending to Avebury the mist had given way to bright sunshine, the Downs were sprinkled with angular rocks, scattered like eco-protesters in the path of any plough, and the Skylarks were celebrating in anachronistic numbers. Now, I'm not completely sure what a ley line is, but it felt like we were following one.

On a muddy farm track I fell in step with the distant pagan drums of the spring solstice and the stone-worshippers gathering at the Pig and Whistle. Then a sound from the farmyard brought me to a halt. A stray chirp had given the game away. A sparrow chirp all right, but with a subtle difference. I had recently learned to recognise this from my BTO cassette of winter farmland bird calls, when swotting up for my surveys. I broke from the group to investigate.

The farmyard I crept into was a treasure trove in its own right, neglected, but all the more alive for that. Not sofas and wardrobes but clumps of vegetation, rusting machinery, Hawthorns and Elders growing free. And at the back, the prize among the clutter: the skulking bird. I could just make out its chestnut cap and black 'ear', before it slipped out of range. Rumbled. Further reconnaissance revealed more of its comrades. I had found a safe house for a colony of Tree Sparrows. A rural refuge.

Monday at work I wasted no time in filing a report to Richard Winspear, then co-ordinator of the RSPB's work on Tree Sparrows. If anyone would know, he would know. 'Yes, I know about those ones,' he replied. 'That colony is part of our intervention project.' Intervention was the RSPB's name for emergency action to keep remnant populations alive. Conservation is usually about holistic treatments. Intervention is a sticking plaster.

I suppose part of me was disappointed. It would have been cool to have discovered a new population of Tree Sparrows; unknown, at least officially. But on the other hand it was reassuring to know that these birds hadn't been overlooked; that they were already being, if not quite looked after, then at least looked at. On reflection I realise it was foolish of me to even imagine these to be uncharted. Between us we can't really miss something so valuable in our crowded island: so few places to hide, so many browsers in the ancient curiosity shop.

Seventeen out of 20 Tree Sparrows had gone from the UK since that *Hamlyn Guide* was published, since Abigail threw her party. That same book described House Sparrows as 'abundant'. They were now two-thirds less so. So I stopped taking them for granted.

In spring, three of my House Martin nests were reoccupied, and the birds seemed to be casing other bits of the wall, chattering excitedly. They were even shaping up to next door's eaves. And sure enough, at midsummer construction began on two nests next door – the first Martins there in 50 years, according to Dorothy, who to be fair needed a bit of convincing that the droppings they left would be worth it.

Swallow declines were being reported in 26 out of 35 countries across Europe. A BTO study suggested that in spite of fluctuations in the meantime, the Swallow had not declined nationally since the sixties. But at county level, losses were being routinely described – a bit of a conundrum. The RSPB sponsored a thesis at Oxford University to delve deeper, to unravel the mystery. Forty or so Oxfordshire farms took part in the study. Early indications were of high productivity and nesting success. Swallows catch insects in flight, finding them over pasture rather than arable fields.

As if things weren't tricky enough, the challenges of genetic modification arrived. The RSPB was calling for thorough checks on these crops before any were authorised for release into the environment. They must be shown to be safe. If not, they should be banned. Government rejected the idea of a three-year moratorium on commercial release, even though English Nature, its own adviser, was among those recommending it. Government argued that this would be against world trade rules. It might even spark off a costly trade war with the USA. While there would be studies of the ecological impacts of these crops, and the changes in crop management they would require, it seemed likely that at least one genetically modified (GM) crop could be released after just a year of scrutiny.

The media was full of stories about GM foods – or Frankenstein foods, as they were dubbed by the tabloids. There were many issues wrapped up in the whole business of genetic modification, and the RSPB had to concentrate on just one – the likely environmental impact of releasing new GM crops. The primary concern was that crops could be modified to make them resistant to certain herbicides. This seemed likely to make even more powerful chemicals useable in the field, with even more pressure on other plants of the farmed landscape, and the insects and birds that depend on them. The RSPB was part of the committee monitoring the crop trials.

Meantime, anti-GM protestors were intent on demolishing the trial plots. Some took the view that the trials themselves could not be safe, and represented de facto release. Plant genes could 'leak' into other plants, via pollen, after all. The trials were due to run until the end of 2002. Few can have predicted the extent of public unrest about genetic modification, this side of the Atlantic. Certainly the companies behind GM products seemed to be caught unawares, as were the governments prepared to let them in. It was assumed that, between them, industrialists, scientists and legislators would be trusted to act responsibly.

As we ended the millennium, the public had wearied of food scares, and promises of life-enhancing technology, by word games and compromised politicians. Trust had been stretched to breaking point. The press, quick to latch onto and reinforce this public mood of defiance, let the column inches on genetic modification run to feet and metres.

The realisation then spread that we were already eating GM food. Sometimes it was labelled as such, sometimes not. And we found out that GM crops were already being grown in the UK, albeit not commercially, and that pollen 'barriers' were required to be no more than six metres wide. You didn't need a science degree, just a passing interest in pollination, or hay fever, or the weather, to wonder if six metres was really a safe distance. And so the trenches were dug between kitchen and field. Shoppers, clutching trolleys and toting loyalty cards, were regrouping round the produce marked 'organic', advancing on the checkouts, and lobbing questions into the information desks that even a biochemist would struggle to answer with any certainty.

If we could allow ourselves to imagine that the experts and decision-makers could be trusted, and that any genetically modified organism (GMO) that the international authorities chose to let loose in our farmed environment – and thereafter on our digestive systems – had to be shown to be of no demonstrable risk to health, and that any GMO must be shown to pose no threat to wild flora through cross-pollination, what then were the risks to the environment of that GMO?

The risk was the loss of even more biodiversity. The RSPB had insisted on testing of the environmental impact of GMOs, and did so before this was front-page news. The likelihood seemed that such tests would show that any given GM crop can be even freer of weeds and insects than its non-GM equivalent already is, because that is partly the point of modifying it in the first place.

What then? Would the government ban it? Even in an age of global free trade agreements, with pressure coming from countries in which tests have been non-existent, never mind rigorous, government would be expected to honour its obligations to biodiversity. Consumers and conservationists would insist that it did.

It was the 20th anniversary of the Birds Directive, and time for a review. Only Belgium and Denmark had protected all the places that they and Europe believed required protection. France, meanwhile, was still permitting the hunting of migrant birds in spring.

Attempts were made to reform the CAP in time for the new millennium's overall plan for Europe's budget, and for economic, social and environmental progress. The RSPB called the outcome of the final negotiations an 'untidy political fix'. The loss of wildlife, destruction of the countryside and erosion of rural communities looked set to continue. The Common Fisheries Policy was also under scrutiny. Seabirds have always been a good indicator of where the fish are, and where they're not. Terns of several species were in long-term decline.

In Wales, 98% of wildflower-rich meadows had gone. Mixed crop farming had all but ceased, taking many wild birds with it. Most damp pastures had been drained. Half the heather moors were gone too. The hills had been grazed to the quick by millions of sheep – nearly doubling in number to 11 million since the early seventies. This was three times as many as recommended, if you wanted to avoid environmental damage. Eight bird species had declined by up to 80%.

Lapwings hit the headlines again in the spring. The situation was now 'dire' in Wales, according to former RSPB man-turned-broadcaster Iolo Williams. It was the same story in south-west England, traditional stronghold for these damp pasture-loving birds. Wet grass is surprisingly important for wildlife, but it's not exactly rainforest in terms of public appeal. No one ever bought or wore a wet grasslands sweatshirt. Conservationists attempted to make them a bit more appealing by calling them 'silver meadows' – which might, to some, sound a bit like a downmarket motel.

A Lapwing hotline was set up in Dorset, where the birds had declined by half in less than a decade. Callers could use this to seek emergency help where nesting birds were threatened; odd to think that not so long ago Lapwing nests weren't even protected in law. A small surviving colony chose a farm field next to an RSPB nature reserve in south-west England. This was about a quarter of the population hanging on in Devon. The farm manager was in a hurry to plough and plant. Each nest was painstakingly lifted five times in the course of these operations, attracting sympathetic interest from national as well as local media. It was a story with a happy ending, as not only did the adult birds tolerate the disruption, but nearly all the young birds survived to adulthood.

The tenth anniversary of the Red Kite's reintroduction to England was reached, and nearly 150 young were raised in 1999 by the English population. North Scotland's more recently returned kites reared nearly 50. Between them, these two newly established groups of kites were now more productive than the relic Welsh population. The scheme could now be declared a success, despite continued setbacks and losses of birds to poisoning. Further reintroduction sites were being prepared.

What is it with Scots and managing football clubs? More by accident than design I found myself organising the RSPB team – the Birdmen – which meant at least that I always got a game, and a favourable write-up. OK, I was also the reporter. We set up an annual fixture with our friends at the RSPCA, allies in so many campaigns, and a great set of blokes doing often difficult and dangerous work tracking criminals. We hosted them for the inaugural game, a pulsating three-all draw. Looking back through the match reports, I note that the pick of the goals was probably the penalty kick despatched by, well, me.

The Large Blue butterfly came back from the dead. Five colonies were now re-established, the species having become extinct in the UK in 1979. Meantime, four other butterfly species were listed as threatened. The RSPB was now leading on more biodiversity action species, including two rare bees, two hoverflies and a Mason Bee, a moth, two lichens and a moss.

The Song Thrush study was revealing a marked difference in the fortunes of these birds in two areas. In mixed farmland in a southern county the birds were faring well, with two or three nests per pair in a season, and young birds surviving to breed in later years. In east coast arable country, by contrast, the birds were making only one nesting attempt and no youngsters appeared to survive to return the following spring.

The RSPB continued to call for a tax on pesticides, so that the price of the products reflected environmental impacts better, and cut the costs of removing them from drinking water, estimated at around £130 million per year. Government was consulting on how such a tax might be structured, with the option of more hazardous products being put in a higher tax bracket. Government had also begun to take steps on climate change, with taxes on business energy use, plans for renewable energy and a public campaign encouraging everyone to do their bit.

Government also issued proposals in August to strengthen the measures to protect SSSIs following a sustained campaign by the RSPB and its partners, which culminated in sacks of signed Lapwing-shaped pledge cards being delivered to Deputy Prime Minister John Prescott.

The Queen unveiled a statue of Eric Morecambe, complete with binoculars, in his home town of Morecambe as part of an art and education project celebrating the bird life of the bay. The RSPB was urging government that environmental education and the teaching of sustainable development should be a feature of the curriculum in all countries of the UK, and be part of more of the subjects taught.

Conservation took a fresh turn. Until now, buying and managing nature reserves had been very much a matter of securing the best bits, the hotspots, the places that were already valuable, full of rare and threatened species, and securing them; not just trusting to fate or the goodwill of other owners, or the planners. Now, it would also be about restoration – putting life *back*, creating nature reserves from scratch. It was in this spirit that work began at Lakenheath – to put the fen back in fenland. It was scheduled to take ten years to create a mosaic of reedbeds, marshes and water channels, and a home for species like the rare Bittern, the fortunes of which were being turned around, when UK extinction had looked inevitable.

Nature reserves were also now coming closer to centres of population. The future of Rainham Marshes was finally secured with its purchase from the Ministry of Defence. London would now have a nature reserve on its doorstep larger in area than Hampstead Heath.

In mid-December the oil tanker *Erika* ran aground and split in half on the Brittany coast. For seabird deaths it was the worst oil disaster ever known on the Atlantic coast of Europe. It was thought that as many as 300,000 seabirds might have died from the oiling. The blighted beaches of France were combed by mask-wearing volunteers mobilised by the French BirdLife partner. The RSPB urged Europe to hasten the move once and for all to double-hulled tankers.

Conservation could point to numerous success stories, where effort had been targeted at saving or reintroducing a declining species in a particular place. But it was increasingly being realised that we faced the loss of once-common species from entire regions or even countries. The Corn Bunting's continued existence in Wales looked shaky, for example, and there were genuine fears for the future of the Yellowhammer in Northern Ireland, where 'giant bird-tables' would be tried on farms, as a last-ditch effort to keep the species going. Saving widespread species in long-term decline was going to require a different approach. We would have to turn our attention to the landscape as a whole, and to how we all live our lives.

2000

'Any bits of warm life preserved by the pen are trophies snatched from the dark, are branches of leaves fished out of the flood, are tiny arrests of mortality,' Laurie Lee had written. I went on his trail. He famously walked out one midsummer morning, in 1936. The older I get the less time ago that seems, in the odd way that ageing has of altering your perception of time's length. It makes the past seem more recent, more real, more linked to now.

Lee ended up, on his walk, in Andalucía, southern Spain, as civil war broke out. Inspired by his adventures, I headed there too. Unlike him, I went in springtime, with just a week's leave to squeeze in before the end of the financial year. Given the limitations on my time (oh, to live in a time less frenetic) it made sense to fly-drive – which isn't to say there wasn't still a good deal of romance associated with my trip. And not a little guilt at the emissions involved, which I would like to hope this little extract might go some way to offsetting.

The *finca* I stayed in is two days on mule-back from Almería. Or two hours by economy-class hire car. The village of which it is part sticks to an enclosed hillside like an overheating iced cake, glinting magnolia-white in the spring sunshine, tucked away from the Mediterranean side by one ridge, and from the high, snow-capped sierras to the north by another.

Sleet-stacked cloud loomed over the higher valleys as I left the village for the coast. Savouring the atmosphere I lay, warming gently in the coastal sun, on the grey shingle, a thin strand in front of the today quiet coastal village of Castillo del Ferro, soothed by the slumbering pull of the breakers dragging pebbles languidly into the sea, like the inhalations of a giant, harmonising smoothly with the twittering, nasal twangs of a Greenfinch in the palms behind.

I didn't realise, until I reacquainted myself with the *finca*'s copy of Laurie Lee's book, that Castillo was one of the villages in which the author and traveller lived. On this very beach, one evening in 1937, locals gathered to watch a destroyer that had anchored offshore, baffled as to why it was panning a great spotlight along the coast. It then, for reasons they also couldn't fathom, opened up on them with a deafening and ground-juddering salvo of deadly shells. Amid the collective astonishment and terror, and as they fled for cover, it dawned on them that their village had been mistaken for one occupied by fascists a short distance along the coast.

A British naval vessel picked Laurie Lee up from this battered shoreline some days later, along with other UK nationals, and his walk was over.

I read all this, and of Lee's attempts to return to Spain in winter on foot through the Pyrenees, by the whispering log fire of the *finca*. Further inspired, the next day I resolved to try to reach the empty farmhouse on the opposite side of the valley, at a distance difficult to judge, but a few miles as the migrant Wheatear would fly. Unlike the Wheatear, of course, to reach it I would have to go down through the village, picking my way through its grungy assemblage of dogs and their deposits, to the streambed, and up again through the almond groves; hardly on a par with a midwinter trans-Pyrenean sortie.

I left it late to set out and was up against the clock, as the sun had already dropped close to the top of the ridge. I got there while the last rays still lit the tiles, intact on the roof of this long-abandoned house. The windows were shuttered, although one upstairs had been blown open in a bygone gale. The doorways were engulfed in briers, a discarded tin teapot had rusted through on the floor below the tangle. I fished it clear, and wedged it into a wall recess, for a nest-box, to tempt some life back. Then I made my way back in the gathering darkness.

I travel, with the time available to me, in search of wildness now lacking at home in the garden of England and large parts of her British Isles siblings. I guess like many people I'm after a reconnection with the earth and a way of life that provides for the 'deeper needs of human nature', that 'nourishes the sense for poetry and reality' described by Gerald Brenan, who wrote of pre-war Andalucía, before the tarmac roads came. These, he believes, more than anything else marked the end of the 'primitive community feeling' that made these mountain villages so different and distinct from the world beyond, a world of which they had little need or for which they had little regard.

I guess I was seeking an echo of this in my journey to the boarded-up farmhouse, empty more than anything because it is on a north-facing slope, disowned for its lack of sunshine, and because there is no road to it. Its spring seeps bitter tears of water that cannot be drunk, the locals told me later.

I think the easier and more convenient life gets, the less interesting it is in danger of becoming. Well, it may be true of recreational travel, at least. I've come to rue missing out on the time before paths became roads, and midsummer morning walks became short-haul plane journeys, although of course there are, for now at least, a few consolations.

At a meeting in Canada in January governments discussed GM crops, and regulations on their export and spread. The RSPB was in the thick of it, advocating strenuously for governments to have the right to restrict the movement of GMOs as a precaution, to protect wildlife. The USA and Canada were strongly against tough restrictions. The agreement finally reached did allow for a precautionary approach to be adopted, if a government so chose. It would apply from mid-year.

The RSPB renewed the campaign to put the life back in the farmed countryside. Reform of the CAP remained pivotal. I wrote at the time that 'until the next talks in 2006, we have a system that will continue to subsidise over-production of some produce. It gives 75% of the money to the 25% biggest farm owners, to produce food on an industrial scale, using methods that remove the variety from the farmed landscape and which continue to do little to support rural communities.'

The RSPB had an ace up its sleeve. It had hit on the idea of buying a farm of its own. Not the first farm ever bought that would be run for conservation reasons, of course, but this farm would aim to be 'real'; an average-sized, mainly arable operation in an everyday chunk of countryside – definitely not a nature reserve; nothing scenic, or even especially public. A worked example that farm owners would have difficulty dismissing as irrelevant, unrealistic or impractical.

The very farm was found, in a village not far from my own, a place I happened to know, close to the ancient woodland I'd worked in a few years earlier. The appeal to buy Hope Farm caught the public imagination and raised £1.4 million, smashing its target. It had been a mixed farm until the fifties, worked by generations of the same family. By the seventies it had, typically of its type and in this part of the world, switched to solely arable production – bigger fields, no livestock, fewer landmarks. Photographed from the air, it looked almost entirely featureless.

The Countryside and Rights of Way (or CRoW) Act introduced in the spring also offered a bit of cheer. And there was some other encouraging news on the funding front – European money was being redirected from damaging subsidies, alongside new money from government.

The charity Plantlife organised a national Cowslip survey in the spring, to form a picture of how many of these plants survived in the landscape. I found some dredged from a ditch, after the drainage board earth mover had been through. They had been dumped with the sludge onto the adjacent crop field. The ditch bank had been scoured to a steep, bare, near-vertical wall – creating a trench, where had been a stream-bank. With the owner's permission I chiselled a couple of the Cowslips free from the rock-hardened mud to take home, knowing that they would soon be sprayed off and ploughed in (which they had been, the next time I walked this bridleway, wheat fields stretching to the horizon). A decade later those Cowslips are multiplying in my front garden. Each spring I can now count more than a hundred flowering stems in a 'lawn' that I judge according to its plant diversity, its bees and grasshoppers.

Not far away on a new nature reserve created on former carrot fields, a plant once thought gone was also being brought back. Fen Ragwort was declared extinct in 1857 after drainage of the fens. It was rediscovered in 1972 in a Cambridgeshire ditch. Seedlings were now being raised and plants introduced at Lakenheath. They would soon begin to flower spectacularly.

I had noticed that in the one year in four that the field at the end of my back garden was sown with oilseed rape, Linnets seemed to be present in decent numbers, twanging from the wires, swirling around in little parties. I thought they might even be nesting in my neighbour's hedge, or at least the farm hedge beyond the track used by the cows. I was also pleased to learn how important clumps of Gorse can be for Linnets, which can nest in loose colonies in these prickly sanctuaries, and forage far and wide from there. Perhaps we could all make more room for thickets of Gorse, with its glowing yellow flowers, even in late winter. The Sandy heath used to be so coated in Gorse this was harvested as a fuel crop. The Lodge reserve now had just one solitary surviving bush. I had planted some Gorse whips in my front garden, from cuttings I took from a friend's garden up on the greensand ridge. It rooted well, and I added these to the hedgerow mix, although not right in the middle – more on the edge. I remembered my uncle, who still farms in Ireland, telling me that Gorse didn't do in a hedge, as it would tend to sprawl and create gaps.

No one could yet explain the disappearance of House Sparrows from urban areas and cities, as well as their perhaps less mystifying decline in rural places. The *Today* programme on BBC Radio 4 asked people to volunteer to help, and realised they'd opened a can of worms when 30,000 listeners came forward on day one. There may have been as many as 10 million House Sparrows in the years before *Silent Spring*. Now, just a fifth of that number remained. In 1974 there were more than 500 House Sparrows in Kensington Gardens, London. In 2000, just eight were counted. The mystery was deepened by the apparent continued success of House Sparrows in cities like Paris.

Sparrows or no Sparrows, a message was sent to Europe and to French government, about what the public thought of them fostering illegal hunting of migrant birds. A petition with 2.2 million signatures had been pulled together, half a million of them from the UK.

Conservationists pushed for legal underpinning of the biodiversity action process – to make the plans binding. The plans needed to be kept up-to-date, and publicly funded organisations needed to be answerable for achieving them. MPs of all parties supported the idea. There were calls for a doubling of heathland by 2010, and a fifth of farm subsidies to be directed to environmental and social benefits. A project called Bird Aid was set up, to provide emergency winter food for birds on farms, to see if this could help stem the declines. Corn Buntings had already become extinct in Northern Ireland.

The RSPB had been calling for a ban on peat extraction from SSSIs by this year, and on commercial cutting and use of peat by 2005. The National Trust announced that it would soon stop using peat. Celebrity gardener Monty Don backed the campaign, even if some other high-profile gardeners refused to do so. As Don put it, digging up peat bogs for gardens was no more justifiable than digging up rare plants from the wild to put in a flower bed.

You could be forgiven for thinking that a warming planet's overall climate chaos contribution to the UK's weather was washout summers. Flooding in April and May inundated the nests of hundreds of ground-nesting birds on the floodplains of the Great Ouse, the river that flows past my village, carrying the rainwater of its catchment to deposit on the washes, and sometimes – when it has rained *a lot* – in built-up areas.

At the start of the year, President Clinton had made a bold declaration: 'We have, I hope, finally put to rest the false choice between the economy and the environment, for we have perhaps the strongest economy in our history, with a cleaner environment.' Clinton's maximum permitted two terms of office drew to a close at the year's end. George W. Bush would now take office, defeating Al Gore in a close-run and ultimately controversial election. A photograph of Rachel Carson had hung on Gore's office wall. He had been greatly influenced by the author, calling *Silent Spring* 'a cry in the wilderness that changed the course of history'.

In November, further climate talks at The Hague collapsed without agreement. They took place against the backdrop of protests about the price of fuel across Europe. Climate change was now being described as the greatest threat to wildlife, if not the world as a whole. It was also the wettest autumn in the UK for three centuries. Nearly £1 billion in insurance claims were submitted for property damage, to put the seal on a miserable year.

Fittingly, the late nineties was an era of melancholic anthems on the music front. It seemed that you couldn't go anywhere, home or abroad, without hearing David Gray's sombre *White Ladder* album. And then there was Coldplay's paean to pain 'Trouble', when it wasn't Moby's pleading, or the Verve, or Radiohead. All affecting tunes, contributing to the prevailing sense that something was ending.

I found a new kind of music and musician when I went to London to meet the composer Dominic Crawford Collins. He was creating a work combining classical music with wild sounds, and keen to donate some of the proceeds to the RSPB. He has a thing about Curlews.

'How many bits of Curlew do you think I listened to before I got the bit I wanted?' he asked me (I was supposed to be interviewing him). 'This year, when I didn't hear the Curlew – and I went out every morning at dawn – when I didn't hear it I had such a sense of loss. I love the way bird calls announce that you have arrived at another place,' he went on. 'Oystercatchers, for example. It's the soundtrack of real life. I think that the song of certain birds in a particular location provides a kind of fifth dimension to your experience of a place – a kind of euphoria.'

Dominic's work, *Birdsong*, is a journey that begins in London, with its often stress-inducing and discordant noises. 'London's different areas have their own kind of music. One sound made a great impression on me: the Starlings in Leicester Square captured the mood of the city – its multitudes, its noise, its busyness, its pace, its power, its overwhelmingness, its sinister undercurrent, its presence. They have gone – it fills me with great sadness to know they will not be there – that along the ledges and cornices of the great buildings which they once used to fill, there will be nothing.'

Birdsong moves out of London, through the farmed landscape, ending in the wilds of the Hebrides. 'Through their song, birds can strengthen our experience of a place – of a moment in our lives,' Dominic enthused. 'The sound of gulls triggers your memory of the sea, the seaside and holidays. For anyone whose childhood summers were filled with the sound of the Corncrake, the effect of hearing its call must be such a strong evocation of past experience.'

Inspired in part by Dominic's evocation of the isles I booked a new year (new millennium, more like) week on the island of Rum, in search of the White-tailed Eagle (aka Sea Eagle), to fulfil a long-held wish. Back in May, it had been noticed that the first of the reintroduced females to rear young in the mid-eighties had gone missing. It was with a palpable sense of bereavement that the great bird's remains were found the following month. She had raised 15 young over the years since her release on the island, playing her part in making this scheme work, and creating a more secure future for a species that had been absent for far too long.

I didn't let myself believe I would ever actually get to Rum until we were on the ferry that morning. Not because among our group Maceo was so jinxed, but because Rum simply takes quite a bit of getting to. It is at least three hours, snow permitting, from Glasgow north to Mallaig, the ferry port. If the sea is rough the ferry doesn't sail; and it wouldn't sail on the Sabbath. So, aiming to cross on the Saturday before new year is not without its risks.

As well as its eagles, Rum is best known for its Red Deer, its castle, and occasional suggestions that it might be the venue for bringing Wolves back to this country. It used to be known as the 'Island of Goblins', because at night, in June, an under-worldly giggling echoes in its mountains. Nowadays we know that this sound is produced by 60,000 Manx Shearwaters, coming from the south Atlantic to breed in burrows. The island is a nature reserve, state-run since 1957 when the owners passed it – and the castle – over to the nation. It is now managed by Scottish Natural Heritage, the government agency.

'What are the chances of seeing a Sea Eagle then?' I asked the warden, on the boat. 'Not bad, really,' he answered, non-committal.

The ferry moors in a sea loch, where visitors are transferred to a smaller craft that can get onto the slipway. There is a delay while the small boat returns to the ferry to fetch the bags. From here we could survey the wide sweep of the bay, with the fabled castle centre stage, half a mile away. Our timing was perfect. As we huddled awaiting our bags, the Sea Eagle made its dramatic entrance, as though to greet us, to introduce the show, amid our *oohs* and *aahs*. It came in low over the headland, beating heavily out over the ferry, as though to inspect the contents. As it circled, we could see that its wingspan really does have the dimensions of a door. It exited the way it had come in. I half expected a floor manager to appear to initiate a round of applause.

The reintroduction of Sea Eagles had begun back in 1975. Young birds were brought from the thriving Scandinavian population to replace those exterminated about a century earlier, around the time that Kinloch Castle was built. We had rooms in the old servants' quarters. It felt much more lived in than most of the grand houses I have visited. It's almost as though its owners, the Bulloughs, left six months ago. Besides the trappings of their wealth and the souvenirs of empire, a strong sense of their character lingers.

We dropped by the island's only shop, between castle gate and shoreline, to buy provisions, and found ourselves having a dram with the man who runs it, over the counter. Before long he was reading his poetry to us, while his little daughter eyed these strangers suspiciously, over fiery cheeks.

At high tide the shop is a matter of yards from the lapping sea loch. At Hogmanay snow coated the ground right up to the water's edge, stars dusted the heavens in clear skies, and full moonbeams glinted off the snow and ice, where the shopkeeper poet and I teetered, tipsy, he terrified of breaking a limb. It was neither the time nor the place to be needing an ambulance, in fairness. The jewel-shaped island fairly sparkled then, and after midnight we all gathered outside the village hall for a few fireworks, and our host recited another of his spirited poems.

The 21st Century

2001

Soon after dawn on New Year's Day the warden drove a group of us across the island at not much more than walking pace. He packed us tight in his Land Rover in a vain attempt to prevent us jarring our heads on the ceiling as we rocked along on the rutted track. I imagined the laird buzzing along this very same road on smooth tarmac in his Bentley, top down, gloved and goggled, scarf flapping over leather seats. I wonder how quickly he tired of that run. The rusting chassis of one of his sports cars nestles in the castle's kitchen garden.

Deposited on the western coastline, we searched for Otters. A flotilla of Shags indicated rich pickings among the submerged rocks. The odd diver (or loon) bobbed and craned further offshore. We sat on the foundations of a fishing village, now buried in clods of moss and tussocks of Deer Grass. We sang 'The Bear Necessities', and dolphins appeared, perhaps coincidentally, smooth shapes arcing through the angular waves. Grungy feral goats gathered on the tideline, kelp dribbling down their beards, long coats trailing on the beached flotsam. They moved away in a dignified retreat as we approached, hopping up the basalt seams in the sand. Ravens croaked and rolled overhead.

The first day of the new year seemed unusually long, with so much sky – so much Skye, in fact – hogging the northern horizon, its Cuillins snowbound, draped, like the castle's upholstery, in an ivory dust cover. Some of the earliest settlers known in Scotland set up camp on Rum, of all the places they could have chosen. We know this from buried remains. Perhaps they landed in this very bay. The passing of more recent crofting and fishing communities is marked by mossy boulders. It brought to mind Charles Ryder revisiting Brideshead, in Evelyn Waugh's novel: his nostalgia without regret; his strong sense of what is spiritually renewable.

By the time our driver returned with the Land Rover we had watched the sun sink behind the 12 columns of the Grecian temple in which the Bulloughs are interred, in stout marble chests. And although there were no more appearances by the eagles, on a hillside facing the sea we discovered one of the crates from which fledged Norwegian eaglets were released a quarter of a century ago. A touching if inadvertent monument in its own right, to nature restored to its rightful place.

The Countryside and Rights of Way (CRoW) Act had become law in England and Wales at the start of December. It would give a legal backbone to the biodiversity process. The new millennium had an inauspicious start. Winter brought more urban flooding. Then disaster struck. No sooner it seemed had the CRoW Act allowed some wider freedoms to wander in certain types of open country than the countryside was closed. Foot-and-mouth disease had set in, and most of the farmed landscape was shut, including nature reserves. Television was full of images of anguished farmers and burning cattle; funeral pyres to a failing system, smoke signals across the land telling that something was badly wrong. Amid the widespread disruption to rural life, ecological surveys and vital conservation work were put on hold.

Over at Hope Farm, bare patches had been left in two places in the crops planted, to see if these would attract Skylarks to nest a second or third time in the crop. It was known that when a crop gets beyond a certain height, it is of little use for larks, which can only access the vehicle tramlines. A simple idea, and a low-cost one. But would the Skylarks *get* it? Research had also shown that insecticides used on crops in spring probably affected Skylarks and Yellowhammers trying to feed their young on insects. Birds were also found to prefer hay fields, as these are allowed to mature and are cut later, giving plants a chance to set seeds that birds might be able to pick up. Silage crops are cut early, and leave little behind for the birds. Hay-making is now much reduced as a practice. In its first year, the 450 acres of crops at Hope Farm produced a profit of £36,000, after receipt of a subsidy cheque for £40,000.

A commission under Professor Don Curry was set up to consider and advise on the future of food and farming. In due course it would recommend an environmental scheme for farmers throughout England, and the Treasury announced that £500 million would be made available. It was expected to be in place by 2006. Farmers would now be paid for leaving winter stubble fields, creating headlands – unsprayed or less sprayed areas – and wildflower mixes, to provide nectar in summer and seeds in winter. A novel scheme was brought in to rank supermarkets on environmental performance, and the green credentials of the food they sold. It formed part of wider moves to encourage shoppers to buy local food from wildlife-friendly sources, and support farms that were doing the right thing.

International Dawn Chorus Day was trumpeted on Radio 4 at the start of May. Later in the month the RSPB staged Wake up to Birds Week, encouraging the world to celebrate birdsong and the dawn chorus. 'Wake up to the idea that birds can help us to survive the modern world, too,' was the call. Dawn chorus events were held wherever they could be, across the countries. 'For three glorious hours we were taken on a wonderful guided tour by the wardens,' wrote one satisfied visitor. 'Expert, but admitting that even they sometimes confused some songs, so there is hope for us amateurs yet.'

Foot-and-mouth forced the general election to be moved from May to June. The RSPB staged a vote of its own, asking the public to vote for their favourite bird songster. The media picked up on the election link, although the general consensus was that the environment had barely featured among the issues debated and promoted by politicians. This was despite the Vote Environment campaign, which tried to persuade the parties, among other things, to set ambitious targets for cutting carbon emissions, which would involve investment in new, clean technologies and the jobs they would create. There was an ambitious call for 100,000 photovoltaic panels to be installed on house roofs, to generate heat and energy from daylight.

The campaign had also called for the phasing out of all known hormone-disrupting chemicals and pesticides that accumulate in the environment, and any other toxic chemicals, by 2005. Representatives from each of the three main parties had pledged to adopt these measures in their manifestos.

There was great excitement when the Osprey, having spread once again to reclaim most of Scotland, crossed the border to nest again in northern England. A scheme set up at Rutland Water reservoir, not far from my village, had established a small satellite population of Ospreys in the south. The annual Birdfair is held nearby, and an Osprey or two usually puts in a guest appearance. One of them did a fly-past as we lined up for the annual Conservation Cup football tournament, staged in a sheep meadow-turned-car park on the Saturday evening after the vehicles had been cleared. We'd won it three times, and got to keep the original trophy, which now adorns my attic. Despite being favourites, my RSPB team, dubbed the 'Man U of Environmentalism', crashed out in the semi this time, to Brazil, and I spent the night in Peterborough Infirmary with a busted knee. I can place this incident in time because I was in a Bedford hospital a short while later having physiotherapy when news of the terror attack on the World Trade Center came through. The world wouldn't feel quite the same again.

As part of its renewed efforts to tackle issues for the farmed environment, the RSPB increased its participation in agriculture shows, including a return to the Royal, the biggest of all. We enlisted support from the world of showbiz, producing a set of eye-catching scarecrows dressed in clothing donated by celebrities. These included the rubber dress worn by Denise van Outen when she presented the Brit Awards, Ali G's bright yellow shell suit, a Johnny Vaughan lumberjack shirt, Linford Christie's Olympic leggings, and contributions from conservation stalwarts Susan Hampshire, Robin Gibb, Sir Stirling Moss and Daley Thompson, among many others.

Prince Charles picked up a copy of *Futurescapes* at the show, the RSPB's blueprint for recreating natural habitats on a landscape scale – pioneering stuff. It also brought in issues of public health, and how a little bit of investment in a better, wildlife-rich environment, with access for the public, could reduce the vast sums spent by government on remedial treatment for health issues such as strokes, the risks of which were said to be increased three-fold by lack of exercise. The Futurescapes programme was costed at just 50p per year per taxpayer.

It was now hoped that commercial peat extraction could be phased out in the next ten years. What had yet to become clear was just how much carbon is locked up in peatlands.

Climate talks were held in Bonn in July. Governments from 178 countries agreed on how to tackle the challenge of cutting greenhouse gas emissions. Crucially, the USA held back. Further talks were held in Morocco in November.

We might never replace all 118,000 miles of hedge that were wrenched from the landscape since 1950, the year my house was built, but we can compensate as far as possible. I was itching to plant a mixed hedge in my back garden, but there was a row of *Cypress leylandii* in the way. When I arrived to live here, it was already a monotonous green textured wall, running almost the length of one side of the garden. It was exceeding optimal height for these things – around seven feet – and formed a solid boundary barrier between this garden and next door's.

According to the previous owner, barrier was its primary purpose. He'd planted it basically to assert the privacy of his domain, a small domestic echo of the 18th- and 19th-century enclosure of common land. There's often politics, as well as wildlife, in a hedgerow. The meaning of gardens has changed. These may have been smallholdings and drying greens for the war generation, social spaces for the exchange of local gossip and root vegetables, but then came the eighties. Private ownership had arrived. Shrub roses were replacing vegetable plots, twirly washing lines were being planted, and regiments of Cypress were supplanting rows of carrot.

I quite liked the privacy too, but wanted a proper hedge. I hit on a compromise solution. I would phase it out and phase in the new hedge. So, late in the year I began my own back-door habitat restoration scheme, a tiny domestic echo of the RSPB's in the Flow Country, extracting modern spruce plantations from ancient bogland. In the first tentative thinning of the Cypress hedge, I removed every second tree, to be used as biofuel (some people still call this firewood). And so began the phasing in of the new hedge mix.

2002

Over the winter at Hope Farm, a small area of wheat, kale and mustard seed plants was left uncut. A few more seeds from the wheat harvest and the oilseed rape were sprinkled amongst it. As a result, a flock of Yellowhammers had stayed all winter. The winter before, there had been none of these flocks of seed-eating birds.

My latest domestic hedge restoration scheme out the back was making slow progress. The remaining Cypresses spread themselves into the gaps. To hasten the progress of the mix, I removed all the Cypress branches on the near side. It now looked like a weird cross-section of a hedge – a bit like Damien Hirst's pickled shark, really – but I figured that the surgery would lessen its competitive edge, maintaining the windbreak while giving the new whip mix a better share of the sunlight. As the young mix inched higher, I bit the bullet and stripped the Cypresses of their remaining branches, leaving the wood-ribbed, nobbly trunks in place as posts, as markers, dead wood, climbing frames for creepers, whatever. The back garden was now laid largely bare again for the neighbours to see, inspect, comment on, gossip into.

The latest of a recent series of wet summers provided some respite for Song Thrushes, including the pair that nested in – and officially launched, as I saw it – the flourishing front-garden hedgerow.

Conservationists had begun to talk more about 'ecological services': the value that an intact and coherent water catchment system could provide, for example. These were things like cleansing water, reducing flood risk and preventing drought from damaging the land. A state investment of just £20 million per year would enable massive gains to be made in restoring heathland, chalk downland, woods and saltmarshes. After all, pesticides and inorganic fertilisers had to be paid for again, in the cost of removing them from water.

A survey was carried out of breeding waders on wet meadows, revisiting places looked at 20 years earlier. Researchers found just three Snipe in all of the East Midlands. Birds like the Lapwing and Redshank were in retreat now to nature reserves, all but vanished from vast areas, unable to survive in the wider landscape. Species like these would also be especially vulnerable to climate change.

Evidence began to coalesce that climate change was already affecting the life cycles and distribution of plants and animals. From this year, energy producers were duty-bound to include renewables in their plans. The Kyoto Summit climate talks were staged in the autumn. Most scientists by now agreed that the targets tabled for Kyoto would not be enough to prevent serious climate change. It was hoped that new targets could be set, to give some chance of meeting the aims agreed in the first place, and signed up to by all countries, that there would be 'stabilisation of greenhouse gas concentrations in the atmosphere ... within a timeframe sufficient to allow ecosystems to adapt naturally'.

The Kyoto Protocol required countries to reduce greenhouse gases by 5.2% of 1990 levels by 2012. The era of the wind-farm proposal had arrived, and the era of conservation efforts to make sure that even more wildlife losses were not the collateral damage of any headlong rush to put wind farms in places that would disrupt or even kill birds, and ruin the ground beneath and around them where extensive concrete bases and access tracks needed to be built.

Ten years on from the Earth Summit in Rio, it was time to reconvene in Johannesburg, South Africa. An interim summit had been held in New York in 1997, providing a mid-term report, and worrying conclusions. Rio had produced conventions on biodiversity and climate, a declaration about forest conservation, and the Agenda 21 charter for the 21st century. Johannesburg placed more emphasis on development to reduce poverty. It didn't all happen in the rarefied atmosphere of the summit itself. There had been months of preparation and meetings, so it was also clear well in advance that governments were a long way from agreeing how to tackle the challenges facing the world, and balancing continued growth with sustainability. The RSPB and Cambridge University launched a report on the eve of the summit that attempted to set out the true economic value of biodiversity.

Media coverage was widely critical of the lack of commitment reached in Johannesburg, and the amount spent on running the event. But it was at least acknowledged that to meet the 2010 target of reducing the loss of wildlife globally would require more and different resources being provided from rich countries to poor.

A quarter of a century after his death, Elvis Presley occupied the number one slot for a month in the summer, his 18th chart-topper in this country edging him ahead of the Beatles. It could have been interpreted as a message from the grave for politicians from 'the King', the song in question being 'A Little Less Conversation'...

Despite the increasing international pressure to cut emissions, and whatever Elvis might have been advocating, the airport threat resurfaced. Government announced that the marshes of north Kent at the mouth of the Thames were again being considered as the site for a huge new airport development, despite this area by now having every conservation designation in the book. It also happens to include three RSPB nature reserves. Even by the normal standards of these things this was a salvo by government and developers across the bows of the environmental movement, many of whose representatives might have challenged the building of such an airport anywhere, let alone here. Conservationists prepared to do battle; if this place could be concreted over, then nowhere was safe. 'If an airport were built at Cliffe, it would be the single biggest act of environmental vandalism ever condoned by government,' the RSPB declared.

The wild bird figures for 2002 – the so-called 'Skylark Index' indicator of government performance – showed birds of farmed habitats a depressing 60% down, and woodland birds also declining, the latter now also giving cause for genuine concern. Species like the Marsh Tit, Willow Tit, Hawfinch and Lesser Spotted Woodpecker were now posted missing from many of their former woodland haunts.

State of the UK's Birds was published, and would become annual. Among the shock headlines, just one in five Spotted Flycatchers survived from the population at the start of the seventies. Less well publicised was the demise of the Ring Ouzel on Exmoor in Devon, where they bred for the last time. There were consolations. The charismatic, cliff-nesting Chough bred in Cornwall for the first time in 50 years. The species had abandoned the county of which it is an emblem altogether in the mid-seventies.

The unfortunately named ship *Prestige* disintegrated off Spain in November, and an estimated 200,000 seabirds died from the resultant pollution. But efforts to strengthen protection for the seas suffered a setback when a private members' bill to create marine conservation law was derailed in the House of Lords by a handful of peers.

It was increasingly busy on the international front, as the RSPB and its BirdLife partners turned their attention to the rainforests of Indonesia, which was now rivalling Amazonia as the tropical forested region in most desperate need of intervention. Television news had been full of apocalyptic images of entire landscapes on fire and smouldering for weeks on end, enshrouding the region in a choking gloom. A campaign was launched to find a way of saving some of what was left of these once-teeming lowland forests, which have more species than almost anywhere else on Earth. These include 600 types of bird, many whose continued existence on the planet was threatened, as the native forest around them was systematically cut and taken away on logging trucks, to be replaced with oil-palm plantation monocultures.

A milestone in conservation for Africa was reached with the publication of a huge directory itemising in detail the continent's Important Bird Areas, including, I noted, around 30 in Uganda. Across the Atlantic, a report was issued by the National Audubon Society. It revealed that a quarter of all bird species in the USA had declined since the seventies. It seemed the spring, if not exactly silenced, was worryingly diminished.

With the steady expansion of the RSPB's programme to 'build capacity' in partners overseas, my own thoughts also turned abroad, and the dilemma of which of the RSPB's partner organisations to join on sabbatical. I spoke to our Canadian partner, and to Audubon in New York, and our Programme Manager for East Africa, but in the end an invitation from New Zealand was too tempting to resist. Here was a chance to help combat some serious extinction threats, and maybe even to meet the albatross. So when the dingy, chill days of December arrived I fell through the world and emerged, squinting, in the dazzling sunlight of South Island.

'I only went out for a walk, and finally concluded to stay out until sundown ... for going out, I found, was really going in.'

John Muir

2003

I suspect not many people will have heard of the Rock Wren, even in New Zealand, where it survives. Hardly anyone will have seen one. It is not one of the higher-profile species threatened with extinction. A few trampers might have come across it in the high country, but only if they know what to look out for.

A relative, the Bush Wren, is now extinct. Another, the Stephen's Island Wren, went unrecorded until 1894. In that year the new light-house keeper's cat provided 11 specimens for inspection. The keeper, a Mr Lyall, reported that this Wren ran like a little mouse, and never flew. He saw only two alive, before *Xenicus lyalli* was declared extinct.

The Rock Wren is a bit of a phantom. It inhabits boulder-beds and screes above the treeline, moving lower down in harsh weather. It is tiny and tends not to fly, preferring to run on comically large feet across and under boulders, and has little voice to speak of. Its calls are described as squeaks, inaudible to some. It isn't shy of people, but nor is it especially curious. There's quite a lot that isn't known about its breeding behaviour. What we do know is that it is in serious need of protection. To protect a species, however, first you have to find it.

I trekked to the Rock Wren's habitat with ornithologist Chris Petyt. Reaching the mountaineer's hut requires an afternoon's tramp up the wide valley through ancient, mouldy beech forest and tussocky meadow. The woods were tranquil, but maybe a little too quiet, for the time of year. It took me a while to adjust to the pace. With the weight of an enormous backback on my shoulders and the steady climb upwards – over 16 changes in geology – I had to pause frequently to catch my breath. The air was thinner and the sunshine brighter and somehow sharper than I was used to, and the hut was bathed in it when I was finally able to let the warm balcony take the strain of my backpack.

There was enough daylight left for our first foray up to Rock Wren country that evening, and I felt weightless, freed up from the oppression of that backpack. The landscape is Lilliputian up there, as I waded among low trees stunted by the exposure, bare rocks like scaled-down crags, and alpine plants poking through a very convincing rockery. Hebes sprung from crevices. Lichens hung like sheep wool on barbed wire. Not a typical December evening for me.

A Dunnock warbled; then a Blackbird, the sounds of a British garden in May. I studied the terrain closely for Rock Wrens, expecting at any moment one of the pictures in my mind, based on photographs in books, to come to life on a boulder in front of me. If I were a Rock Wren, I kept asking myself, where would I be? But none materialised. Perhaps we just hadn't got our eye in. We searched until the light faded, and retired to the hut for an early night. I was reminded of that scene in *The Magnificent 7*, when the righteous cowboys who have come on a gallant mission to liberate the village from relentless persecution by bandits find no one at home to welcome them. By way of consolation, a Kiwi blew its whistle, on the stroke of midnight.

Next morning we made an early start to climb high above the treeline. We entered something that felt much more like it could be the Rock Wren's domain – a canyon, on one side a bare rock face with a boulder-strewn slope at its base, where huge slabs had fallen away over the course of time, as though a hurricane had toppled a Stone Age temple. All but the biggest blocks were semi-engulfed in sprawling, twiggy Hebe shrubs. Textbook habitat. We decided to spend a bit of time here, searching thoroughly.

Chris heard a squeak, and made his way round and up to the top of the rock face. I stayed on the boulder-bed. Soon it was my turn to hear a squeak, and I even caught a glimpse of a small bird flitting behind one of the lorry-sized boulders. I couldn't move quickly across this obstacle course of angular rocks and shrubs though, and by the time I got to the boulder to peer round it I was greeted by silence, bar the tinkling of the stream bed and a distant Tui (Blackbird-sized honey-eaters, with cloak-like wings) clanking in the valley, way below the treeline.

I moved up the stream bed and a gentle waterfall to the next level of Rock Wren accommodation. A Dunnock teased me with squeak-like calls, and brief glimpses, turning tail as though inviting me to chase. Chris reappeared higher up: he signalled with a thumbs down. We moved even higher, and as we did so we were quietly enveloped in damp cloud, and rain. We crouched in the lee of a ridge to eat a sandwich, then slipped and slithered on red-raw fingers back down to the shelter of the beech woods. We skirted the edge of Lake Cobb. By mid-afternoon we were back at the hut, and the rain kept us there.

I picked up a back issue of *New Zealand Wilderness*, and saw it had a feature on haunted huts. Against my better judgement, I read it. Our hut was named in memory of one of four friends who died 25 years ago when their hut was blown away in a night-time storm, echoes of which then kept me awake for much of the night.

Morning brought respite and we set off early again to explore around the peak named Xenicus – the scientific name of the Rock Wren. I picked my way across steep screes, and three Keas came swooping across the valley to harangue me on a narrow section of path. And as these strange intermediates between parrot and raptor whirled above me, Hitchcock-style, I overbalanced slightly in a gust. Luckily I regained my footing, and the Keas, perhaps realising they'd been naughty (or because I wasn't now carrion), made off in the direction of Chris. Good old Keas, still flying the flag for native species, along with the occasional Pipit. I hope they are more than just remnants. I was glad of their company, as at that moment, atop this sublime mountainscape, I was really feeling the absence of things, frustrated at our inability to locate the Wrens, mocked by introduced birds like Redpolls calling 'twit' as they passed overhead.

We headed back to Fenella Hut, empty-handed, to write up these notes. It was time to 'go out'. I felt serene, even beatific, the way only settings like this can make you feel. But I'd have felt even more at home if the Wren had been here to welcome us.

I would find ample consolation on Kapiti Island, which lies five kilometres off the coast near Wellington. This is the old New Zealand in microcosm, because conservationists have managed to clear it of introduced species. Since then, the forest has been regenerating madly and the birds are responding in kind.

Not many people get to stay overnight, as I did – too much risk of stowaway mice getting in and wreaking havoc. On arrival I was thoroughly frisked and found to be rodent-free. Kapiti redefines the term bird sanctuary. There are birds everywhere. Wekas (like ancestral Corncrakes) came to greet me as I disembarked on a narrow strand of boulders. Kakas (a kind of parrot) congregated noisily around the deck and roof of the house where I was taken for the introductory talk. Kererus (large pigeons) slapped each other with their wings, and gazed at me expectantly, chins resting on puffed, bibbed bellies. Takahes, like prehistoric Moorhens, high-stepped deliberately across the cropped grass. A large male known as Mr Green came to introduce himself. He had a beak like a bolt-cutter, but he wielded it gently. There are only a couple of hundred of these birds left in New Zealand, and therefore the world, yet their needs don't seem too exacting – here they happily graze the introduced grasses of the former pasture.

These are all 'A-list' celebs in the world of bird-biz, but very down to earth, even vulgar, when you get to know them. It was all a bit like *I'm a Celebrity Bird, Get Me Out of Here.*

Call me obvious, but for me the big prize was to see – or rather meet – a Kiwi, most famous of all, most eccentric (which by local standards is saying something) and most intriguing of NZ birds. It's the national bird, and one that lives in a burrow and is said to sleep on its back with its legs in the air. And this is how it happened ...

Evening came as I sat counting Tui after Tui that had flown across the pasture to roost in the trees of the south-facing valley-side. The Wekas squawked their goodnights, neurotic even here, where the biggest risk to them is someone treading on their toe. The time came for the Kiwis to rouse. Kapiti has so many Little Spotted Kiwis it could be at capacity. It is virtually the entire world population. They are almost extinct on the mainland, having no defence whatsoever against introduced mammals. There are six territories around this small valley, but Kiwis are unpredictable. Meeting one is far from guaranteed.

My fellow overnighters and I waited expectantly on the porch. Before long, the first Kiwi call – the male's – issued from the dark, like a long blast on a referee's whistle. The female replied, slightly less shrill. I think you call it ululating. The four of us tiptoed quietly with a red-tinted torch to see if we could trace the source of the calls. The night was perfectly still. A crescent moon had risen. Visibility was good. After 20 minutes or so of waiting, we finally heard an approaching rustle from the dark wall of bush. It was getting louder, coming through the undergrowth towards our clearing. We held our breaths as not one but *three* little dark shapes emerged, and scuttled into the open, right towards our feet. When they got really close we could see them quite clearly. Ducks.

I laughed aloud, despite myself. But what I didn't realise until later was that we had just found Brown Teal, another unique NZ species that is actually even scarcer than (though clearly not as famous as) the Kiwi, with only five pairs or so here: a really noteworthy discovery. Captive-bred Teal were introduced on Kapiti around the time I was born.

The others called it a night soon after that, but I was happy to stay outside. I explored in the direction of some other calls, prepared for and familiar with (Rock Wren) disappointment. I knew well now what the 'presence of absence' means, the feeling of looking so hard for something you don't see what *is* there any more, only what isn't. And then I realised that this shape, the one that had materialised on the path in front of me now, was a Kiwi. Not a Duck, or Weka, or a Rabbit, but a Little Spotted Kiwi. Not quite as the picture in my head depicted it, but nonetheless a Kiwi. Bold as brass, in the middle of a grassy, pebbly path just above the boulder beach, within hearing range of the occasional lapping wave.

Hello there, I may have whispered. I stopped where I was and it strode over to me, stretching its neck upwards like a puppet, and sniffing audibly – the first time I ever heard a bird sniff – either because I smelt (the backpacker's prerogative) or because my torch looked like a glow worm, which Kiwis like to eat. I guess disappointed, it trotted and snuffled off into the longer grass, much as a Hedgehog might have done.

ECO TERROR POSSUM PLOT! screamed the newsagent billboards back in Wellington, and the headlines in the *Dominion Post*, the daily broadsheet. All the media led with a story about Kapiti, and anonymous 'terror' messages sent to BirdLife partner Forest and Bird saying that non-native predators would be smuggled onto the island and let loose, by disaffected hunting interests. Campaign Manager Eric Pyle was quoted, and in the thick of it. When I went to meet him that afternoon, as per an earlier arrangement, he was a little preoccupied.

He told me he'd never experienced this level of media interest. We chatted about the issues conservationists face here – intensive dairying, albatross deaths on long-line hooks, the struggle against introduced species – between him jumping up to give telephone interviews to Australian journalists and taking calls from hunting organisations anxious to distance themselves from the alleged act of sabotage. I found myself wondering would someone really contemplate letting rats loose on Kapiti if they'd ever been sniffed by moonlight by a Little Spotted Kiwi.

Soon after, it was time to head south. It was time to meet the albatross.

Kaikoura, New Zealand, is a stop-off point on the well-worn groove of global backpacking. It is the place that you *have* to go to see whales. 'The other main reason people visit Kaikoura,' says the *Rough Guide*, 'is to frolic with dolphins. Other activities are simply ways of filling in time until your turn comes.' Albatrosses, like seals and sharks, are lower down the billing at Kaikoura.

The morning was bright and calm, so I went for the early albatross boat. Dolphin fans were shoaling in good numbers at the back of the shop, getting suited up and boarding their bus. For the albatross gig it was just me, and a Professor called Jim – 'from Doblin, but living in Hang Kang,' in his bush hat, clutching binoculars and bird book. This made our sailing quorate, but only just. The driver asked us what we were most interested in seeing. Jim politely gestured to me to go first. I could tell he had his answer already prepared.

'Oh, you know, albatrosses,' I ventured, undemanding. 'And whatever else is out there. Maybe sea mammals?'

Jim's turn. 'I need Western and White-chinned Petrels,' he answered decisively.

'Oh, you'll definitely see those today,' the driver assured him.

'*We will?*' Jim was clearly delighted. He already *had* all the albatrosses, of which there are a number of different species. He had spent quite a bit of time looking for them. Today his wife was shopping in Christchurch. 'She's tired of boats,' he explained.

Gary, our skipper, was soon at full throttle, bouncing us over the gentle swells. We headed for a point where the shelf falls away to the underwater canyons that make these such fertile waters for seeing whales and other marine life so close to shore. Prof Jim and I clung on at the back. My shouts were drowned out by the engine, so I had to tap him on the shoulder when I saw something. He then leant across and yelled a name in my ear, whether I'd identified the bird or not. When he yelled 'GULL!' at one stage I began to doubt Jim. It was clearly not a gull. I tapped him again. Still gull. There was nothing else for it but to look at him funny, and he got his bins on it, and, to my relief, apologised. 'ARCTIC SKUA!' Holding tight to his bush hat, he handed me the bins.

Gary cut the engine and we were adrift, four miles out. He produced breakfast – albatross breakfast, that is: a breeze block of frozen fish liver, inside a thick plastic mesh, on a rope. The gulls were already gathered in raucous numbers as the bait ball splashed off the back. The petrels and shearwaters were gathering too, jostling. They pecked ineffectually at the caged morsel. I now realised that if the albatrosses turned up for this picnic, they'd be really close.

Suddenly, mysteriously, the first of them was with us. Like a delegate to a conference, it slipped quietly in and took a pew at the back, to regard the proceedings. It sailed gently towards the bait, steering with unseen feet across the churning waves. It was a species called the Shy Albatross, and it looked anything but shy as it eased its way past the Black-backed Gulls, dwarfing them, disdaining them and their efforts to make an impression on the bait block. Their beaks simply aren't up to it. This Albatross's bill was about five inches long, and hooked at the end. Below its eye was a line, which at one moment looked like the smile of a dolphin, and in another moment like the scar of a gangster. Surrounded by shearwaters giggling like goblins, it fed alone, but not for long.

More giants materialised from the void of the Southern Ocean horizon. A Wandering Albatross floated in on a nine-foot wingspan, a colossus of a bird, padding on outstretched webs to a halt on the waves, folding its wings in three and cruising in to share the bait.

Gary had been running these trips for five years. I asked him if he'd noticed a change in albatross numbers in that time. 'Definitely,' he replied, 'especially with the Wandering Albatross. They reckon that at the current rate of loss they'll be gone in ten years.'

After an hour or so of lounging in the sun with 13 albatrosses, and with the bait block having dwindled to the size of an orange, Gary pulled it in and tipped it out of the cage. It promptly rolled down the throat of a Wandering Albatross, hardly touching the sides as it went. It was all too easy to picture the same thing happening with a baited hook. I wondered if someone, one day, would drown the last of these birds; and whether the world's fishing ministries would really allow this to happen.

Later in the year the RSPB and its BirdLife partners would launch the Albatross Task Force, to work with and on fishing vessels to find ways to stop the pointless slaughter of albatrosses and other 'by-catch'. This would be another long game, involving some heroic instructors with strong sea-legs and bags of dedication.

Back home, government came up with a site to offer to conservation by way of the compensation it was legally obliged to provide after allowing Lappel Bank to be sacrificed to development. The case had been taken all the way to the European Court of Justice. A major conservation project to make the best of this compensatory site was now on the horizon.

A study by the RSPB looked at the effects of pesticides on Yellowhammers. It found that use of these chemicals in the breeding season reduced the amount of invertebrates that the birds could find for their chicks. The chicks near sprayed fields were found to weigh less and even to starve more often. It provided evidence that any ways of reducing the use of these pesticides might improve the fortunes of Yellowhammers in farmland. Another study confirmed that late grass crops on farms producing silage should be allowed to produce seeds, rather than being cut before the grasses had ripened. This would help birds like Sparrows, Yellowhammers and Reed Buntings survive the winter, because they would have seeds to eat. The trick would now be to try to find a way of making this possible for birds on more farms.

Genetic modification continued to make the headlines. Government launched an official public consultation, inviting the public to air their views and concerns. Public opinion had no doubt been distorted by press hysteria, but there were genuine grounds for concern. Gene scientists didn't help their cause by performing stunts like placing genes for luminescence from deep-sea organisms into plants, to make them glow. The intention had been to show what was possible in an eye-catching way, but the interpretation of this kind of work reinforced a view that much of this science might be reckless, pointless, gimmicky and maybe even dangerous. People instinctively feared where all this swapping around of genes might take us. Dolly the Sheep's unedifying story was wrapped up in the whole circus, and prompted philosophical and theological arguments about 'playing God'. Where would all this cloning take us?

Crop trials were ongoing, and it seemed a little premature to ask the public for their views in advance of the results. Advocates for GM technology were making the same sort of claims made about pesticides 50 years before; namely that they would increase farm production, incomes, and provide more food for the world. The parallels were obvious – we needed to be aware of the possible other, unintended, consequences of unleashing this new technology on the wider environment. Except this time, it might be harder to get the gene 'genie' back in the bottle. Impossible, even.

When they finally came, the results of the trials showed that GM oilseed rape and sugar beet were more problematic for biodiversity than conventional crops, as the herbicides that could be applied to them now that they were product-resistant were harder on the other plants and invertebrates in and around the crops. It was sufficient evidence for conservationists to call for a ban on the commercial release of the crops.

'In 25 years will we look back on the GM debate and think that it was a lot of fuss about nothing?' Graham Wynne wondered. 'Or will we see it as a crucial turning point in the relationship between farming and wildlife?'

It was tempting to conclude that even without genetic modification, crop and agrochemical developments would continue to result in even 'cleaner' crops, for as long as that remained the focus of crop development. Technology, whether it is genetic modification or ever-larger combine harvesters, would continue to make the production of food more efficient and less supportive of biodiversity, unless there were compensatory measures; unless all interested parties could work together to deliver a multi-functional farmed environment, in which food production is just one component of a diverse landscape supporting many interests. Conservationists had to help those who control food production to concentrate on putting the life back in the proportion of our landscape that is needed to support human beings, ecosystems, natural processes, aesthetic values and amenity for the people whose taxes underwrite it.

This couldn't be left to chance or the possible goodwill of farmers and their suppliers, and especially not to businesses intent on controlling not only the supply of seed, but the chemicals needed to grow it. The public had learned already that when producers are remote from the places where they produce, they are more likely to behave unsustainably – as it is when consumers become increasingly disconnected from the origins of food.

Lessons came from the GM controversy. More people had come to realise that the price of so-called progress can be too high, and what we lose we may never get back. For the time being, at least, no one could force consumers to buy GM products. Nor did anyone have to grow them or, if the labelling is clear, eat them. As consumers, we could but hope that there would always be a choice.

A number of pesticides and herbicides were banned this year. This included 81 different products sold to gardeners. As of July, they could no longer be bought, and any supplies in the garden shed had to be disposed of by the end of the year. From next April it would be against the law even to still have them. The majority of the products were herbicides, containing the now banned active ingredient dichlorprop. This and several other active ingredients had been banned throughout Europe.

Max Nicholson died, aged 98. He had been one of the great figures of 20th-century conservation. A sundial was installed at The Lodge in his honour. I am sure he would have approved as the RSPB bit the bullet on tropical forest destruction and looked hard at the possibility of acquiring the rights to log a vast area of lowland rainforest in Sumatra. And of course not exercise the right; just own it, and preserve the forest.

At midsummer, I set out on a midnight mission to find one of our rarest and most threatened birds, to write about an attempt to bring it back to England. I found myself in almost total darkness, standing in a field. The grass around my boots was damp with gathering dew. I could feel and taste the breath of cows on my face and neck. I was surrounded by them, and their thick smell. All I had for protection was a preparedness to stay calm – they were only cows, after all (I think) – and Gwyn Williams, the RSPB's Head of Reserves and Protected Areas. An image of General Custer and the Little Big Horn was conjured. I dispelled it. When you have a ring of cattle around you it is best not to think about any kind of horns, little or big.

To explain why we were here, I need to recap. There's a bird that, until a few decades ago, was found on almost every farm in the land. Almost anyone alive in rural Britain in the early part of the 20th century knew this bird's unique voice. Today, it is almost nowhere. Perhaps no other common UK species and its song has been so thoroughly (but inadvertently) removed from our landscape. It is a bird that lives in long grass and nettle beds, field margins and hedge bottoms. Its needs are basic.

This bird is the Corncrake, an intriguing creature. Built like a Moorhen, but land-living and with the colours of a sparrow, it skulks in the undergrowth. It is rarely seen, but makes its presence felt at night with its guttural *crek-crek*. It is a sound that is almost reptilian, a throwback to a stage of evolution when the birds, no longer reptiles, began to expand their vocal range but hadn't yet developed the notes or the pitch. It's what a large lizard might sound like, under stress.

Each autumn the humble Crake leaves its little runways among the waving grass and takes wing, legs trailing behind it, to cross the

Channel and continent for Africa. Exactly where, scientists weren't entirely sure until recently. They are difficult birds to find, in fairness, especially when not doing the night-time rasp.

I know that agriculture has advanced beyond recognition in the developed world, but it still amazes me that the loss of the Corncrake can have been so comprehensive. I've quizzed scientists about it. Surely, I plead, a few Crakes would have survived, in a forgotten corner here, or a neglected paddock there, as machinery churned inexorably through the larger fields nearby? Has our entire farmed landscape been so thoroughly tidied, put so far beyond the use of this modest little species? I should add here that Corncrakes survive in the Western and Northern Isles, and here and there in Ireland, thanks to crofters and conservationists getting their collective acts together, but let's concentrate on mainland UK for now.

How exactly it happened, however it was that the population dynamic of the Corncrake unravelled, practically all of them disappeared, from Dover to Dounreay. To summarise their particular problem: they nest in loose groups in hay and silage fields, usually, and these fields are cut, sooner, more often and more quickly than they used to be (substitute chap with scythe for large mower). Result: Corncrake nest failure, and the death of adult birds, on a nationwide scale, season after season.

It is clear that to have any chance of restoring the Corncrake, you'd need a very large area under management sympathetic to their needs – primarily, their need to not be chopped up while nesting. The RSPB believed it had created such a place – at the Nene Washes, in East Anglia. So, how to tempt the Corncrakes back? They would have to be helped along. Mercifully, they can be readily captive-bred. The challenging bit is to make sure they are introduced to their new home as very young chicks. Otherwise, they will regard the incubator, wherever that might be, as home. They will attempt to return there next spring after (hopefully) negotiating the return trip to deepest Africa.

To begin with, the project partners released 52 young birds – tiny, black, fluffy and impossibly photogenic – to the verdant pastures and long grasses of the Nene Washes the previous midsummer. They were now on their own. A group of us volunteered to go there to see if any of these Crakes had made it back. We would only know about any returning males. It is only the males that call. And of course we had to go at night. Which brings me back to the beginning: midnight at the Corncrake oasis that ought to be the Nene.

The cows soon lost interest in Gwyn and me, and we were free to continue our trudge along the raised river bank, listening intently for any distant – or close – trace of the raucous rasp. I scarcely dared to hope. On the one hand I felt poised on the edge of history. Any Crake we heard would quite possibly be the first in these parts since before World War II. It would be quite a milestone in conservation; a wonderful justification for the time and effort that has gone into the reintroduction programme so far. To not hear one? A crushing disappointment, obviously.

We heard Lapwings whine, and Redshanks complain, and ducks mutter. But there was no rasping. The only air movement had been issuing from cows, occasionally lightening our mood. As we trudged, and as our conversation became less optimistic, the silences longer, our effort to hear more strained, I cast my mind to the odds against any of 50 of these birds surviving not only the journeys, but also just one summer out there in this wild environment. Well, you probably wouldn't bet money on them, would you? How magical it would be if one would just announce its survival.

The statisticians had estimated a survival rate that should have given us several calling males. By the time we had regrouped with the other search parties, we feared the worst. Someone would have phoned us, to share news of the first Crake. And, well, we could have heard a Corncrake at two miles, in these calm, close conditions.

'Do they know how to sing?' I asked, clutching at straws, slightly, but wondering if perhaps our Crakes actually were out there, just mute, having no experience of other, older Corncrakes teaching them the words, so to speak. There's a well-rehearsed experiment showing how some male songbirds reared in isolation lack the full phraseology of their wild-living counterparts, although they do attempt some vocalisation. The consensus was that the Crake-rasp is 'hard-wired'. They don't need lessons. The clutched straws broke free in my grasp. We called it a night and headed for home, and bed, and dreams of Corncrakes, missing in action. I will return to this story.

Even allowing for the distorting filters and editing suite of memory, it's pretty clear to most people that there are many fewer butterflies around than in the past. The same is true of those other big and obvious insects, the bumblebees. Of 19 UK species, eight are in serious decline and three have been completely extirpated. An RSPB supporter wrote in to make the point that, these days, 'hardly any tiny insects splatter against the windscreen' in the course of a long car journey. 'Twenty or 30 years ago it would have been thickly covered along with other parts of the car with these and some bigger ones: especially moths after dark. What has become of these?'

A lot of people remark on this phenomenon of the now unknown, 'bug-splatted' windscreen. Did cars just become more aerodynamic, or are there really so many fewer insects about nowadays? To try to test the theory, a Big Bug Count was organised, the first to involve the public in trying to work out more about insect populations. Participants were asked to record numbers of insects and other small life forms (now dead forms, of course, and not always insects) stuck to their registration plates after car journeys. It was a valiant attempt, but perhaps one of the more eccentric 'citizen science' projects to have been attempted. Quite how it would produce anything reliable eluded me, much as I would love to know some precise answers to the question of what happened to the insects. My instinct is that this one is key to the wider question of what has happened to our songbirds.

In the autumn I visited Cyprus, at the outset of a project that would seek to address the problem of illegal killing of mostly migrant birds there, which had been an issue for decades and wasn't going away. An estimated 10 million or more birds were being netted on the island each year, mainly in the autumn, as they stream south from Europe to Africa. The scale of the practice had become by now industrial. Huge mist-nets were being slung across specially planted avenues of acacia, and tapes of bird calls played in the darkened early hours to lure passing birds to their doom. Fruit-fattened warblers like Blackcaps and Whitethroats are the preferred quarry; other species are killed and discarded.

Trapped birds are pickled and sold in jars or in restaurants as a delicacy. With Cyprus shaping up to join the EU, conservation could not afford to allow this illicit trade to continue unchecked. It could undermine the credibility of the Birds Directive and its application in other member states, where illegal hunting remained an issue and hunting lobbies are ever-powerful.

In December, government withdrew its proposal to replace the marshes of north Kent with an airport. It was a huge victory for conservation and reprieve for this important wildlife site. It was also a victory for common sense, but government was sticking to its intention of expanding airport capacity, although this seemed to contradict its obligation to cut carbon and other greenhouse gas emissions.

2004

The Starling was still the most recorded bird in the Big Garden Birdwatch held each January, and now participated in by close on half a million people. But this year it was only a third as numerous as in 1979, when the survey began. House Sparrows, meanwhile, had declined by half. One participant in the survey reflected that in the fifties there were still 'sparrow clubs' in Kent villages, with prizes annually not for birds seen, but for the most Sparrows killed. A year later the House Sparrow would overtake the Starling as the bird most commonly seen in gardens. Both species were now red-listed for danger because of the rate of their decline. In February, government announced that both would be taken off most of the general licences that had allowed culling where they were causing a health nuisance or damage to crops.

House Sparrows remain a familiar feature of life in my village, although nowhere near as numerous as in Old Fred's day. The estate that still owns much of the land around, and the farms, rather than selling these off, has let them to family tenants with a tradition of livestock farming. It's a bit of a throwback to an earlier age, and it makes for a diverse landscape. The birds respond in kind. So I've always thought my village a little bit special for wild birds – a chance sanctuary for many of the species in trouble in the wider landscape.

The Tree Sparrow used to be common and widespread, but disappeared from entire regions in just two decades. It was with a peculiar mixture of pride and regret that I now learned from someone who has lived locally all his life, much of it spent searching for birds, that my road was the last place in Bedfordshire where a small colony survived. They held on while entire populations of their kind simply vanished from the surrounding landscape. This refugee population finally dwindled to nought in the early nineties, a few years before I got here. Not that I could have done much to help, I think.

At the start of the year I received some intriguing news: Tree Sparrows had been seen again in the village. They were visiting bird-feeders in gardens in January, including next door. They had also been seen at the disused airfield in a decent-sized flock, and in other nearby locations. Would they be able to recover as a breeding species here? They nest in tree-holes, and will take readily to nest-boxes of suitable size. To help them, a group of us put up about two dozen boxes in a local spinney. We also set up feeders. The spinney is mainly thorn scrub, with some fairly well-developed Ash trees. There are almost no natural nest-holes in the whole area. Tree Sparrows need nest-holes, as a rule, preferably in groups. They also seem to like being near bodies of open water. We aren't too far from the rivers and gravel pits here. So it was just a question of waiting to see if what we had provided would make the difference, and get our Tree Sparrows back where they belong.

Spring marked the 25th anniversary of the Birds Directive. In that time it had put in place a network of 3,000 specially protected areas across the continent, and protected millions of birds from excessive and indiscriminate killing by hunters and trappers. It had come to the rescue of many places which had endured the shadow of destruction hanging over them: a kind of Euro cavalry waiting just over the hill to ride to the rescue at the sounding of an environmentalist's bugle. The EU was growing, with ten more countries joining in May. They too would have to honour this conservation law. All eyes were on Malta and Cyprus, in particular. Indiscriminate shooting and trapping in Malta had caused the extinction of half the island's breeding bird species. Since 1980, 24 bird species had declined by a third across Europe.

Reforms of the CAP were continuing to address some of these losses. All farmers could now access environmental funding to do things like create more unploughed and unsprayed strips of land along hedges and ditches. Hedges would be left to grow between the beginning of March and the end of July. There were measures to stop agrochemicals getting into streams, rivers and other watercourses.

The RSPB reached its centenary in Scotland, and a fitting milestone – Paddy's Milestone – was reached when that landmark became an RSPB nature reserve under an agreement with its owner, the Marquis of Ailsa. It has tens of thousands of Gannets and other nesting seabirds, which had experienced a disastrous breeding season around the UK's coasts. A huge petition was handed in to Downing Street in June calling for better legal protection of the marine environment.

The Scottish centenary had another feather for its cap when more than a thousand Corncrakes were counted in the isles. They had more than doubled since conservation effort kicked in, and most were on nature reserves or land in which farmers and crofters were working to help them. But what of the reintroduction scheme to bring them back to England? A female bird had been seen in June, near a pen in which male birds were being kept, and which were calling. She had evidently been attracted by their calls, enabling the project staff to catch glimpses of her. But would she or any other of the released

Corncrakes be out there, hidden in the thick grasses of the floodplain, actually nesting? And then ... a breakthrough. In August, three juvenile birds were seen together at the release site, indicating that Corncrakes had in fact bred here for the first time in 50 years. More were hatched and released. Later in summer they would attempt the long flight to Africa for the winter, and their return next spring would be anxiously awaited.

The EU turned down an application to grow a GM crop on the continent; a spring oilseed rape plant that had been modified to survive dousing in herbicide. Trials had shown that this crop and its associated herbicide had been bad for wildlife. The USA, Canada and Argentina challenged Europe over its ban on GM crop release into the environment. A panel of experts from the World Trade Organization sat to adjudicate. In politics, George W. Bush defeated Al Gore to retain the US Presidency. Gore was now freed up to pursue his interest in environmental issues.

On Christmas Day 2004 not many people could have told you what a tsunami was. On Boxing Day an earthquake somewhere below the Indian Ocean created the giant waves that devastated coastal regions of Indonesia, India and islands across the region. A week later I was in the middle of this ocean, to work for a year with the RSPB's partner organisation in Seychelles.

I signed up for this posting partly because I wanted to know how a country really works, at a scale I could grasp. And maybe also then how the world works. How the world *could* work, living within its means. Seychelles has an impressive environmental track record. It still looks intact, ecologically. It has saved some species from the brink of extinction. It is a developing country, with an enviable record in health care, literacy and standards of living. It has to do this sustainably; everyone there can see the physical limits of their environment. I wanted to know more.

2005

New year dawn broke over the Indian Ocean and I blew in as might a vagrant bird on the north-west monsoon: the weather system that prevails between October and April. It provides a tailwind if you happen to be heading this way from Europe in this half of the year. Seychelles is well outside the flight path of most migrant birds, which tend to stick quite sensibly to major land masses like Africa and minimise sea-crossing distances. But a few species think nothing of the hop to Seychelles, and a few others turn up randomly, having been blown off course or perhaps had some failure of their navigational instrumentation, as yet not fully comprehended by humanity.

I descended on the main island Mahe between towers of tropical rain cloud swaddling the mountains. Dazzled and dazed in the airport queue, I defrosted in the greenhouse warmth. Sun shafts pierced the cloud, and raindrops glistened on waxy leaves. Granite monoliths glinted, projecting above the forest canopy, curved and fluted, melted by millennia, dark and streaky, like fibreglass props from a low-budget B-movie set in the land that time forgot. A tiny, orange-red bird with dark glasses flitted onto a banana leaf beyond the glass. Madagascar Fody, long since through this immigration lark.

A T-shirt stood out in the duty-free queue. *Saving the Seychelles Magpie-robin*, it read. *BirdLife Seychelles*. Bizarrely, I produced that garment nearly 10 years ago, in my first job with the RSPB. Not the wordiest editing job in the world, I reflected; but less, as they say, is more. And less then is certainly more now, where Magpie-robins are concerned. I hoped that T-shirt has played its part in the recovery. I couldn't wait to meet these birds, and all the others, and help them some more. I first got to know about the Seychelles environment as a volunteer newsletter editor at the Cambridge office of BirdLife, back in 1994, when I produced the bilingual *Bulletin Afrique*, pulling together reports from different partners in Africa, including here, and Uganda.

We took the steep former coastal road that links the airport, constructed in 1971 on reclaimed land in the south-east of the island, to the main and practically only town, Victoria. The main road that makes this link had been closed. I could soon see why. The tsunami's backwash had sucked the foundations from under the road bridge across the main channel that links the man-made lagoon with the open ocean. The wreckage was spectacular. The streets of the town were still littered with ocean debris – lumps of coral and strands of weed – where the waves had gone walkabout, mercifully just a few feet high by the time they reached here.

I would hear many tales of the tsunami in the days ahead. The night before, my colleagues on the small offshore islands, including Cousin, had noticed lizards and hermit crabs climbing into trees. In the morning, the sea mysteriously retreated, to the bewilderment of everyone. Most people's instinct was to stay clear of the beaches, but some went out to collect stranded fish, or for the unique opportunity to examine and photograph exposed corals. It seems obvious now, but the sea of course was soon to come back. It returned in a sequence of remorseless waves, none of them with anything like the power and height unleashed on Indonesia, for example, but nevertheless extensive damage was done to boats, vehicles, properties near the shoreline. Some people here died from their injuries. It was a chilling reminder of nature's raw and unpredictable power, and the fragility of economies like this one.

Ten thousand years aren't many, in the context of a planet aged 4.6 billion years. It's the bat of an eye in the context of a lifetime. And it is within that eye-bat that Britain has become isles, since the last ice age, the thawing of which created the English Channel. In the same meagre geological period, Seychelles has gone from having a land area larger than the British Isles to its current scattering in the middle of the Indian Ocean.

The largest of its islands, Mahe, spans five miles at its widest, by 20 miles north to south. That it is a kilometre high at its peak gives it its larger feel, gives it more land area, more diversity, more rain, and so much more than the beaches and palms that are the most – and sometimes, you feel, only – projected image of the country.

These last peaks of the former land mass are a thousand miles from other lands, and many thousands of years, in evolutionary terms, from the land masses they used to join, that now compose India, Madagascar and Africa. These factors contribute to making Seychelles so unusual, with many unique specimens within its flora and fauna. They also contribute to its having limited resources and a precarious existence. The population of 80,000 is less than that of Grimsby.

Most of these people live on Mahe, but there are around 40 other inner granitic islands, so-called because of their base of continental rock – another feature making it unique among oceanic islands. One of these other islands is Cousin, where it all began here for RSPB/BirdLife. Cousin was purchased in the late sixties, after that appeal to raise £50,000. This was done to save unique species on the very brink of extinction.

My year in Seychelles conservation would make a book in its own right, if I ever have time to write it. Of the 100,000 words I compiled as a blog for the RSPB through the year, I wrote this in my diary:

I washed up on a 'desert' island, dropped here in a boat, on a carefully chosen breaker. The island is two miles across, a kinked hoop of bleached sand separating ocean from forest. It's part of an archipelago, a thousand miles from India, and from Africa. A wake of Ghost Crabs formed and parted as I made my way across hot sand to the top of the beach.

Seychelles. The very word conjures instant images of purity, as though it were selected for its echo of sea breeze, shell sand, surf. In fact, Seychelles was a sailor. It is perhaps for the best that Captain Pugwash didn't get here first.

I reached the trees and found that none are the palms of myth. The one-time coconut plantation has been replaced by native species like Pisonia. And the birds that long depended on this tropical island are now restored to them too. Welcome to Cousin Island.

This was my early glimpse beyond the colour supplement image of paradise. What these can't show is how the tropics seeks to combine your juices with its own, until your mind is in continuum with its slow-cooker heat. Onshore breezes bring scant relief. The air is even thicker amid the greenish tints of the forest interior. The aroma is physical, taste-able, like a pet shop: part sweat, part dung, part pheromone. It sounds like a pet shop too, oscillating at the edge of vision. The ground around my sandals converged, as hermit crabs and skinks tiptoed and sashayed towards me.

A Giant Tortoise staggered forward, a living link between geology and biology: animate boulder, time-smoothed, sun-dried lump of the granite mountain top beneath us, with sprouted tanned leather neck and limb. It peered weepily, mouthing noiselessly, like the toothless, mummified ghost of the succession of human forms it has encountered here in the last two centuries: navigators, pirates, castaways, smugglers, plantation workers, conservation volunteers, eco-tourists ... While the Tortoise moved in slow motion, the nesting Fairy Terns and Tropicbirds just looked knackered.

I stumbled on a scattered party of Ruddy Turnstones poking around in the flaky leaf-litter – the very same scurrying, plover-like birds that feed and breed on the brutal, rugged coastlines of northern Europe. Who knew? It's like I'd rumbled them, on a crafty holiday, on the skive. I bet they hadn't turned a stone since they got here.

I met the fabled Magpie-robin, the nearly-Dodo, one of the great success stories of conservation, of extinction averted. It's a species that was reduced to almost single figures on just one island here. A few were moved to the restored Cousin, and have thrived. Restoration also involved removal of anything mammalian – rats, mainly – against which these docile, trusting natives have no chance.

Like its fellow islanders, *Pi Santez* – as it's known in Kreol – came to check me out. Perched there in black and white, it was all too easy to imagine it as a museum exhibit, in this dingy, stuffy archive of a place. But then life ignited: the Magpie-robin angled its head, riffled its tail, then arrowed down to my feet, snatched an insect and returned to its perch.

But the best, most Alice-in-Wonderland moment, was yet to come. I stepped over a tree trunk and an animal – by this I mean a hairy animal – bolted from under my feet, and slalomed off through the trees.

What the ...?

It was the only furred, fast and running away thing I've encountered. Surely not a rat? Not that big? That would be a disastrous development. No, if I'd had to stick my neck out on this, I'd say it was, of all things, a hare.

I replayed the befuddling image of the streaking beast in my head as I walked back to the volunteer hut. I wondered whether I should even mention this to anyone. They might think I'd got the fever, the *grippe*.

I could just hear them. 'You think you saw a *hare*? On a *desert island*?'

Choosing my moment, I had a quiet word with Catherina, who leads eco-tours.

'Ah yes!' she laughed. 'There are some castaway hares still out there. We don't talk much about them. You were lucky – not many people have ever seen one!'

Alice in Wonderland did say, that of all her tea party guests, 'The March Hare will be much the most interesting. And perhaps,' she added, 'as this is May, it won't be raving mad – at least not so mad as it was in March.'

Or as mad – I might add – as it looked in paradise. Hares, I learned, were imported as a source of food for plantation workers, decades ago. They have survived all the restoration work since. I still smile to recall that Robinson Crusoe hare. You'd think by now, in paradise restored, it might have learned to relax a little.

I returned to the UK for three weeks in May, which meant I could vote in the general election. Tony Blair's Labour government was duly elected for its third and what would be final term of office. Britain had already started to look different to me although I'd only been in the tropics for four months. I had a new appreciation for its cool, fresh air, its seasonal uncertainties. To be suddenly dropped into the month of May – always my favourite month – was a special treat. The sound of a Wren singing lustily, and unseen, in a north London street in the half-light of dawn on the first day back will stay with me for a long time. I had encountered many special birds abroad, but the sounds of a northern springtime, the defining cues of the seasons, I had missed in fundamental ways. I understood what playwright Dennis Potter meant when he spoke about finally, really, 'seeing the blossom' – in his case he never truly saw it, appreciated it, he acknowledged, until he knew he was dying.

I visited family in Scotland and in a Perthshire glen I stopped on my bike as Swallows swooped northward on a fresh breeze, a Cuckoo wobbled on an overhead wire, a Stonechat abused it and, to cap it all, a Red Kite cruised overhead, glinting auburn in the sun, the first I'd seen of these birds reintroduced in this, my old stamping ground. And in that moment I felt more strongly than ever that I was doing something worthwhile with my life.

On the way back to Seychelles I spent a few days in Nairobi with our partner organisation Nature Kenya working on projects there. There was time for a short tour of the National Park on the fringes of the sprawling city. May is rainy season, and the cool temperatures and spits of rain, while refreshing for me, were enough to keep the Lions and other mega-fauna tucked away, out of sight. We passed trucks-full of bemused tourists. 'Have you seen anything?' they would ask us, glumly. But the conditions made for a feast of birds – Kenya has around 2,000 species.

So what had been happening back home? With the coming of spring, for the first time all farmers in England could access funds to help wildlife on farms. But there was bad news too. It was reported that genes from the GM crop trials of two years earlier had leaked into the environment. In a follow-up study, modified genes from the trial crops were found to be present in the wild plant Charlock, in a field used for the trials. The affected plants were visibly different from the other Charlock plants around them. Furthermore, when the relevant weed-killer was applied to them, they didn't flinch.

Seeds from other plant species were collected and raised as plants in a laboratory, as scientists carried out further tests on possible gene leakage. Two of these were also found to be resistant to the herbicides. Charlock seeds can lie dormant in soil for decades, and would therefore be practically impossible to control as a 'super-weed' if present in the environment.

Canada was said at this time to be beset with 'super-weed' problems. There, modified oilseed rape plants had spilled out into the wider countryside and other crops. Having cross-pollinated with different varieties of modified plants, they had inherited resistance to as many as three types of herbicide. Controlling them outside of their field of origin had become impossible, except when the old-school, highly toxic herbicides were brought back and redeployed. It seemed that GM technology was turning the clock back, and creating as many, if not more, problems for agriculture as it was solving.

The loss of natural services globally was reckoned to be costing the planet 250 billion dollars a year. More effort was needed to meet targets to cut emissions. The 15 years since 1990 had included the ten warmest years on record. There were strong symptoms of the change in the behaviour of birds, which were by now breeding an average of eight days earlier than around the time of *Silent Spring*. North American Swallows were arriving 12 days earlier than as recently as 1980.

The UK was one of just a few countries that met the original 2000 target for emissions reductions set at Rio in 1992. New targets had been set in 1997, however, when it became clear that this wouldn't be enough, with mounting evidence that the pace of warming might be faster than previously thought. Effects on wildlife were already being detected. Meltdown of Greenland and Antarctic ice sheets seemed more likely, with possible knock-on effects on the oceanic currents and airstreams that moderate the climate of the UK and Europe. This protocol came into force in February after Russia signed up in December, joining the EU, Japan and Canada.

Charities pooled resources and formed a united front on climate change campaigning. Stop Climate Chaos was formed, combining environmental organisations with new partners including Oxfam, Christian Aid and the Women's Institute. The G8 Summit was held at the Gleneagles Hotel in Perthshire, Scotland. It produced little tangible progress on tackling emissions.

International media headlines surrounded an outbreak of bird flu in Asia, associated with domestic and other captive birds. The spread of the virus to Eastern Europe could also be linked to the movement of livestock. Nevertheless, some people were quick to point the finger at wild birds, and to call for controls on the movement of migrant birds too. Wild birds and their movements are visible, of course. What most people would have no idea of was the extent of the international movement of birds in crates and cages, from poultry to wild-caught birds. Even governments seemed to be having difficulty in keeping tabs on the extent of this trade. With the industry now under close scrutiny, it was a little troubling that conservationists seemed to know more about the movements of migrant wild birds than the authorities did about the transportation of those in vehicles.

With attention firmly fixed on them, it became apparent how much of a threat the wild-bird trade was still posing, and now to human as well as avian health. Logic suggests that sick wild birds might struggle to travel any great distance. Nature also has some quick and effective ways of removing birds from the environment as soon as they aren't quite at it – via predation, for example. Sick birds in cages, meanwhile, can traverse the globe in a matter of hours.

A small number of finch-like birds from Taiwan were thought to have brought bird flu to the UK. These were just one tiny example of the million or more wild-caught birds still being brought into the EU every year. There were restrictions on the species that could be bought and sold this way, but many of those being traded were still being taken with little regard to or monitoring of the impact this was having on wild populations.

There were outbreaks of bird flu in Africa and in India, each case linked to poultry movements. The bird flu factor added another strong reason for banning the wild bird trade altogether, on top of the welfare and conservation arguments. The UK government supported a temporary ban on the import of wild birds to the EU. Could the ban be made permanent? 'Shining a light on the trade in wild birds has made governments think again about why they permit such a squalid industry,' the RSPB reflected.

Word was coming through that the beautiful Bali Starling, formerly known as Rothschild's Mynah, had become extinct in the wild. Its beauty had made it much coveted as a cage bird. Now there were only caged ones in existence. Forest birds in places like Indonesia are often hard to see, because of where they live and how they live. They are not so hard to hear, however, other than against the din of other birds also singing and calling. But this was one less voice in the chorus of the forests.

* * *

One of the birds you find in Seychelles and nowhere else – if you are lucky, and up late – is its Scops Owl, in the high mist-forests. Locals call it the *Syer* – which means 'woodcutter' – because it makes a spooky, nocturnal sawing sound, a ghostly echo of early colonists. They have a saying here: 'You don't saw the branch you sit on.' Early settlers tried deforestation. The steep mountainsides promptly shed their soil in the tropical downpours. Today the trees are back – not, in many cases, the original species, but soil-stabilising trees nonetheless. Like the Magpie-robin, the *Syer*'s situation is no longer classed as critical.

Like the Warbler and Robin populations we worked to save, Nature Seychelles has grown steadily in recent years. It had recently moved to its new Environment and Education Centre just south of Victoria, the capital. A medicinal plants garden and nursery was being developed, and beyond the wall a wetland sanctuary. It had been a little neglected, but we were sorting it out for wildlife and visitors – safe access, interpretation, and viewing facilities. We shared the base with the Wildlife Clubs of Seychelles, which has over 30 clubs, and growing. With growth of this kind comes a commitment to finding cash, a serious challenge for non-government organisations in uncertain economic times.

Eleven per cent of the world's bird species are classed as endangered. The success stories in Seychelles, the world in microcosm, have offered hope and inspiration against this bleak backdrop. The continued existence of Magpie-robins, Hawksbill Turtles, other marine life, is living proof of a kind that it is living sustainably. The one major blight here is the damage that has been done to its coral reefs, bleached and disintegrated by sea-warming events over which it has no control, and which reflect global changes. The RSPB and its BirdLife partners are doing all they can to ensure that the bigger world is watching, and taking note.

Elsewhere, heightened fears had begun to be expressed about what was happening to our younger generations, and their increasing dislocation from the natural world, from an outdoors no longer accessible to many, or not considered worthy of exploration, or safe to inhabit. An important book was published in the USA about this gathering disconnection of children from the natural environment in the modern world. *Last Child in the Woods*, by Richard Louw, coined a new term for this phenomenon – Nature Deficit Disorder. James R. Miller applied the term 'shifting baseline syndrome' to an 'environmental generational amnesia' – each generation knowing less about what it had lost or was losing than the last. This leads to a 'continual ratcheting down of expectations', and ultimately to the 'extinction of experience'. Some said that kids in inner-city America might be more likely to identify a gun from its report than a bird by its call.

A far cry from Seychelles. As my year here neared its end I was invited to the International School one morning to address the assembly. I was to talk to the children about birds, and conservation. This was quite a big crowd, by local standards, and I gave the assignment due preparation, with a carefully constructed presentation, and a few note-cards for reference. I arrived bright and early, and a little apprehensive, to set up. In due course a school-full of pupils had filed in, and taken up position on the floor of the hall. There were children of all ages and nationalities, pre-school to about 12, I estimated. Sue the Head Teacher brought the throng to attention, and I was introduced.

It can be difficult to judge the level at which to pitch a presentation. The range of ages now in front of me emphasised this point, so I tried to assume no knowledge in my audience; make it accessible, usually a smart idea. I was backed up by some visual aids, and began by clicking through some appealing images of local wildlife, asking questions of the onlookers, gauging what they knew. Up came the Magpie-robin picture.

'Anyone know what this one is?' I ventured. One of the older children put her hand up. 'Magpie-robin!' she announced, happily, and of course accurately. 'Very good!' I replied, encouragingly. This was going OK. If in doubt, have a quiz. I carried on with the Q&A format.

'OK, who knows what the word "extinct" means?' I asked. There was a little boy near the front, I'd guess about four years old. He had been putting his hand up each time, fit to burst, not quite clicking his fingers, the way kids used to do at my school, much to the chagrin of my old teachers, but not far off.

'What's your name?' I asked him.

'Nelson!' he screeched.

'OK, Nelson,' I replied. 'What do we mean when we call something extinct?'

Nelson didn't hesitate. 'Dead!' he yelled.

'Ha ha! Ya, good,' I replied to the group. 'But it's more than that. More than just dead. What is it?' His hand shot up again. I glanced at Sue. She looked a bit uneasy. But I had to give Nelson another crack.

'OK, you again, Nelson.'

'Really, really SMELLY!'

Things unravelled a little after that. Some kids were now standing up and starting to mill around a bit. Sue intervened. Like a hypnotist, she snapped the throng back to attention in a handclap. Standing at the front, she assumed the position, arms bent at her sides, and – flapping – launched into song.

'Chick-chick-chick-chick chick-ennn, lay a little egg for me ...'

The assembly, to a child, was instantly on its feet, singing along, wafting elbows.

My work here was finished.

A short time later, hall now empty, I packed up, still chuckling, life affirmed. *Teach Your Child to Wonder*, Rachel Carson called another of her books. I returned to the office hoping – just hoping – that I'd helped teach a few children to wonder.

2006

Early in the new year I left Seychelles behind, with a fortnight to revisit East Africa. The dawn brought with it a profound feeling of relief and liberation. It carried a sense of homecoming too, for me. We think of Africa as resolutely hot but I woke in a room that had the delicious sensation of great space and of coolness, of heavy blankets, and freshness, after the perpetual cloying air of the Seychellois tropics. It had rained almost constantly for the last monsoon month. I felt as though I might decompose there. Now I was in a house called Trees, high on a plateau overlooking the Rift Valley; beyond it in the haze, somewhere to the west, my Ugandan birthplace. Between me and it lay a carefully tended garden, a row of spectacular flowers beyond a lawn, busy with sunbirds, and on the grass a bird that lingered long enough to permit me time to find it in the book. A Cape Robin Chat. The first new bird I'd met in months. Seychelles has one type of sunbird, Kenya about three dozen. I felt a little like I'd been freed from house arrest.

I'd been brought by colleagues from Nature Kenya. We came here from Nairobi in the dead of night, to huddle round a fire. You can regulate a cold body. It isn't always possible to cool a hot one, as I'd found in Seychelles. I went with Joshua Wambugu to visit a project in the local town. Project Leader Simon Joachim guided us on foot across what felt like half the plateau. It is a part agricultural landscape with figures, a pre-industrial scene, with people cycling, carrying branches in baskets, walking with carts and animals. There were birds galore, including Widow-birds with enormous streamer tails draped across brush, Fiscal Shrikes, and a bird we are trying to save here – Sharp's Longclaw, a species on the edge of extinction.

I moved closer to Uganda – a tented site at Crater Lake. A sleeping volcano forms a natural amphitheatre, a forest and green lake within a perfect bowl, spangled with Flamingos and presided over by magisterial Fish Eagles. But that's as close to my birthplace as time and my budget would allow. I visited Lake Naivasha a short distance away, where agrochemicals from the local market gardens supplying Europe with cut flowers were threatening to ruin the very lake that is the lifeblood here. Feelings were running high, and in recent days an activist had been murdered.

My return to Britain coincided with the circus surrounding the arrival of a US vagrant – an American Robin, supporting the theory that everything's bigger in the USA, even the robins. Over-sized (we're talking Blackbird-scale), over-fed, perhaps, and now, you've guessed it, over here. Ladies and gentlemen, y'all welcome … the American Robin. Just arrived in sarf London.

It recalled for me the mechanical Robin that made a cameo appearance at the end of David Lynch's film *Blue Velvet*. It landed on the windowsill of Jeffrey's kitchen. It had a live beetle writhing in its bill; an enduring image and, like many of Lynch's movie moments, a slightly puzzling, unsettling one.

Jeffrey's girlfriend Sandy in the movie had dreamed of Robins coming down to Earth from the heavens, as salvation of a kind, so I suppose Lynch's faux Robin represented a synthetic happy ending to a very disturbing run of events in Lumberton, which began with Jeffrey's discovery of an ear in a patch of waste ground. You could say that it was something of a London birder's dream that one of these birds – a real one – turned up in Peckham.

I've never been moved to go and see a bird that is lost. Mostly I feel a bit sorry for it, and hope that those who turn out for 'twitches' are motivated partly by compassion. But by anyone's definition of interestingness, it's pretty interesting when an American Robin turns up in London. It's so interesting, in fact, that even the tabloid news desks were animated by the happening. It's not like them to do ornithology, as a rule, but on this occasion they worked out that not only was this a once-in-a-lifetime event – the first American Robin ever recorded in London – but it also attracted a large number of ripe-for-ridicule 'twitcher' types to Peckham Rye seeking to add the bird – *Turdus migratorius* (puh-lease) – to their lists.

I returned to the RSPB to resume duties. The loggers had moved in and begun to harvest the conifer tree plantations around The Lodge, the RSPB having at last been able to purchase this land after an appeal and Lottery funding, and add it to the nature reserve. I was pitched straight back into the ceaseless quest for grant funding of this kind from trusts and foundations. This included raising some of the money needed to buy a piece of the Norfolk Broads – one of the most biodiverse places in the UK. It is also one of the places most threatened by rising sea levels. Salt-water inundation might change it beyond recognition, rendering it uninhabitable for the species that make it so unique. We secured it, and announced this gem of a place, where Cranes were returning to breed after centuries of absence, as the RSPB's 200th nature reserve.

Ten years had elapsed since the year I spent in the previous village I called home, and 100 since *Wind in the Willows*. I went back there to see if the Water Voles had survived, one bright, breezy day in early April. Ten years is a long time in weed-growth terms. This year's surge of nettles had just started, through a tangle of dry stems. So, plenty of vole cover at least. I carefully walked the bank, and could see on the opposite side what looked like vole tracks, droppings – and yes, even burrow entrances, both in the mud of the brook itself, and higher up. And then a tell-tale splosh, and a swish of mud, and the distinctive shadow of a vole shooting downstream.

That was my only glimpse, but I'm delighted to report that the banks on both sides were once again pockmarked with holes and laced with vole pathways. There is something about this little stretch of brook that works for Water Voles, and keeps them going when they have gone completely from all but one in ten of their former haunts. Water Voles occur on a fifth of the RSPB's nature reserves, and thrive in carefully managed reedbeds. From such safe havens they might be able to spread and recolonise well-managed wetland systems elsewhere. I was also very pleased to note on my visit a little plume of smoke from up by the cottage, issuing from the unmistakeable form of Old Frank. No sign of the cat, mind you.

It also meant a chance to check out the hedgerow I had planted back then. I was thrilled to find that it dwarfed me. I walked its length, examining its colourful medley of leaf types, stems and barks. Its Hawthorn buds were set to burst, the Mayflower having become the Aprilflower in times of climate change. A skittish Yellowhammer was absorbed in its midst.

Hand-reared Cirl Buntings were released in Cornwall, to try to re-establish the species there. I went to Devon, to look at some land we hoped to purchase there as a reserve for the species. The name Labrador Bay doesn't really prepare you for the landscape ahead. I had images of exuberant canines bounding through sandy shallows, and the curve of a bleached strand. The road to it is flanked by trees that screen the clifftops and disguise the drop to the exposed rocks and grits of the Jurassic shoreline way below.

A car park with an optimistic ice-cream vendor overlooked the pasture, thin hedges and barley, and the ocean beyond. It was an intermittently rain-swept afternoon, and I enjoyed discovering the dramatic folds and slopes of the landscape between here and the cliff edge. I ducked squalls of rain thrown from seaward in the lee of hedges, which were themselves in places bent in a permanent gesture of submission. I was joined in sheltering by one of the Cirl Buntings. They like it here, although the rest of southern England has pretty much lost their interest. It is the Yellowhammer's cousin, with spicier colours and a bolder headdress. Familiar in Tuscany, still, if no longer on these shores. I was chided by it, churlishly so. I was obviously less objectionable than the passing squall. 'Cirl' comes from the Italian 'cirlar' – to chirp. Squall passed, it surfed off on the wind.

A pair of Kestrels continued to hunt, poignant against the grey-jade sea, pinned to the gale. A Buzzard rode it out too, then buckled like a sheet of card, then regained control. A bulky Sycamore clung to the clifftop, low-forked trunks adding girth, scars of a mouse's incisors perhaps when this monster was a seedling. Perhaps by now, with the surf crashing way below beyond the verdure, the clifftop was clinging to it.

I hadn't picked a typical day for this visit to the south-west. It was another very dry summer, with water shortages and impacts on wetlands. A series of extreme weather events (New Orleans was still reeling from Hurricane Katrina) and furnace-hot summers in the midwestern USA made timely the release of the film of Al Gore's book – *An Inconvenient Truth*. 'What changed in the United States with Hurricane Katrina was a feeling that we have entered a period of consequences,' he said. It was getting warmer everywhere: every year since 1997 had been among the warmest recorded for the planet as a whole.

Pressure was mounting to harness more wind energy, but it was critical that turbines should only be constructed in appropriate places. The RSPB had involvement with 430 wind-farm proposals, objecting to much less than a tenth of them. It would be self-defeating to ruin important wildlife sites in the rush to erect turbines. Wind-farm developments in Norway, for example, were known to have killed several White-tailed Eagles and caused others to desert their traditional territories.

And what of protected areas? With three years to go these were roughly three-quarters of the way to achieving the 2010 target set to get these places back into favourable condition in England. In Wales the picture was much less encouraging, with only around a third having been restored. Scotland's target was to have 80% favourable by 2008. With two years to go they'd reached 67%. Figures weren't yet available for Northern Ireland.

Progress was being made on the great House Sparrow mystery. A study revealed that many young Sparrows were starving in the nest in summer, hinting at a scarcity of insect food like beetles, crane flies and aphids. Nothing fancy, just the kind of beasts you find where there is grass, broadleaf plants and shrubs. These simple but vital fragments of nature are lost to creeping urbanisation and the effacement of garden space to new builds and car parks. I see it happening everywhere. One day the slabs and piles of sand arrive, and the skip. The pavement kerb is dropped, the front garden is dug out and the carport put in. Piece by piece the ground is lost to the worship of the motor vehicle, nature is quietly entombed and smothered.

In the autumn I visited friends in New York and Boston, to witness the astonishing 'fall' of migrant birds funnelling down the eastern seaboard and through Central Park. I saw Peregrine Falcons among the avian multitude, restored now not only to this wild coast and its vast wetlands through which the NYC–Boston train passes, but also to the cities themselves. I looked out across the Sound of Maine, towards the rocky coastline at Newagen, unaware at the time that it was here Rachel Carson's ashes had been cast to the wind.

2007

We had reached the centenary of Rachel Carson's birth. Edward O. Wilson gave the keynote speech at a special conference held in Pittsburgh in her honour. There were many other centennial initiatives in the States to mark and celebrate the moment. But not everyone joined in. When a Democrat Senator tried to submit a resolution celebrating Carson's legacy, the move was blocked by a Republican opponent on the grounds of what he called 'the junk science and stigma surrounding DDT'.

A mere ten years had passed since I moved to this village. Ten years aren't many, in the context of a planet 4.6 billion years old. But when you consider that it has taken just 200 or so years – as that Greenpeace leaflet put it – for 'modern man to make a rubbish tip of paradise', then a decade starts to feel a little more significant; especially in terms of the restoration of that paradise, piece by piece.

This truth hit me between the eyes when I unearthed photographs taken ten years before, in my first year. It's always instructive to revisit such moments 'frozen' in time. The memory can't really be relied upon, after all. I may know that the front garden was then a carport – and goodness knows I got well enough acquainted with it in the course of its restoration to garden – but pictures really bring home what's changed.

I wrote about the launch of this modest garden restoration scheme back then, under the heading 'Putting the life back'. My aim at the time of designing and planting was simply to create a hedge-lined enclave of flower-rich lawn/meadow, with wild borders of plants like Lavender, Hollyhock, Ox-eye and Red Campion. I loved the idea of lifting the lid on the oppressed soil below, liberating it and the seeds within, and guiding the progress of the plants. A piece of the countryside, in miniature, would emerge: idealised, perhaps, but why not. I trained climbers against the house, and over an archway to the front door, which now frames the narrow entrance to the scene. And yes, it is transformed again to something wildlife can inhabit, and that soothes the senses and the mind when gazed at or walked among.

So far, it has afforded safe nesting places for Robins in most years, as well as Blackbird, Song Thrush and Blue Tit. The Hawthorn hedgerows down each side, already bearing autumn fruit, will soon be stout enough for Chaffinch, Dunnock, Long-tailed tit and others to build in. I began the delicate task of laying the hedges, cutting the stems part-way through, to lay the plants at an angle, making a denser core, a better structure for wildlife. Several Ash trees have risen from the front hedge, which is mixed. I hang feeders off one, where Sparrows and finches hold conference.

Hedgehogs have been regular evening visitors, and I have watched Bank Voles, Wood Mice, Weasels, and once a young Brown Hare, which crouched in refuge as dog walkers passed by on the pavement side. And some kind of milestone was passed when the garden hosted a very cute and tiny Rabbit for a few weeks.

Back in the photo album, I was delighted to note that the fields opposite are also different now. And it occurred to me that as well as the direct impact I've been able to make at a micro, domestic level, as any wildlife gardener might, I had also effected – albeit less directly – some of the macro changes beyond the hedge. The same claim can be made – quite justifiably and proudly – by any RSPB staff member, volunteer and supporter. I am all three, as it happens. The fact that the field opposite now had a 6-metre margin all around it, and burgeoning hedgerows, to name just two features of green farming subsidy schemes that we have worked so long and hard to establish, is in large part down to the likes of us, alongside our partners in farming, of whom there is now a small army.

Further afield there were saplings rising, hedges sprouting, beetle banks, ditch-banks, buffer strips, new ponds, set-aside fields, and stubbles in winter: all features that have been tailored to provide for the needs of threatened birds – the need for food and water, year-round, and safe places to breed. There might even be patches left bare in the crops for Skylarks and others to nest in. It was hard to tell, from the edges, but I hoped so. Conservationists have shown that these work, and cost little.

A Corn Bunting has jangled each spring from a neighbouring wire throughout the past decade. Yellowhammer, Turtle Dove, Grey Partridge, Yellow Wagtail, Cuckoo, Bullfinch, Lapwing: I could still hear them all locally, clinging on. And, the one I was still daring to hope would come back to breed – the Tree Sparrow. They had now been turning up in our gardens, sharing the seed dispensers with the resident species. Another pair had stayed until early springtime, but departed then to wherever it is they still and currently bred.

At roughly a hundred square metres, this revived patch of the Earth's skin wasn't on its own going to halt climate change, or prevent flooding, or local extinctions. But I remained optimistic that, between us – those who manage landscapes, and those of us who merely garden – we could make it all fit for Tree Sparrows once again; and if we could sort them out, why not the Linnets too, and the Spotted Flycatchers, and the rest.

The Biodiversity Action Plan had also passed its tenth anniversary. Its list of species was revised. There had been 26 bird species on the original list, the new list had 59. House Sparrow, Starling, Lesser Spotted Woodpecker and Cuckoo were among the new species now requiring special attention.

After decades of slog and controversy, the import of wild birds for the pet trade was finally banned in July, from all 27 countries in the EU. The decision was taken largely because of bird flu. The decision would boost the conservation of as many as 55 species as a result, and put an end to the suffering and enormous loss of life of these and many other bird species in transit. It was thought that as many as 2 million wild birds might now avoid the fate of being trapped, caged and exported, as a result of the ban. Tony Blair had been a keen supporter of the ban, in one of his last acts as Prime Minister. Chancellor Gordon Brown became Prime Minister following Blair's resignation after ten years at the top. The words 'credit crunch' were about to enter the vocabulary, with the collapse of some prominent banking institutions.

European law remained fundamental to tackling unlawful hunting in the Mediterranean. It seemed ironic therefore that there were more recorded crimes against wildlife in the UK in the middle years of this decade than ever before. This included some very high-profile cases, which caused great controversy and no little embarrassment on the estates in question.

It was the 15th anniversary of the Habitats Directive, a chance for a modest celebration of the network of protected areas it had created across Europe. It had enabled a number of battles to be fought and won to protect the best sites from destruction and loss. It had also made funds available to protect species like Corncrake and Bittern, and to work on priority habitats like native pine forests, heaths and reedbeds. Of course not everyone was supportive of these very effective measures to protect the environment. There was pressure from some sectors of industry and governments to weaken the directive.

Government figures on bird populations were released which showed a 'north–south divide' emerging in England. But unlike the economic schism that was much talked about in Thatcher's eighties, this one had riches split the opposite way. South-east England was bottom of the regional league table. Wild birds on farmland there had declined by more than a quarter in just three years. Hearteningly, the north and east had actually recorded some modest increases.

A taxi driver asked me about these headlines. He had recently sold up his pub business in east London, having witnessed the steady decline of the family-run pub, and bought a place in Norfolk. His love of nature, dormant for years, was now flourishing, he told me, grinning. He had picked up on the north–south divide coverage, and wanted to know what was behind it. The figures more or less reflected the presence or otherwise of high-productivity arable farmland. There was also thought to be a trace of climate change behind them. Overall figures now showed that wild birds breeding on farmland in England had reached an all-time low. And there was further disturbing news, as Europe announced the abolition of the set-aside scheme. This had required all arable farms to leave some fields out of production. Nothing was being put in place to compensate wildlife for the loss of the relative benefits set-aside had offered.

Bali hosted the latest climate conference. Twenty years on from Live Aid, the Live Earth benefit concerts were held in different places, attempting to limit the carbon 'footprint' of the event, and offset these in some way. Scientists predicted that, without action to reduce global emissions, a quarter of the world's land-living species would be committed to extinction by 2050. The *Climatic Atlas of European Breeding Birds* was published, showing how populations would be affected by changing temperatures and weather patterns. A Climate Change Bill was announced in the Queen's Speech.

2008

All the world's governments had committed themselves to slowing or halting biodiversity loss by 2010. But the reluctance to commit trivial sums in the context of national budgets meant a growing recognition that these targets were almost certain to be missed. To maintain the protected area network needed to safeguard 90% of Africa's biodiversity would cost less than one billion dollars a year. In a typical year the global community was providing less than a third of this amount.

There was a stark message at the heart of *State of the World's Birds*, published at BirdLife International's World Conference in Buenos Aires. 'Because birds are found almost everywhere on earth, they can act as our eyes and ears, and what they are telling us is that the deterioration in biodiversity and the environment is accelerating, not slowing,' Dr Mike Rands, BirdLife's Chief Executive, announced.

The landscape of Northern Ireland is laced with hedgerows at much greater density than we are now used to elsewhere. Within them, the reseeded pasture greens remain fresh in late summer, under regular rains that frame respites of warm sunlight. Ruined farms dot the scene with history, eyeless husk monuments to our forebears, sometimes still slate-roofed and modest in scale beside the relative sprawl of pale, pebble-dashed bungalows.

I was back for a family gathering. The hillside here steamed gently as I picked my way around the 'sheugch' – a word Dad and Mum have always used for the mixture of cowpat, rainwater and mud that inhabits such terrain, and lays in wait for the unwary boot. The onomatopoeia of entrapment and release is clear, and evocative. Dad often spoke fondly about the Mountains of the Moon, and the Mourne Mountains, and as a young child I thought them one and the same mythical place. The former I now know to be the Rwenzoris of Uganda. The Mournes, meanwhile, hug the southern horizon here, as though bursting clear of the patchwork bedspread around them.

Somewhere between me and there, two dozen juvenile Red Kites had just been released to the winds, to a landscape that hasn't included them for many decades. I scanned the sky, in vain hope of an early glimpse. The throaty croak of two Ravens tumbling was some kind of reward.

The crumbling cottage on this hill's crest was my great-great-uncle's. It has been in the family since the mid-eighteenth century, when it was tenanted. My maternal grandfather was born here about a century ago. Empty since the war, it has withstood the western elements impressively well. Staircase, windowsill, upper floorboards and kitchen grate remain. Jackdaws and Swallows are today's tenants. Stoats lurk in the brier-embraced adjoining byre, where the roof is no more. I explored carefully with nephews and nieces, Natasha and Ben with their butterfly net, trying to get a closer look at the Red Admirals, me trying to gently impress on them the significance of the spot, recalling how it all seemed to me at their age, when I was visiting cousins.

We couldn't linger long. Marc and Owen had discovered sheugch the hard way, and Uncle Conor had a small flip-flop to rinse in the burn, before we could return to the family gathering in the warmth of a long white house far below.

I visited the old cottage again on my own, for a meditative hour. It slowly dawned on me that there were other occupants of the old place, a pair of birds regarding me nervously from the nearby Sycamores, behaving very much as birds do when near a nest they wish to keep secret. I moved behind an Ash, out of sight, and after a few minutes one of the birds flew to the chimney stack and disappeared into a crevice. It re-emerged soon after, and made off. I couldn't get close enough to view them without spooking them, so I walked back down the hill to borrow binoculars from my aunt and uncle. It was worth the effort. Back in position, I didn't have long to wait for the birds to reappear, and straight away I could see what they were – Tree Sparrows.

A massive wind-farm proposal was seen off on the island of Lewis. And there were major issues with the proposed barrage across the Severn Estuary. At face value it might have looked as though no form of energy generation works for conservation-minded people, and this might have been how some developers liked to characterise these thorns in their flesh. But in fact viable and workable alternative places were being proposed – avoiding important places and rare species.

Some people may have hoped that the so-called biofuels might offer a green alternative to fossil fuels, but conservationists now had their work cut out to disabuse them of this notion. However it might be that the world could reduce its reliance on fossil fuels to make its wheels turn, biofuels were not the answer. The idea of growing crops to use as fuel had appealed at first glance to those keen to cash in on demand for greener sources of energy. But the impact this was going to have, and indeed was already having, on habitats, and on food crops, and grasslands, was potentially disastrous. And nor had the case been made that these crops would actually reduce greenhouse gas emissions.

The RSPB was supporting its partner Nature Uganda to head off a plan that would destroy the Mabira Forest and replace it with a sugar cane biofuel crop. In Kenya, there were proposals to grow 80 square miles of sugar cane on a river delta that teemed with life – local communities, 350 species of birds as well as the mega-fauna once typical of vast areas of wild Kenya, including Elephants and Lions.

On the domestic front, it began to emerge that woodland birds like the Willow Tit, Spotted Flycatcher, Wood Warbler and Pied Flycatcher were taking over as the fastest-declining species, having shown the most dramatic decreases in the last decade or more. Were insect declines behind this, or was a problem developing in their African wintering grounds?

To find out more about insect monitoring, and what unseen gems might lurk in my neighbourhood, I borrowed a moth trap, and left it out on a suitably warm and humid summer night. In the morning I lifted the egg boxes one at a time from the large basin into which the night-flying beasts are lured by the high-powered spotlight, to rest unharmed till morning. It was like finding living, vivid fossils, a procession of stunning specimens I could link in the book to their beautiful, poetic names, before releasing them to wherever it is they hid by day. I read that two-thirds of our moth species are in decline. The giant moth trap at Rothamsted has been running since the sixties, and was now catching a third fewer moths than it did back then.

Nine years on, the Birdmen played our friends and rivals the RSPCA for the tenth time. We needed a win to level the series, to make it four wins all and two draws. Them being at home, and bigger than us, we went into the match as underdogs. But we got the win, so it was honours even, and we called it a day on the fixture after that. There were suggestions that I dived to win a vital early penalty, but there was definitely contact. But they do say history is written by the winners, and those holding the pen.

Winds of change were blowing across the Atlantic, as Barack Obama was elected US President, and, amid the jubilation that surrounded his victory, declared that future generations would remember this as 'the moment when the rise of the oceans began to slow and our planet began to heal'. We could only hope this proved right.

> Till a' the seas gang dry, my dear,
> And the rocks melt wi' the sun
>
> Robert Burns

2009

Sudden and unexpected heavy snow in February decimated Dartford Warblers in the heathlands of southern England. The thousand pairs present just a year earlier were reduced to about a hundred. It underlined just how vulnerable birds like this are to hard and unpredictable weather.

I now work in a building that screams as you arrive in the morning. It fools me most times, and has me craning my neck looking for the birds producing the sound. It's quite a novel way to be welcomed to work, all in all, although I have to share this ovation with the colleagues, all 150 of them, with whom I share this two-storey office. It's called the Avocet building, and it's one of the newer parts of The Lodge.

The screams are oddly disembodied. They are actually tape recordings of the raucous, slightly nasal contact calls of Swifts, familiar to many, but to which others find it surprisingly easy to appear oblivious, of a summer's day or evening.

Even allowing for the fact that this is 'Bird Central', you might think it a tad eccentric for us to be playing these calls from the rooftops here. But the idea is that the recorded calls will attract the real thing – actual Swifts – to come and have a look at the special nest-boxes we've installed for them.

At the time the Avocet was built in the mid-nineties, I spoke to a few people about the option of leaving nesting cavities for Swifts. There were logistical reasons why it couldn't be done then. It's been done now as it becomes ever clearer that Swifts are in urgent need of help. Despite the fact that these masters of flight hardly ever have need to touch the Earth that we walk upon they have gone into a worrying decline. One of the reasons could be a loss of places to nest – the sort of places that newish buildings, like the Avocet here, tend to have less of than old ones – hence the boxes now fixed into the recesses, and the tape-lures.

Swifts only really touch down when they come to nest-sites, otherwise they do pretty much all their living on the wing – eating, mating, gathering nest material and even sleeping up there, somewhere. They migrate to southern Africa and back each year, and clock up quite some mileage in the course of the few years that is their average lifespan.

There was some encouragement that we might be getting the long-lost Nightjar back, ahead of schedule, the heathland restoration being still very much in its formative stages. More than three decades had passed since Nightjars last bred here. An excited visitor arrived in the shop to announce that he'd found one sitting on a tree stump. Word filtered through and at lunchtime I went up there with a few others to have a look. Sure enough, right by the path, just the other side of a protective wire fence, near the main entrance to the nature reserve, on a lovely sunny morning in June, was a Nightjar. Here was this scarce, rarely seen, nocturnal, enigmatic, log-coloured bird sitting there in the sun, plain as day (once it was pointed out), eyes open just a crafty crack, with the hint of a benign, Mona Lisa smile on its bristly beak, thinking no one could see it, roosting through the day with the warm rays of the sun on its back. A peculiar-looking beast, and one that anyone who saw it would have to admit was worth the effort of walking about half a mile to see, in pleasant surroundings.

One visitor sent me a short note later: 'Obviously everyone at RSPB is doing a sterling job in creating the right habitat and bringing rarer birds to Sandy Lodge ... allowing the general public with a real interest in birds the privilege of seeing one. On our way home tonight about 8.30pm there was still a good crowd of people intently watching. Fantastic. I echo you with a well done to everyone.'

I might have been part of the group she saw, having brought my partner Sara to see the mysterious Nightjar later in the day. By this time it had moved, finally roused from its suspended animation when someone on a mountain bike braked too hard when approaching the scene. The screech of brakes was enough to spook the hitherto unflappable Nightjar, which flew up onto the low branches of a nearby tree. Luckily, it could still be seen there. The thought occurred to me that we could have been surrounded by Nightjars in such repose, and been none the wiser.

Sara and I met when we were students at Stirling, and re-met many years later, having always kept in touch. In late summer we returned to 'Osprey island', in the middle of that quiet loch where once upon a time I discovered the secret Osprey. We were married on a rare sunlit morning there amid the ruins of the ancient priory, where once Mary Queen of Scots found refuge. No doubt like us she had Ospreys soaring, whistling, plunging all around. I recited a piece by John Clare, accompanied by a bumblebee that happened to be passing at that moment:

> I hid my love in field and town
> Till e'en the breeze would knock me down;
> The bees seemed singing ballads o'er,
> The fly's bass turned to lion's roar;
> And even the silence found a tongue,
> To haunt me all the summer long;
> The riddle nature could not prove
> Was nothing else but secret love.

Some high-profile development threats underlined the fact that nowhere was totally safe, even places with all the environmental designations in the book. Donald Trump's golf course and housing development was permitted on a unique dune system in north Scotland, in a case attracting international coverage. High-profile schemes were mooted for new airports and additional runways at existing airports, and a barrage scheme that threatened to destroy the Severn Estuary when an environmental alternative appeared not to be favoured. On top of this, a new report revealed that only 19% of our rivers were in good condition.

There was a huge victory for conservation in Europe when, after seven years of campaigning, it was announced that the major road planned to link Helsinki with Warsaw would be rerouted to avoid wrecking protected areas. Our Polish colleague Malgorzata Gorska won the Goldman Prize – the 'Nobel Prize for the Environment' – for her work to coordinate this campaign: a true conservation hero. Now we would try to avert a similar disaster befalling the celebrated Serengeti Plains in Tanzania.

Long-distance migrants like the Cuckoo, Yellow Wagtail and Wood Warbler were added to the Red List of birds of highest concern. While most migrant birds had been returning earlier, the Wood Warbler and Spotted Flycatcher had apparently not adapted their arrival times. Was this significant? Were they now out of synch with what is happening here? More than 50 species were now on the Red List, up by 12 since 2002. Eighteen had been added and six, now considered less urgent, were moved to the Amber List.

The previous year had proved another bad one for seabirds, but at last the Marine and Coastal Access Act became law in November, for England and Wales. Scotland and Northern Ireland were working on similar legislation. Having laws in place is one thing, however. Making them work is the next challenge. Getting this far had been a long slog, with many false dawns, and getting the act passed was a major milestone in conservation history. My colleagues in the Marine Unit, and their predecessors who had come and gone, were entitled to be elated at this result. The focus was now on putting in place a network of protected areas at sea, by 2012. The same need had long been identified for Scottish waters. Scotland has nearly half of all Europe's breeding seabirds. Its seas are administered in part by the Scottish government, and in part from London. A campaign was also in progress to end the killing of 200,000 of these seabirds by fishing vessels each year in Europe.

In a report, economist Sir Nicholas Stern advocated stimulating the low-carbon economy. This meant government investing in renewable energy and technologies to cut carbon emissions. An estimated £14 billion would be needed to help make this happen. And it could and should all be done without compromising the best places for wildlife, or what remains of them. Copenhagen hosted the UN Climate Summit in December, at the end of a year of campaigning and marches through major cities, the so-called Wave. It produced much talk and more disappointment. There would be more talks.

One of the highlights of the year for me was the unexpected dump of snow that came in December. I can barely recall ever having serious snow before Christmas in the lowlands of the UK, and waking up to blue skies and a foot of pristine, sparkling snow, and yomping to work through it, was a day that glitters in the memory. I sensed Mother Earth gently reasserting her power, and her beauty, dazzling us with ice-crystal jewels, both to disrupt our comfort zones – and certainly our reliance on road transport – and any complacency we might have about who, ultimately, is in charge round here. I love the way snow softens the hard straight lines with which we score our world in contravention of one of nature's basic laws.

It was a resounding re-statement of nature's capacity to surprise, to send us a serious winter day in an age when climate change has neutralised so many of our recent winters. Days like these are so rare that when they come they are de facto national holidays, giving children and families an unexpected chance to embrace the outdoors. Hard to believe that an average schoolday could offer so much formative benefit. Perhaps we should think of such days as a chance to celebrate the Earth, the weather, the season, again.

Without proper winter, there can be no magical days like this, and maybe no proper spring. I was taking the long view. Spring would be along soon enough, and with any luck its birds – and maybe its butterflies too – would still be with it, or ahead of it. Nature, meanwhile, waits in the earth, biding its time.

2010

We had probably all got used to the idea that long, cold winters were a thing of the past. And then the snows came, and came again, and the cold winds and frosts persisted right through March. Inevitably, small birds suffered. I'm sure my parents were missed by their local birds, as they'd escaped the freeze and taken off to see the world in a cruise ship. Back home, we had the consolation of some unusual birds that began turning up in gardens. The Fieldfare was one, surprising a few people when they encountered this large, colourful thrush up close, a regular visitor in winter flocks from Scandinavia.

The cold weather delayed the return of our Corn Buntings to the village fields. But I was pleased when, as in most years since I've lived here, the blue-grass twang of the singing male rang across the pasture once again, in late March. Corn Buntings have disappeared from wide areas of the countryside, and are now gone from Wales, for example, and been put on the Red List. There was media coverage locally and nationally of the enormous winter flock of them that gathered at a farm not far from us. There were 800 buntings at one stage, and they stayed for days, demonstrating their dependence on stubble fields. Perhaps our own village's Corn Buntings were part of that gathering.

Work was stepped up to help endangered insects. Field Crickets were reintroduced to nature reserves in Sussex and Surrey, and the Short-haired Bumblebee was brought back from exile in New Zealand, whence it had been taken by settlers, and where it had thrived. Meantime, ours had become extinct. A reintroduction scheme was being attempted in Kent. Work began to prepare the ground for release of Pine Hoverflies at Abernethy, and the Dark-bordered Beauty moth at another site in Scotland.

Honeybees had long been in the headlines. People were starting to wonder if something else was debilitating bees, and making them more vulnerable to attack from different sources. A new generation of insecticides was introduced to public debate – the so-called neonicotinoids. Dr Hennk Tennekes made the case that these products might be behind the dramatic decline of bees that had been noted across Europe. And bees may not be the only victims. Almost 50 years since the collateral damage of *Silent Spring*, was this a case of history repeating itself?

These substances are often used as seed dressing for crops like maize, sunflowers and the oilseed rapes. They are said to get into the whole system of a plant, including its nectar and pollen. Some scientists also think they leach into soil and underground water tables, where they persist. There was growing evidence of negative impacts on the abundance and behaviour of earthworms, mites, beetles, ladybirds, crustaceans, honeybees, bumblebees, solitary bees and some aquatic invertebrates. Much of the evidence has come from laboratory studies, some has been field-based. It isn't yet certain that these substances are causing the loss of insect-eating birds, but a number of organisations called for a precautionary suspension of products containing neonicotinoids for outdoor use until thorough testing had been done.

An online petition has been signed by more than a million people, calling for a ban on neonicotinoids in both the UK and the USA.

Former RSPB Chairman Professor John Lawton led a review for government and issued a report called *Making Space for Nature*, on the state of protected areas in England. He called it a 'repair manual to help re-build nature'. It pointed up the pressing need for bigger and better connected areas, to make ecosystems viable and joined up. It made plain, in short, the need to begin to properly tackle conservation on a landscape scale. The true cost of 'natural debt' was beginning to become clear. RSPB Chief Executive Graham Wynne – now Sir Graham – moved on in May. He spoke of the RSPB's 'modest little mission of saving the world through birds'. Operations Director Dr Mike Clarke stepped up to take the reins.

The National Ecosystem Assessment was published, showing how the natural environment is essential to quality of life. Despite all that was going on around it, the general election left a sense that conservation was lower in the political consciousness than for many years. 'Vote blue to go green' was the slogan, as Labour's 13-year reign came to an end. New Conservative Prime Minister David Cameron pledged to make the coalition formed with the Lib Dems 'the greenest government ever'.

As the extent of the nation's budget deficit became apparent, government reviewed spending plans in the autumn. Some extra money was found for climate change issues, and environmental farming schemes. But the prevailing theme was cuts. There was also the renewed prospect of state-owned forests and nature reserves being unloaded onto other owners. Eyebrows were raised about the fate of these reserves, and a storm of controversy followed the announcement of a consultation period about selling off the nation's forests, a story that caused Mum and her walking friends some anxiety amid an extraordinary and spontaneous public backlash at the very idea.

Hope Farm celebrated its tenth anniversary with a three-fold increase in the number of farm-dependent wild birds achieved in that time, without affecting profitability. Lapwings, Grey Partridges and Yellow Wagtails had all been able to establish breeding populations. Skylarks, Starlings, Linnets and Reed Buntings had at least quadrupled, and Yellowhammers more than doubled. It showed that with as little as 3 or 4% of an arable farm's area managed carefully as habitat, the declines of farm-dependent birds could be reversed.

And a bird came back. The Red-backed Shrike, extinct as a breeding bird in this country since the late eighties, returned to south-west

England. A pair was discovered nesting, and a round-the-clock vigil was set up, as known eggers lurked nearby. Unlike the birds, the old threats hadn't gone away. The birds raised young, and all departed in late summer for southern warmth. Their return next spring would be anxiously awaited.

Dad died after a summer in hospital, battling as ever, determined to get out of there. He got home, to be assessed for care there, but his mobility had gone, and I think in his heart of hearts he knew that it wasn't going to work. Two days later he had ceased to be able to communicate, and a few days after that he let go. He had reached a good age and had a full life. He was by turns shy, stubborn, hard-working, principled, sometimes reclusive, care-worn, uncompromising, controlling but decent, unassuming. Geographer and mathematician, teacher in Ugandan and Scottish schools, a liberal and an autocrat, a rebel with hard and fast rules, resister of prejudice, proud and sometimes fierce, a man of closely guarded emotions. In retirement he had grown increasingly attached to his garden birds, and had a cottage industry going at home to keep them supplied with blended bread, seeds and nuts. I sometimes had to check with him which was our muesli, and which was theirs. I think his ability to enjoy birds had been affected by his impaired hearing from quite a young age, which seemed to curtail his love of music prematurely and could make him feel isolated.

We said farewell at an Edinburgh crematorium. I read a short poem by W. B. Yeats, the first few lines of which are below. Dad spent time in recent years finding his forebears, including in the County Sligo cemetery where Yeats rests too.

> When you are old and grey and full of sleep,
> And nodding by the fire, take down this book,
> And slowly read, and dream of the soft look
> Your eyes had once, and of their shadows deep.

From Edinburgh I headed back to Stirlingshire, to walk in Hermitage Wood and the hills again. I was pleased to see that an official Environment and Media Course is now established in my old department. The environmental movement needs all the media expertise and science communicators it can muster: to keep the pressure on politicians, to win support, to make people care enough to do their bit for conservation.

I noted too how the rhododendrons have advanced on the woods, despite conservation work party efforts to keep them from swamping all. How the Rabbits – also aliens – have multiplied to almost absurd, *Father Ted* proportions. And how the Buzzards, no doubt partly in response, and relatively free from persecution – are back in the skies over the Carlin Crag, where I spent many happy days contemplating the view, engaged in that all-important mental preparation for essays and exams. Well, sometimes.

I struck lucky when a piece about the Goshawk for *BBC Wildlife* magazine won me a place on an Earthwatch expedition to the upper reaches of the Peruvian Amazon, to some of the remotest swamp forests. It was a glimpse of paradise, two weeks immersed in nothing but forest and rivers. They say Amazonia is the lungs of the planet. Most days began at dawn, with sunrise bird calls and the firing-up of the generator replacing the night-time chorus of frogs, crickets and owls. With the moon receding, and butterflies taking wing, we would sit quietly in the open boat against the bank, recording macaws, often seeing dozens in the space of a few hours, their dinosaur squawks ringing across the canopy as they shuttled over the wide, languid river. Between macaws, ornithologist Alfredo would confirm the identity of the many other bird species calling, flitting and swooping around us, and Pink River-dolphins idling alongside the boat.

We set up a study of White-winged Swallows led by Princeton University in the USA, installing around 50 nest-boxes on poles, trees and emergent stumps at the edge of lakes and river channels. If the Swallows adopt these, researchers can record the box contents, leading to a better understanding of how this species lives and breeds across Amazonia. First, our boxes would have to survive the imminent wet season. Water levels would rise by about 15 feet here, judging by the tidemark on many of the tree trunks. The Swallows will also have to interpret these strange square objects as suitable nest sites. It was pioneering stuff.

You might say returning to another December arctic front in Europe and the concrete canyons of Madrid airport was a bit of a shock to the system.

2011

'The bird migration thing. It fazes me to think of it. Really think of it, as I lie back on the grass at the front and try to make sense of the society above me. Today Bedfordshire. Tomorrow Bordeaux?

Thursday Andalucía? Friday Mauretania? Saturday Gabon? ... Uganda? Next spring, these eaves again? Life would certainly be poorer if they didn't come back,' I wrote ten years ago, about my House Martins. Of course they aren't mine, and never were. They can come and go as they please. And so they went.

Reflecting on it now, it pains me to report that they aren't back. Of course I noticed this as it happened, how four nests dwindled to two, then one, then none. I installed artificial nests for them, after the old soffits, with their coffee-stain rings of House Martin nest, and lumps of mud, had to come down. I even put one on next door's eaves, as a gift. And from time to time House Martins have investigated these potential nest sites. This year there's been very little evidence of them. April was so parched the Martins hardly seemed to have come back at all. When they did come back, there was no mud for them to use.

I visited friends who farm livestock just along the road, to give them a Kestrel nest-box I'd made from an antique commode, and to help them install it in a suitable place. There was a leaking standpipe in the farmyard, and what a magnet for birds that was proving, in these peculiar, drought-stricken times of spring. With the first day of proper rain the Martins were noticeably animated, gathering round the puddles, and swooping up to the window. But they didn't occupy the woodcrete artificial cups, or build their own. I see Wrens and Blue Tits sometimes go there at dusk to roost. But something about them may not be to the Martins' taste. I will fit something non-synthetic over the soffits, to which mud might stick more easily.

There is better news at The Lodge, where I have been greatly consoled to note that real Swifts have started taking notice, and coming in to have a closer listen at our screaming building, to bang on the box fronts to see who is at home. Oddly for quite a small bird, they don't breed until their third year. These juveniles have a bit of time to find a new breeding site. It feels like only a matter of time before they take up the offer, and the screams as we arrive for work of a summer morning may start to be for real. Maybe next year ...

Some of my local migrant bird voices have fallen silent this year. I haven't heard a Cuckoo or a Turtle Dove around the village. Even since I've been here, Spotted Flycatchers have given up on some of their former local haunts. Of the residents, the pair of Lapwings that held on for years, and that I would see and hear each morning as I cycled to work in spring, appear now to have given up, moved on, with no Lapwings to succeed them. I can still hear Nightingales from the garden after dark in May, but the man who lives in one of the remoter cottages in the village tells me they have gone from the copse behind his house. Our Corn Buntings still sing from the wires beyond the end of the back garden, but I fear for them too. The Tree Sparrows flattered to deceive, and haven't been seen, even in winter, for a year or two now.

A project was launched last year in this part of the country to try to help the Turtle Dove, in what may be a last-ditch effort. Some of the birds would be fitted with radio tags, the technology now sufficiently 'nano' that we can track even small and lightweight birds to find out where they go. Essentially there were ten times as many Turtle Doves in 1970 as there are now. We use 1970 as the baseline because we know roughly how many there were around that time. In all probability there were very many more in the decade preceding that, where this story began. I thought I'd lost mine locally but there was a glimmer of hope when a bird flew into the mist-net of the ringers just a mile from the village.

Effort has also been stepped up to find out what is happening to more of our migrant birds when they are in Africa, particularly species like the Cuckoo, Spotted Flycatcher, Wood Warbler and Wheatear. You wonder how we could ever find them in the forests and great plains of this vast continent. The gadgetry helps of course, but I remembered finding a Grey Wagtail in the steamy mist-forests of Seychelles. I heard it calling, by a mountain stream, before tracking it down. A familiar voice, a long, long way from home. My colleague Duncan McNiven provided another insight into how 'our' UK summer warblers appear in an African context during the much greater part of the year they spend 'down south'. Working with partners in Cameroon, Duncan was catching and ringing birds during a study of migration. Among the general din of birds and all things living in the forest, he would notice a burst of song, maddeningly familiar, yet impossible to place. After a few days of this, the mystery bird sang again, and for longer, until it finally dawned on Duncan what it was: a tiny Wood Warbler. Soon there were more of them, all singing, and singing more lustily each day. And one day later they were silent: all off north to relocate to the northern Beech and oak woods of Europe.

The Red-backed Shrikes returned, and now there were two pairs. The round-the-clock guard was resumed, and both pairs raised healthy broods. There is also a happier ending – so far – to the Corncrake tale. The team has carried on with the project, releasing more chicks each spring in Cambridgeshire. Fourteen territories were recorded in those darkening meadows this summer. Slowly but surely they are recolonising; the project so far is working. Somewhere out there, among the irises and sedges, the rushes and grasses, they are now in a position to make their two nesting attempts, free from the threat of mower blades. It is still early days, but if this reintroduction works, it will be a testament to the tenacity of the birds, and of course to those doing the hard work with partners and supporters.

Most people are too young to have noticed that the Corncrake has been absent from the midnight choir. We can only hope that one day more people will have the privilege of being kept awake by a Corncrake, or perhaps serenaded by one in dreams of adventure, and bigger, wilder landscapes.

At the end of October, world population was said to have reached 7 billion, up from 3 billion in 1960. Promoting women's rights in developing countries to manage their own fertility is likely to be key to addressing the social consequences of this growing population pressure. Recent humanitarian disasters linked to drought and conflict in north-eastern Africa and flooding in Pakistan are exacerbated by population growth, and resultant pressure on resources locally. Developed nations like ours, where human population is relatively small and stable, produce almost half of the world's climate emissions. The latest UK census estimates a population here of 60+ million, now rising more rapidly.

There were two surprise visitors in November. A first-year Osprey decided to loiter for a couple of weeks, roosting in pines on the edge of the new heath at The Lodge, and fishing at the gravel pits at the base of the ridge. Sara and I caught up with it one brisk Sunday morning as it cruised over the trout-filled pits, gulls following calmly in its wake as they might a trawler, anticipating scraps. Later that day it finally departed south. This lingering Osprey was a first for The Lodge – a sort of homecoming, I thought, for this iconic bird of nature recovered – and a last for the year: the latest dawdling Osprey yet recorded, which reflects the unusual mildness of the autumn.

The second surprise was a note from Nick, my old mucker from Stirling DJ-ing, football and ornithological days: '25 years on, the Hog's Head turns up at the RSPB', it read. He got that nickname from something he did a long time ago at a bad taste party, which can't be revisited here. He was now managing nature reserves in Kent. Better late than never, I told him.

BirdLife staged an exhibition in London called *Ghosts of Gone Birds*, with artists depicting a hundred or more species now lost to the world. The event was masterminded by film-maker Ceri Levy, who came late in life to a love of birds and concern for their well-being. BirdLife Rare Bird Club President Margaret Atwood knitted a Great Auk for the occasion, which may yet cross the Atlantic to raise funds there, towards the prevention of any more extinctions.

I had been co-opted to my village parish council, I think unofficially as the local bird man, the 'green' representative. We began to discuss ways of giving the local kids a bigger share of the space around us, for recreation. A piece of land was being looked at, and I realised this little corner of a field is the very spot where the Tree Sparrows had last hung on in the county. Perhaps if we can put the kids back in countryside fit for them, the Tree Sparrows will follow soon enough. We talk a lot about the disconnection of children. At work, I had begun coordinating a project funded by the Gulbenkian Foundation to look at ways of measuring the extent of Nature Deficit Disorder in the UK. For me, this is more than just a lifestyle thing. It is partly to do with the physical limits we have imposed on public access to the landscape, for children and for adults too. It is also about creating a countryside worth visiting, and repopulating it with people as well as its former features of interest, and its birds.

US academics R. M. Pyle and later James R. Miller have described a 'cycle of impoverishment' caused by 'homogenisation and reduction of local flora and fauna, followed by disaffection and apathy'. An awful lot of public funding has so far largely failed to adequately rectify this creeping phenomenon in the UK. I resolved to kick-start a conservation team in the village, to start work on managing the hedgerows and newt ponds put in ten years ago as mitigation for a local road development, and left untended since. The ponds are long since choked with weed and the hedges need to be laid, and relieved from the plastic shackles that have strangled some of the trees. We may have to do all the work ourselves, in the spirit of localness.

Old Fred's widow Dorothy passed away, having been in failing health for some months. She was laid to rest beside Fred, in the churchyard of St Peter's. The autumn sun shone brightly on us as the coffin was lowered, and three generations of her extended family, and neighbours, paid our respects. There was bite in the gusting wind, the Sycamores swished noisily, drowning out the A1, busy beyond the Great North Road it replaced in the sixties, and which now lies quiet between us and it. The gusts also interrupted most, for me, of the vicar's words, as I looked on from the edge of the crowd. Thirteen years to the day had passed since old Fred fell at his back door that icily cold Sunday morning.

The service was moving, mostly where it was touchingly funny, the sweet eulogies of Dorothy's granddaughters read by the vicar. For music, Dorothy, to reflect the family's love of Scotland, and their happy memories of the annual summer break in the Highlands, had asked for the organist to pick Scottish tunes. So we entered the church to Robert Burns, and 'The Bonnie Banks of Loch Lomond', and departed to 'Will Ye No' Come Back Again?' Between times we sang of flowers and birds, in 'All Things Bright and Beautiful', and 'The Lord Is My Shepherd'; fitting, of course, for the pastoral thread that runs through their and so many families' history.

We heard how Dorothy had been working in a London bakery when war broke out. She had a choice between the munitions factory there, or the Land Army here. No contest. She lodged in the village, trained nearby, and then found herself on the Bettles' family farm, where she met Fred, where he kept a 'beady eye' on the feisty young Cockney lass's work. They married soon after war ended. And when the dust had settled, they moved into this row of houses newly built for rural workers such as them, to raise their children. Dorothy had helped out on the farm for as long as such work was needed, milking and harvesting, then in a local market garden and flower-grower's. She was very proud of her neat front garden, and we shared a garden path, where the encroachments of my Lavender, Hollyhocks and Wisteria would be monitored closely. 'I don't mind them,' she would tell me, 'except when it's wet.'

They never bought their house, when the Thatcher years exhorted owner-occupation. So now with Dorothy's passing they were clearing everything out. I helped to dismantle Old Fred's sheds at the end of the back garden, among his apple trees, a birch, a spruce and a larch, trees he'd raised from seed or seedlings, little souvenirs of Scotland brought back from those Highland holidays. The matured fruit trees and Scots Pine in my own garden were also gifts from Fred to an earlier occupant. Our orchard has been shared. Plums, pears and apples have been traded. I trimmed off some dead wood from their trees, neglected in recent years.

I salvaged what was salvageable, for firewood and for re-use – solid old doors and posts, bits of roofing, windows. I raked in the sawdust of decades of workshop activity, conscious all the while that an era had ended. Old Mont from the farm up the road was now in care, no longer to be seen on his walking frame, making his way painstakingly down the road as far as our houses, and maybe a bit further. I found out he'd planted the willows opposite, at the time of the Frog Hall pond. They were the war generation, the last to work the land that way, when this county was known as England's market garden, piling produce onto trains and lorries for London. The last to live through the transition from hands-on – literally – field workers, to civvy street. I made a deal with Fred's son Chris that, come the spring, we'd seek permission to walk some of the woods he used to explore as a child. Perhaps there might still be Turtle Doves there that I'd missed.

The front of the house faces south, and from where I write the late-year sun backlights the sparrows in the front garden. The effect can be dazzling, as the boisterous flock battles for pole position on the feeders, or gathers at the centre-stage bird bath 'lido' for a communal water fight, to throw liquid sparks into the air to catch the rays. Only shadowy sparrows, but the glittering show can be stunning. Just everyday birds, doing what birds do, enlivening the scene, bringing beauty, movement, catching the light and the air, making lots of reassuring noise.

They are garden birds now. The food is here. Across the road, the fields don't have House Sparrows any more. But I still find signs of encouragement there. I walked my local paths with colleagues from The Lodge agriculture team. The field margins and the bigger hedgerows resulting from agriculture policy reforms are still there. The Bullfinches came back with the burgeoning hedges. I watched a pair in a tall thorn one morning, working together: he keeping watch, resplendent with the sun on his crimson chest, she working the branches, eating her fill. Meadow Pipits and Yellowhammers have responded to the wider margins. These 'unfarmed features' could be better, richer in plant species, but they have undoubtedly helped. But their future is precarious and remains at the whim of politicians, and of more discussions.

As the year neared its end, the latest climate talks were held in Durban. A deal was finally struck in the early hours of the morning, towards a new, legally binding commitment to reducing emissions. Next up, and 20 years on from Rio's first Earth Summit, the Rio+20 Conference, in June 2012, aims to 'secure renewed political commitment for sustainable development' and review progress made till now. It looks like our PM won't be able to attend, due to a diary clash with the Queen's Diamond Jubilee. David Attenborough lent his support to the climate cause in the final episode of the latest BBC natural history epic series, *Frozen Planet*. It would be shown later on the Discovery Channel in the USA.

The lyric of Band Aid's ubiquitous and recurring Christmas hit assured us there would be no snow in Africa at Christmas. The line is becoming increasingly and worryingly accurate. I realised this as I looked at photographs a friend had taken when she climbed Kilimanjaro for charity, and was struck by the apparent absence of snow from the iconic mountain's summit. The same is true of the Rwenzoris in Uganda – the ancient Greeks' Mountains of the Moon, fabled source of the Nile – their glaciers steadily receding.

There was no snow this year to soften the hard lines of the eastern landscape as Sara's family gathered for Christmas in Suffolk. Our journey takes us through some remorselessly bleak Cambridgeshire arable land: featureless, empty, exposed, soulless, gigantic fields of unrelieved winter wheat, the occasional grain-silo installation; hedgerows often beaten to sporadic, gappy tufts, the prairie effect relieved in places only by roadside saplings in synthetic tubes.

We passed one rare stretch of mature hedge that looked as though it had been shredded by a hurricane, attacked in anger by something with a blunt instrument, for having the temerity to flourish so close to a road. Up ahead, the guiltless machine, lights flashing its apparent rage, resting between bouts of this dirty protest against the walls of the cell. The kind of ill-considered, brute assault on the nature of our waysides we're supposed to have grown out of. In our village we're nurturing these hedgerows, trimming them carefully, coaxing their shapes to our needs, seeking to involve the community in their care.

The folds of rural Suffolk bring some respite from the vacant plains. The absence of snow and ice at least made carol singing on Christmas Eve in Sara's home village less hazardous than in recent years. I got chatting to a fellow caroller over mulled wine and mince pies in a darkened garden. By curious coincidence he used to work as an ecologist for the RSPB, and at the Rothamsted Research Centre not far away, where the long-term studies of invertebrate populations have been done. It seems that lack of insects, linked to loss of wildflowers, could be key to what's happening to birds and birdsong. Instinct tells me this too, but it's a very tricky thing to prove conclusively. He told me his honeybees had 'sudden death' syndrome, he thinks because of pesticides.

* * *

We spent new year on the north Norfolk coast. Fieldfares and Redwings toured the fields, our islands still their Africa, for the winter. We watched snaking threads of geese come in high at sunset, clanking like distant freight trains, and flights of Wigeon take off as early evening fireworks crackled behind the church at Cley. A shadowy Redshank piped, irate at our intrusion, as any true 'sentinel of the marshes' ought to be. Pipits squeaked and Lapwings whined, settling for the night. A tiny warbler skittered off and careered into a safer part of the reeds. On the dunes, a wartime pillbox was struggling to keep its sand-filled eyes on the horizon, where a tanker sat, ablaze with festive lights in the North Sea gloom. Fittingly, in the antique bookshop there I found a copy of another Rachel Carson book, *The Edge of the Sea*.

When Carson's ashes were cast to the ocean, her friend Dorothy Freeman read some lines from T. S. Eliot's *The Four Quartets*, as the author had asked her to do – a haunting work, too long to do justice to here.

2012

> How can ye chaunt, ye warblin' birds
> And I sae weary, fu' o' care.
> Ye'll break my heart, ye warblin' birds
> That wanton through the flowery thorn
> Thou mind me o' departed joys
> Departed never to return.
>
> 'Ye Banks and Braes', Robert Burns

The government is missing its 2012 deadline to designate a network of Marine Protected Areas. It could be years before the internationally important protected areas are finally designated. It is already 30 years since the original deadline set for doing this.

The term 'shifting baseline syndrome' was first coined in connection with fisheries, and the changing perception of fishers of what is a healthy norm for fish stocks. It is now applied more widely to our expectations of what wildlife should be in our worlds, changing and lowering, from generation to generation. The fear is that young people don't and increasingly won't miss what they've never known. Researching locally, I came across some old notes that made me suddenly aware of the extent to which this has already happened – has happened to me.

There's an estate near here that I've got to know really well since I've lived in lowland England. It's been a kind of sanctuary for me, a bolt-hole, an oasis and a shelter, when I've needed it; a place of sustenance and refreshment, when the arable plains beyond have seemed too harsh, too exposed and too confining in their thin, often feature-less pathways. Much of the wildlife I see – the Rabbits, Pheasants, Red-legged Partridges, Grey Squirrels, Muntjac Deer – is non-native, most of it quarry for the gun. Amid all this the estate has been a place of reconnection. It has mature oaks, pines and birches, quiet glades, bits of pasture, formal gardens, the odd surviving pond and open, scrubby area. There used to be shooting of Pheasants and more here, but that fizzled out a few years ago, leaving only spent cartridges, oil drums, plastic sacks and chicken wire as mementoes.

Its hundred or so acres have had liberal-minded owners sympathetic to the wildlife interest of the place, and to public access. It has had knowledgeable estate workers too. I'd long thought it a haven for birds, and mammals, reptiles and amphibians, locally. It is, like most places now that offer refuge for reasonable assemblages of wildlife, well covered and recorded by naturalists. There's not much that will be missed, and anything out of the ordinary attracts an eager crowd of onlookers in no time at all.

I've seen and heard quite a lot here over the years, while walking and cycling. I have known that, in common with most places, it has lost some of the more celebrated species, the specialist rarities renowned for their scarcity, their choosiness, perhaps, and their demise from all but the most carefully maintained of special sites elsewhere. These are often in the margins of the land; species like the Nightjar, the Woodlark, the Tree Sparrow; gone from here, gone from most of the countryside and the now absent heaths.

I've noticed some losses for myself, not just of birds, but more specifically, more definitely, of its breeding Common Frogs, which used to form a stew of writhing limbs and spawn in early spring in one pond, but which now are gone. The pond sits quiet now in March, the surface undisturbed. The Common Frog doesn't come here any more. Common Toads too, in a deeper pond, would produce each year a procession of dispersing toadlets. Garden staff would put notices out asking people to avoid treading on them, and drivers to look out for them on the driveway. I used to hear and see Common Lizards on certain sunny banks, but I don't any more. Grass Snakes too, I would guess, are all but absent now, as a result.

The Adder was hunted to extinction in the county by bounty hunters years before.

Talking to the grounds staff recently I was intrigued to learn that they have a small archive of breeding bird records for the estate, carefully kept and neatly typed in the sixties. I explained my interest in all life since *Silent Spring* and they were kind enough to share these records with me. I looked through them with great interest, but with a mounting sense of dismay; mild shock, even. The same sense of shock was shared by others I later spoke to, who I thought might have known, even if I had not. Many of the birds named are now gone, missing in action. Besides the missing Nightjar, Woodlark, Tree Sparrow and Tree Pipit – the last of these I noticed dwindling each year until all were silenced – there are other species on that list, compiled each spring and summer from the mid-sixties to the early seventies, that no longer breed here.

Some of the losses could be explained by local changes in the landscape – Mallard and Little Grebe perhaps vanished along with the larger ponds of old. Swallows, Pied Wagtails, Little Owls and Barn Owls probably relied on the now demolished outbuildings for nest sites. Sand Martins and Kingfishers chiselled nest-holes in the quarry, before it became overgrown. Skylarks needed the wider spaces; Whitethroat and Lesser Whitethroat the open and scrubbier spaces before these became too enclosed for their needs.

The missing Jay, Siskin and Crossbill nests are difficult to explain. They aren't declining nationally, they just don't nest here any more, only visiting now outside the breeding season. Other absentee nesters I think reflect the wider demise of their kind – the Grey Partridge, Woodcock, Turtle Dove, Collared Dove, Cuckoo, Lesser Spotted Woodpecker, Marsh Tit, Willow Tit, Redstart, Nightingale, Starling, even Greenfinch, Linnet, Redpoll, Bullfinch, Yellowhammer, Reed Bunting, Hawfinch and yes, even the humble House Sparrow. These are no longer nesting, or singing.

It's not just the species but the volumes of some of them that are astonishing. House Sparrows had been so numerous here back in the late sixties and early seventies that in most years their numbers weren't even estimated. Perhaps it was difficult to know exactly how many there were in the various roof spaces and eaves they prefer. Fifteen House Sparrow nests were counted in 1968 by someone dedicated enough to look more closely. In 1972, an astonishing 32 Tree Sparrow nests were counted, the birds and the counters aided by nest-boxes that were actually intended for other, 'nicer' birds. But the statistic that I think stunned me most of all is this: 50 Willow Warblers were recorded holding territories in 1970.

Willow Warblers aren't rare birds yet, by any means. They are still probably the most abundant of our summer visitors to these islands. No one thinks they are in danger. But they don't breed in this enclave now. But what's sinister is that very few people would nowadays think that Willow Warblers ought to breed here, or therefore think the species is in any sense missing. It's just not really Willow Warbler habitat, they would say – it's too dry, too wooded, on the whole. Even allowing that 40 years ago the lie of the land was a little different, with young plantation trees, perhaps, it still seems incredible that there can have been 50 Willow Warblers performing their gentle, falling Satie-esque song all around this estate on an April morning. That there are none today is sobering.

It is discovering the silent, steady, unseen and mostly unremarked withdrawal of this chorus line within a choir that I have found most unsettling. And this is just the recently shifted baseline. I can think of other birds that were probably nesting here before these records began to be kept in the sixties. The Cirl Bunting, Whinchat, Stonechat, Wryneck, Wood Warbler, Corncrake: all long gone. Taken as a whole, this isn't just a handful of birds, and their songs and calls and colours and movements, now absent in springtime. This is around 40 species. Silent.

In this context there seems no doubt that the silenced spring is happening under our noses. Of course Rachel Carson was right to draw attention to the harm that excessive use of particularly noxious agrochemicals were doing to birds, to wildlife in general, and quite likely to ourselves in the process. She was right that had measures not been taken, the spring would have been comprehensively silenced a long time ago. In large part thanks to her we began to address those particular issues, in the USA and beyond. We have been quite effective, on the whole, at tackling the most visible ecological problems that we have created. They are, by definition, easy to identify, object to and redress in tangible ways. Human beings as a rule don't like to see fellow creatures in unnecessary distress. We especially dislike the idea of directly lethal toxins.

Nature, as a general rule, has astonishing powers of recovery. It is pretty good at bouncing back from things that kill it, if the killing stops before it's too late, or is reduced to sustainable levels. What it's not so good at is recovering when the very ground beneath it is altered, where it no longer has a home or a source of food. Sometimes these changes are visible, but often they are not. The birds, the other life, just stops coming back, stops singing. If we have our wits about us we may notice. If not, we don't notice. It can be hard to see something that isn't there, impossible to hear nothing.

Are we silencing the spring more generally? If we take the birds that are affected by agrochemicals and agricultural landscapes, the answer, sadly, is still yes. More recently, the serious observed declines in woodland species too indicate the problem is widening, perhaps now linked to changes in Africa and lands in between. Seabird breeding success has fluctuated wildly in response to a depleted marine environment. But there are isolated beacons of hope. Some species have come back, usually with dedicated help. Climatic changes have made it possible for others to colonise, to augment the orchestra in certain places, though this should not distract attention from underlying issues.

In Carson's homeland, the answer is also yes. BirdLife's US partner Audubon reports that: 'Since 1967 the average population of the common birds in steepest decline has fallen by 68 percent; some individual species nose-dived as much as 80 percent. All 20 birds on the national Common Birds in Decline list lost at least half their populations in just four decades. The findings point to serious problems with both local habitats and national environmental trends. Only citizen action can make a difference for the birds and the state of our future.'

According to the *New York Times*, which serialised *Silent Spring*, Rachel Carson 'owed her love of nature in large measure to her mother, who once wrote … that she had taught her daughter "as a tiny child joy in the out-of-doors and the lore of birds, insects, and residents of streams and ponds".' Carson had no children of her own, although she fostered her niece's young son after his mother died.

Not long after Dad died, Mum was sorting through all the things that have to be sorted through; to be kept, handed down, given to charity. In the midst of this, two boxes of photographic slides emerged from the loft, and I took these, at some later stage to look at them, maybe have them scanned. Most of the pictures were taken in Uganda, by Mum, and some by Dad, in the early sixties. 'I haven't looked at them in decades,' she told me, although very keen on the idea of them being viewable once more. As I neared completion of this story, and realised that there wouldn't be time to revisit Uganda in person, to find my birthplace, perhaps offer my services to Nature

Uganda, I dusted off the boxes, borrowed a projector, and sat down to go through the contents.

There's a peculiar atmosphere attaches to this, with the darkened room and the hum of the machine, a whiff of burning dust, the vague keyhole glimpse of the image as you hold it to the light, the further clue to its content in the neat, tight, period handwriting of my parents on the frame, and the sudden, life-size appearance of the image, smudged in places with mould and dust, but colours still vivid, the past springing onto the living room wall.

Here is East Africa again, its steamy upland forests and its dusty plains, the frothing Nile and its glistening Hippos; the mountains, acacia scrub, the salt-white beaches of Zanzibar. Against this tapestry the people – Leso and Karanjong – the smiling young couple and their toddling children: Kevin, Neal, Clare; like me but not me. Many of the images are of landforms, no doubt used to illustrate lessons: erosion, hydro dams, cotton farming, mines, markets. There are schools and colleges, parades, *Macbeth* being performed on an open-air stage, beaming pupils graduating.

With a loud click suddenly the landscape changes. We are in Ireland, on Donegal's craggy coast, the yawning arcs of its bleached bays. The only things that date the landscapes of both places are the small, pleasingly curvy cars within it, Mum's dresses.

As chance would have it the very last set I load and view reveals Mum, Kevin perched on her shoulder, at Sorote rail station, at 3,757 feet according to the sign, with Joan her best friend, and her children, the family I landed next to in Cambridge. And, as a fitting finale, there is Dad's sequence of shots as he sets out to climb Kilimanjaro, which some believe means 'that which is impossible for the bird'. Each stage of the walk is neatly labelled, each hut of tin, each biogeographic phase of the ascent, through forest, then stands of Giant Groundsel, to moorland, to desert col, or pass, to the snout of the now-dwindling glacier at Kibo (the 'house of God') Summit. He isn't in them, but his guides are. He never liked having his photo taken in later life. But then he is there, not at the peak itself, but back at Bismarck Hut, with his guides. *With* the mountain, not on it. Grinning broadly, he has been 'garlanded', a crown of wildflowers around his brow.

Early in the new year a Song Thrush adopted the back garden for a stage. Robert Burns knew this bird as the 'Mavis'. It's apt that this old name is feminine – I have been pleased to discover that female thrushes have songs too. On one icy morning, after the most penetrating of frosty nights, Mavis perched in the dawn spotlight where the arrowing rays caught the topmost branches of the Bird Cherry I planted a decade ago, and piped fit to burst, urgent, some mysterious alchemy giving it the life force and the foresight to claim this patch, and defy the bitter chill. A cameo of spring foretold in a forbidding, wintry setting. The preoccupied bird disregarded me as I passed below. I thought I could see its breath rise on the biting air, or that of the thawing twigs, as I went.

I spoke to Mum on the phone, telling her about the Uganda slides I'd looked at, jogging her memory. She remembered Sorote station, and that she too would have been to Kilimanjaro, had she not been 'watching the weans'.

Later in the conversation, unprompted, she spoke ruefully about the absence of Dippers from the rocky river that flows past her home in the Borders hills. 'It's very worrying,' she said. 'Very worrying indeed.'

Have they gone? I'd be surprised. But then I've been surprised before. I said I'd make a few enquiries. But I hope to get there as soon as I can to help her have another look, and listen, for the bird that whispers to the river.

Postscript

I can end this story on a strong note of hope, and a return to the man and the bird where we began. It is 50 years since the office manager J. A. Baker spent almost all of his spare hours looking for wintering Peregrine Falcons. He did this in a part of coastal Essex, on the upper lip of the mouth of the Thames. More often than not he found what he was looking for.

'For ten years I followed the peregrine,' he wrote. 'I was possessed by it. It was a grail for me.' Peregrines can have a strange effect on people.

He wrote those words in the opening chapter of *The Peregrine*. By the time the book was published in 1967, the Peregrine Falcon, the object of his fixation, was facing extinction in England. It was seldom seen any more in southern counties, apart from stragglers from the north and east in winter, and had long ceased to stay till late spring, or to attempt to breed. Its demise reflected a wider malaise of its world.

'Now it has gone,' wrote Baker. 'The long pursuit is over. Few peregrines are left, there will be fewer. They may not survive.'

The Peregrine Falcon, *Falco peregrinus*, thought to be the fastest animal that ever graced the planet, faced more than its share of challenges down the years. Even by the time Rachel Carson was warning the world that chemical 'biocides' threatened the end of birdsong, it was clear that the Peregrine was undergoing a tragic decline.

Fast-forwarding 40 years since Baker communed with his wintering, Essex Peregrines, it is 2003. I stand, face up, looking skyward at a vertical cliff face. Its summit is 320 feet above me, touching the off-white December sky. Above it hangs a bird, one quite unlike the gulls that drift by. It circles, then drops to a ledge. It fluffs out its plumage and begins to nibble a breast feather. It's a Peregrine Falcon: the traveller. I've seen it for myself. It's back.

The cliff in question is the chimney stack of the Tate Modern art gallery, on London's South Bank. The return of the Peregrine has been one of the great conservation success stories of recent times. It is a cause for celebration for anyone who loves nature at its wildest and most exhilarating. And one of the best things about this comeback is that the Peregrine, having reclaimed much of the rural landscape, is now claiming a share of our towns and cities too.

The Peregrine is symbolic of many things, and now it epitomises the potential for regeneration of our inner cities, and our ability to live side by side with wild nature, even in these environments.

At the time of my 2003 visit, the Tate Peregrines had been hanging around the tower for a year or two. They were thought to be the offspring of a pioneering pair that nested on tall buildings downriver. There were reports in the 1860s that Peregrines nested on St Paul's Cathedral just across the Thames. But the pair that fledged two young on the derelict Spillers Millennium Mills building in the Royal Docks in 1998 was probably the first to breed in London. Battersea Power Station then hosted a pair from 2000.

I was on my way to meet Adrian Hardwicke of the Tate Modern, a manager at the gallery as well as a friend. This was our first chance to discuss installing a nest-box for the birds, and setting up a viewing point for the public. In the end we decided that a nest-box was unnecessary. The birds have other nest-site options nearby and seem content to use the tower as a resting place, a vantage point for surveying their domain. Happily, it was possible to set up the telescopes, and the Tate Peregrines watch-point is still thriving today.

In September 2011 I revisited Adrian, now a director, for a catch-up. I also caught up with the staff and volunteers who show the Peregrines to a largely unsuspecting, passing public: visitors from all over the world. I had a memorable afternoon helping to introduce the world to these birds perched high on the face of the brick column, barely visible to the naked eye, but brought very much into view, larger than life, in the eyepiece of the 'scopes. The typical reaction is disbelief and then delight, bordering on elation. Some people think it must be a contemporary art stunt – performance art of some kind – or that the birds are captive, waiting to be called to a falconer's fist. 'But if they are wild, then how do you know the birds are going to be there?' is a frequently asked question.

The truth is no one can be sure the birds will be there on any given day. But the Tate Modern is a favourite perch for this pair. This is especially so from July, when the young are well grown and the parents can once again spend most of their time away from the nest. The tower is close enough for the adults to keep an eye on the sky for any passing danger, or interlopers. The same pair has been in residence here for six or more years.

I found a note I made at the time of my 2003 reconnaissance visit. After the meeting, and a quick tour of the gallery, as an Edward Hopper twilight settled over the great city and coloured lights wriggled on the churning river, I paused on the Millennium footbridge. A busker strummed 'Waterloo Sunset'. I looked up again to the top of the tower, where the light box (now removed) glowed like the end of a great square cigar. There was the Peregrine, still perched, like a piece of living art in its own right, a jewel in the crown of this great city.

It said much about nature's tenacity, its powers of recovery, its ability to adapt, if we'll let it. Although from that range and in the lessening light I could see little more than a tiny, dark, hunched shape, I took a lot of pleasure in knowing what it was, why it was precious, how it mirrors the cleaning up of the Thames, the changing face of energy production and the rebirth and re-use of buildings, from power stations to art galleries.

I think J. A. Baker, although he could never have guessed it possible, would be thrilled to know that the Peregrine survived and came back, even to central London, as it did to Rachel Carson's US eastern seaboard and to New York City, a few years before that.

* * *

There is something infinitely healing in the repeated refrains of Nature – the assurance that dawn comes after night, and spring after winter … what will sustain me in my final moments is an infinite curiosity as to what wonders will follow.

Rachel Carson

Acknowledgements

The following people have all helped in some way with the content and preparation of this book, and for that I am sincerely grateful. There are many more too numerous to list – you know who you are: Carry Ackroyd, Brigid Allen, Elizabeth Allen, Guy Anderson, Sue Ansell, Julie Bailey, Richard Bashford, Alfredo Begazo, Chris Bettles, Dorothy Bettles, Fred Bettles, Mont Bettles, Lucy Bjorck, Gail Brice, Rachel Bristol, Abi Bunker, Dan Burnstone, Pete Carroll, Clare Chadderton, Liz Charman, Doug Christie, Mark Cocker, Dominic Crawford Collins, Rob Cunningham, Steve Dakin, Ian Dawson, Tim Dee, Paul Donald, Julie Doyle, Euan Dunn, Jenny Dunn, Mark Eaton, Sara Evans, John Eyre, John Fanshawe, Andre Farrar, Rob Field, Helen Flood, Gillian Gilbert, Jenny Green, Richard Gregory, Mark Gurney, Adrian Hardwicke, Richard Hines, Ben Hoare, Sara Hulse, Deirdre Hume, Rob Hume, Robert Hume, Bill Jameson, Kathleen Jameson, Kevin Jameson, Cath Jeffs, Shelley Jofre, Charlie Kitchin, Marcus Kohler, Rob Lambert, Ceri Levi, Helen MacDonald, Mick Marquiss, Jim Martin, Stephen Mason, Anne-Marie McDevitt, Susan McIntyre, Duncan McNiven, Matthew Merritt, Alec Milne, Dominic Mitchell, Darren Moorcroft, Isabel Moorhead, Stephen Moss, Nelson, Ian Newton, Derek Niemann, Sarah Niemann, Peter Oliver, John O'Sullivan, Lyndon Parker, David Payne, Giovanna Pisano, David Pons, Richard Porter, Nigel Redman, Sarah Richards, Roger Riddington, Mari Roberts, Chris Rollie, Steve Rowland, Matt Self, Rosemary Setchfield, Alison Sharpe, Danae Sheehan, Innes Sim, Jen Smart, Helen Snaith, Lucy Stenbeck, Sue Steptoe, Jim Stevenson, Dan Sturdy, Nat Taylor, Russell Thomson, Mike Toms, Ralph Underhill, Roger Upton, Alan Vaughan, Jo-Anne Vaughan, Terence Vel, Paul Walton, Joshua Wambugu, Mark Ward, Alice Ward-Francis, Ellen Williams, Gwyn Williams, Marie Winn, Richard Winspear, Simon Wotton.

Thanks also to the following titles: *BBC Wildlife*; *Birds*; *Birdwatch*; *Birdwatching*; *British Birds*, *The Ecologist*, *www.theecologist.org*; *The Guardian*; *John Lewis Gazette*; *Lost in London*; *Wilderness* magazine, New Zealand; *Wingbeat*; *Regar* newspaper, Seychelles; and to *Seychelles Nation*.

Thanks especially to Sara, for all your love and support.

Further reading

The following is a small sample of the sources mentioned in this story and some useful background reading. Others are mentioned in the text. The date is that of the edition I consulted.

Baker, J. A. 1967. *The Peregrine*. New York Review Books, New York.

Bell, I. 1993. Robert Louis Stevenson: *Dreams of Exile*. Headline, London.

Cameron, A. 1988. *Bare Feet and Tackety Boots*. Luath Press Limited, Edinburgh.

Carson, R. 1962. *Silent Spring*. Houghton Mifflin, Cambridge, Massachusetts.

Carson, R. 1999. *The Edge of the Sea*. Penguin, London.

Cocker, M. and Fanshawe, J. eds. 2011. *The Peregrine, The Hill of Summer and Diaries: The Complete Works of J. A. Baker*. Collins, London.

Dorst, J. 1970. *Before Nature Dies*. Collins, London.

Gibbons, D. W., Reid, J. B., Chapman, R. A. 1993. *The New Atlas of Breeding Birds in Britain and Ireland: 1988–91*. T. & A. D. Poyser, London.

Lear, L. 1998. *Rachel Carson: Witness for Nature*. Allen Lane, London.

Lee, L. 1969. *As I Walked Out One Midsummer Morning*. Deutsch, London.

Lee, L. 1981. *I Can't Stay Long*. Penguin, Great Britain.

Marren, P. 1999. *Britain's Rare Flowers*. T. & A. D. Poyser, London.

McLean, A. 1984. *Night Falls on Ardnamurchan: The Twilight of A Crofting Family*. Gollancz, London.

Muir, J. 1938. *John of The Mountains: The Unpublished Journals of John Muir*. Houghton Mifflin, Boston.

Rackham, O. 1993. *The History of the Countryside*. J. M. Dent, London.

Shoard, M. 1980. *The Theft of the Countryside*. Temple Smith, London.

Steuart, K. 1901. *By Allan Water: The Story of An Old House*. Elliot, Edinburgh.

Wells, H. G. 1948. *The Short Stories of H. G. Wells*. Ernest Benn, London.

Wilson, J. D., Evans, A. D., Grice, P. V. *Bird Conservation And Agriculture*. Cambridge University Press, Cambridge.

Index